S0-AIF-494

GRAFFITI ON MY SOUL

Johanna

Eloquent Books

Copyright © 2010

All rights reserved – Johanna

No part of this book may be reproduced or transmitted in any form or by any means, graphic, electronic, or mechanical, including photocopying, recording, taping, or by any information storage retrieval system, without the permission, in writing, from the publisher.

Eloquent Books
An imprint of Strategic Book Group
P.O. Box 333
Durham CT 06422
www.StrategicBookGroup.com

ISBN: 978-1-60860-961-1

Printed in the United States of America

Book Design: Stacie Tingen

Dedication: To the Light Who fills my darkness.

Acknowledgements

With love and appreciation to my family; to my sons who battled my computer for me at all inconvenient hours, to my daughters and daughter-in-laws whose help and encouragement have buoyed me up, and to my husband whose background presence is my comfort.

I am also grateful to my friends Marie Ross and Glenda Jackson for making time in the midst of their Christmas preparations to hunt down those last minute errors in the galley. Three cheers, as well, to all the girls at Strategic Book Group for patiently travelling this journey with me toward publication. You are all troopers!

CHAPTER 1

It is a $235,000 price on my husband's head. It is an earthquake that has shaken our family apart; ripping our children's net of security and plunging us into a suffocating crevasse of fear.

So much pain! So much pain! Before me soars a wall a thousand feet high. How am I to scale it? How am I to staunch my husband's bleeding anger? How have I come to stand—so unaware, so unprepared—in this place I stand tonight?

God's cathedral of the sky is bright tonight with stars. His light filters through the blackened arms of whispering trees to the prison of my flesh. Is this a furlough? A parole for my night-filled spirit? At least she cannot steal this moment from me. It is mine; God's gift. Her control stops here. The warm night air encircles me with the gentle mercy of a hug; there is a peace here that she has not—cannot—destroy. But tomorrow, in court, it will only be a memory, a taste of balm that will fortify me and mine for another day of suffering.

How can this be? How can this be happening to us? We are such ordinary people, bit players on a quiet suburban stage of North America. We never chose to audition for a nightmare. Normalcy and decency, not horror, have been the focus of our placid days. Can death be worse than this? Can an evil we have never paid homage to strangle us? I have become a creature of craven fear, a dog kicked in the streets. I am the rats I studied in university, zapped sporadically with electric current, urinating and defecating in fear. Now the phone rings and I run for the bathroom; the doorbell goes and I am afraid to answer. Our youngest daughter lifts her frightened blue eyes to mine and asks, "Is that the Judge?" The sight of the mailman grips my gut with icy dread. All doors are locked and barred. Like a robot I do the tasks of every day; fainting before each new threat and fresh offensive. I am a fugitive; trapped, dodging buckshot. My stomach heaves and churns in a never ending round of diarrhea and nausea. My joints lock shut and my head burns.

I must evaluate what is left to me. My home is falling under the long siege. It is no longer a haven of security. My husband is about to lose control and run amok. We have no money, even for food; no means to defend ourselves. Legal aid is broke and cannot handle appeals. I have discovered that justice is a rich man's toy. How do I explain this to my children? Our eldest daughter has perforated ulcers. The others are anxious, unable to concentrate. Their marks in school have dropped from honors to a questionable pass. At one, at two, at four A.M. our sleep is jolted by the ringing of the phone, and when we answer no one ever speaks. And then we struggle anew over the rugged terrain of our fears, praying for the comfort of sleep, only to wrestle again with the specters of our nightmare.

So what is left for us? Pain. Fear. A shattered faith. But also memories. These remain. There is no future. Only the past. That cannot be seized. Memory reminds me that there was a time of normalcy and hope and beginnings. Why is it that of the thousands of days I have lived only a relative few remain, etched like photographs in my mind? Are these the pictures of who I am? Do these lead me somehow to the place where I am today? Is memory just an escape from today's horrors, or does it hold the final meaning of my life?

The raucous cry of crows erupts from the darkened trees and their black silhouettes shoot across the gentle sky.

CHAPTER 2

I was conceived in the sullied womb of war; the individual wars and the Great War that tore the world apart from 1939 to 1945, in the most destructive antagonisms of history.

Fragments of this war are preserved in the rambling memories of my father–others are burned deep in the soul, where the sharp bite of psychological shrapnel continues the frenzy of conflict.

Etched in the sunlight of my kitchen on a day of peace, my father stubs out his cigarette nervously in a shell ashtray, and his eyes see nothing of the red poppies in my garden, or the sun dappled trees brushing my window. He looks, instead, through a window of his own to a vivid world long gone, and to a time I have never known. Still, it is this reality that has framed my existence:

***

"I never knew where it would lead me when I signed the attestation in '37 to go wherever his Majesty sent me. I had to put aside my dreams of going to university because it was the Dirty Thirties. No student loans then. But it was an honor to be accepted into the peacetime forces. After joining the permanent Air Force that May, I was sent on to Camp Borden for technical training and then became part of the #1 Fighter Training Squadron in Trenton. From there I was posted to Calgary. In retrospect, something happened in Calgary that seemed to be the harbinger of all that would come. The old timers used to talk about a sign in the sky, a prophetic warning that would precede the next World War. I never thought much about it, but one warm, clear, glittering night a couple of guys and I were out walking, and about ten p.m. or so we stopped to rest on a grassy hillock.

"Son of a...what is that?" one of the guys whooped.

The whole northern sky had turned blood red, thick, intense. I have never seen a sky like that before or since.

"The prophecy!" I thought instantly, awestruck and chilled to the bone. "Can this be it? The one predicted at Fatima?"

The headlines all over the world the next day recorded the strange inexplicable phenomena. An anomaly of nature, they concluded. It left me with a strange feeling; but soon I had other things to dwell on.

It was August '39 and the orders had come to go West. "Okay", I thought. But, within hours, in one of those subterfuges characteristic of growing hostilities, we were headed East instead. As the train rolled to a stop in Moose Jaw, we saw people were running back and forth, excited, electrified, waving newspapers and holding them up to the windows of the train. In large black print the headlines read: "WAR IS DECLARED!" It's funny, I didn't feel anything at that moment; not excitement, not fear. Only a numb feeling of predestination that we were in it for the long haul.

We always said that we marched in parade behind the boy scouts. The Air Force was new at that time, and our uniforms were so unfamiliar that old ladies thought we were busboys and asked us to carry their bags. On one occasion Ernie McNabb, our squadron leader, was called to Toronto for a high level staff meeting. Ernie was a prince of a guy, always a hundred percent for his men. When he didn't return after four days we began to ask questions. Turns out even some Colonel was making derogatory remarks about the Air Force, and Ernie, who was built like a weight lifter, grabbed him by the throat and threw him through a French door. That was a no-no! Had this been in battle he would have been court-martialed on the spot."

"Well, what happened to him?" I asked.

"He was thrown in jail, of course. But after one or two phone calls he was released. Didn't even get a demotion."

"How did he pull that off? What do you mean 'after a couple of phone calls'?"

"Well, his Dad was the Lieutenant Governor of Saskatchewan," Dad grinned.

"It was at a supper hour at Dartmouth that the call came: 'That's it, fellows. We're going. The contractors are already crating the air craft."

"Oh, oh!" I thought. "Now I'll have to call off our wedding! Who knows when I'll be back...or if..." I hurried to Halifax to wire my fiancé. I felt terrible because I was not allowed to give her any information.

"Hey! That's not fair!" the guys berated me when I got back. "You've got to give her a choice too!"

They were upset with me, and threatened to blackball me if I did not set the matter right. They had a point! So back I went to Halifax the same night to send a second wire:

"If you want to go through with it, come immediately, but be prepared to return at once."

In this way Pauline could surmise that I was about to be shipped overseas without me saying so directly.

She didn't let me down. She left immediately by train for the long ride from Yorkton, Saskatchewan, to Nova Scotia. We were married on May 28, 1940, in a small chapel in Woodside, Nova Scotia, by the RC chaplain, Squadron Leader McCarthy.

On June 7 we set sail for France. Our ship, the Duchess of Athol, was a passenger ship, not yet converted to a troop carrier. Our escort ship was named the Harvester. Dodging German U boats, we changed course to head south of the Azores. Three days from land we were notified by ship radio that France had collapsed, and we would be heading to England instead.

Our #1 RCAF squadron disembarked at Liverpool, and we were taken to an unfinished RAF station at Middle Whallop. Since everything was top secret, it was disconcerting as hell to find out that we had hardly set foot on English soil when our arrival was touted over the air waves by Lord Hawhaw and his spies. And no sooner had we arrived than there was a red alert. An unidentified aircraft was coming in for a landing. Everything had happened so quickly that we didn't even have helmets or rifles yet. But we were ordered to grab hand grenades and surround the plane. Turned out it was a French biplane, bringing some of the top brass who were escaping from France.

The Fifth Column was very active, and the jerries were bold. They made a sport out of bouncing their planes down our runway to let us know they were there. It happened that the runway was next to a swamp, so we decided to get them. The contractors moved the landing lights, which were mounted on stakes, out into the swamp, so it would appear that the runway was located there. The next night when they swooped down, the Germans dropped dummy wooden bombs on our dummy landing strip! At the mouth of the Thames a dummy aircraft carrier had been constructed out of wood, but there too the underground caught on–there were spies everywhere–and it, too, was bombed with wooden bombs!

Our next posting was to the former international airport at Croydon, just outside London. It was here we got our first baptism of fire.

It seemed we were always under red alert, so we soon didn't make much of it. This particular evening, about seven o'clock, I was on duty by the maintenance hangar, preparing an aircraft to be delivered to the dispersal point. Two Hawker Hurricanes were being ground tested nearby. Inadvertently, I happened to glance over my left shoulder and saw a whole swarm of forty nine aircraft bearing down on us. Another senior NCO, Lock Watson, was standing a step in front of me. I tapped him on the shoulder and pointed up.

"I don't think those are ours!" I yelled.

By the time I took a second look, the aircraft had already discharged their bombs. They wobbled down through the air like matchsticks or handfuls of pencils. The roaring of the engines being tested was so loud that we couldn't be heard, so we signaled the ground crew and shook the aelerons to alert the crewmen in the cockpits. Before I took two steps, bombs were exploding all around me, accompanied by steady machine gun fire. It was bedlam! By now we couldn't see a thing because the chalk cliffs had thrown up great opaque clouds of white dust. I tried to run but fell flat on my face, skinning my elbows. I couldn't understand why I fell until I looked down; I saw that the concussion had broken all the stitches on my coveralls, and the loose pieces of material had whipped around my legs like a lasso. I was not conscious of fear, only of an icy hand that drenched the back of my head and neck and soaked me through with a deadly chill. I managed to hobble over to a tin shelter with four other fellows, but hadn't been in there for more than thirty seconds when an officer called us out to a rescue. Central to our operations was a tower that held all our ammunition on the main floor and had our offices above. Fifteen feet away from it, an anti-aircraft installation had been blown sky high with all the people within. The tower was on fire now, and concrete slabs of walls and ceilings were hanging down at rakish angles. We had to get the ammo out before everything else blew. Dodging flames, we grabbed the ropes on the wooden crates of ammo, praying that we would not be the next casualties, and dragged them free of the burning building. Upstairs, later, we found the body of a fine lad I knew. He was crouched under a table, and there was not a scratch on him. The only anomaly in the whole scene was that every stitch in his clothes, and even in his shoes, had been totally disintegrated by the concussion.

The huge tower clock had stopped at just a few minutes after seven. The whole thing had taken only seven minutes. But seventy four ambulances were pulling heads, arms, and legs from the wreckage and heaping them on stretchers. I was numb with shock.

To the left of the field was an aircraft plant. It had not been hit. To the right of me was a huge flat building, the Bourgeois Perfume Factory. As we walked closer we could see it had suffered numerous hits. Beneath the floor of the factory an air raid shelter had been built to house the 326 women workers. A direct hit had gone through the roof, down through the building, right into the center of the shelter, where it had exploded with demonic force. There was nothing salvageable for the ambulance crews. They just covered it up with lime to kill the smell and prevent the spread of disease.

To settle our shattered nerves we headed out to a pub called the Propeller, located about a mile from the station. We were puzzled by the large crowds of children waiting outside the pub. The bartender told us that the children assembled there every day to meet their parents as they returned from their shift at the perfume factory. This was the saddest of all the sights I saw during the war—all those children waiting for the mothers who would never come back.

The raid had taken a huge toll on the civilian population, hitting the residential district first, and then the air raid shelters in the Commons, the park adjacent to the station, before it hit us. Roofs and body parts were strewn everywhere.

The next day my buddies went down to check out the hospital about four miles down the road. It was a big sprawling hospital with a low flat roof on which was painted a huge red cross. The numbers of the wounded there were so great that the hospital personnel had no alternative but to place the overflow patients on row upon row of cots on the grass surrounding the hospital. In the early daylight the Germans returned and strafed the hell out of the hospital and all the surrounding cots.

The Battle of Britain was underway."

***

Dad mops his brow, which is hot with perspiration although the house is cool. Eight mutilated cigarette butts, his daily quota, fill the ashtray. His eyes are red and wet.

***

"The Germans tried everything to break our spirit, to demoralize us, and the civilians too, so that the country would surrender. We were outnumbered four to one in airpower. The guys had to get pretty ingenious. By cover of night a couple of Daks (Dakotas) would act as troop carriers, moving us constantly to new locations where new color bands would be painted nightly on the tails of the Hawker Hurricanes, because each squadron was known by its colors. So the Germans began to think there were a lot more of us than there were. It was like a game of chess. Dummy dispersal points with dummy aircraft were constructed here and there across England, using gunny sacks, canvas and anything that could be painted, anything to give us a larger presence than we had. So much attention was paid to detail, with ladders leaning against the planes and fuel tanks standing by, and tar sprayed on nonexistent landing strips, that surveillance planes were taken in.

A clever strategy was adopted to protect England's cities and industrial areas. Huge barrage balloons were floated above them, and from these balloons hung flexible steel cables that formed a spider web over the city. In attempting to avoid the balloons, German planes would swoop beneath them and end up caught in the cables. The joke was that now we knew what was holding up the island. After all the steel dropped on it by the Germans, the island would have sunk if it hadn't been for the balloons holding it up!

While at Croydon we were billeted in a boys' school which had been evacuated. It was a first class building and even had a pool, which we enjoyed. One night our paymaster got drunker than a skunk and walked straight out of the second story French windows. He landed on his back, winded but unfazed. We told him it was a good thing he was so drunk or he'd have been a goner.

A bluff ran along one side of the station where the dispersal point was. On the other side were a lot of houses that were evacuated, but the boys at the dispersal point noticed chickens still running around the chicken coops. So one day they invited us for a big chicken supper. Under cover of darkness the guys all lined up outside the chicken coops, and one guy would reach in and wring the chicken's neck. With military precision we passed each chicken down the line, plucking feathers and eviscerating as we went. Some of the guys found a vegetable patch, and others found out how to turn the gas back on in the houses so we could cook up the feast; a welcome change from mutton. In about three days the patrol–probably the Home Defense that used to roam the fields with rifles and pitchforks–noticed a lack of chickens, and the gas company got into the act and called our CO, Ernie McNabb, up on the mat. But Ernie was used to being on the mat. He was as cocky as all get out and was always in hot water for something–more often than not for fraternizing with the men. But he was a good guy, the first to shoot down a jerry, and all the guys looked up to him. Anyway, the whole thing soon blew over; the chickens didn't have to be fed anymore, and Ernie got a verse of our squadron song dedicated to him:

***

"Young Ernie leads this bunch of nuts,
Short of stature but long on guts.
He'll take us all throughout this brawl;
We're Canada's fighter squadron."

***

This kind of tomfoolery kept our spirits up and kept us from going over the deep end.

From Croydon we were sent up to Northolt, where we joined a Polish squadron composed of escapees from Poland and Yugoslavia. One day a German bomber landed in a field nearby. The pilot was found sitting calmly on the tail of his plane holding a cigarette. In passable English he asked for a light! We thought it might be a trap and were afraid to approach him at first. He became our first POW. Another time an ME109 (Messerschmitt) landed and was brought into our hangar. Before you knew it, the guys came in with their hacksaws and began cutting it up for souvenirs. But the station authorities appeared and forced them to give back their trophies, and the Messerschmitt was kept for research.

At Northolt we were bombed day and night. You could set your clock by the German planes. One noon hour I heard rapid machine gun fire.

"Those don't sound like Mosquitoes," I shouted, "Those aren't ours!" Running to the mess hall I yelled: "We're under attack!"

Everyone took off for the Anderson huts, and we, senior NCOs, for the hangars. One of the aircraft was hit dead on and debris was everywhere. The guys were crowded around afterwards, trying to assess the damage, when I noticed a round hole in the tarmac. Reaching my hand out toward the hole, I felt heat coming from it.

"Take off!" I shouted, "There's a DA down there!"

A DA is a delayed action bomb. We later had one of these come right through two unoccupied bunks in our bunkhouse.

Despite the danger, King George VI visited us at Northolt on September 26, 1940. There was no mustering, no parades. He just got off his aircraft at our dispersal point and mingled with us, chatting and shaking hands with us. He was quite a guy. It gave us all a boost.

I guess the reason that Northolt was such a popular target was because it was near the beginning of the London subway. We had a favorite pub, the Orchard, about five miles away. One night we headed out to town for the evening. We had a habit of always stopping at a special fish and chip shop on the way. Served English style, wrapped in newspaper, the fish and chips there were really good. But this night we decided to go get a drink first. As we sat, knocking them back in the pub, a whole mess of jerries swooped down and started dropping their payload. The black out curtains were pulled, and every once in awhile they would blow in from the concussion. After the all clear sounded, we started back to the fish and chip shop; only we couldn't find it. We couldn't find anything. The Germans had dropped land mines on parachutes. These landed in trees and houses and sent their blast out horizontally, leveling everything. We crawled over smoldering rubble all the way back to the base, shaken by our close call, and thanking the Providence of God that we had not stopped for our usual fish and chips. Along the way, on an overpass, we found four frightened weeping young women. We took off our protective steel helmets, feeling a little like supermen, and gave them to the girls to wear while we guided them below the underpass to a brick shelter where other survivors waited.

Near Northolt was a town called Hammersmith. It was designated as a demilitarized zone and was inhabited mostly by aged people, women and children. Since it had no strategic importance, life tended to carry on as usual in Hammersmith. One Saturday morning while the people milled around in the streets, doing their shopping, the Germans swung in low over the street and strafed the crowd into oblivion. Our ambulances and motor transport were called in to pick up the bloody fragments of bodies that remained.

The morning I was to leave for a special course on advanced air screws (propellers), we received orders to carry our armaments to our place of duty. We wondered what was up? I boarded my train, armed, and found myself in a compartment across the aisle from a couple of British officers. They waved me over and began to interrogate me intensively. Once satisfied that I was not a subversive, they told me that a sea invasion had been attempted that morning. Wave after wave of German barges, loaded with men and equipment, had pressed toward the coast of England. With a horrendous blast, their first row of barges had hit a line of submerged drums of gas and explosives. Suffering heavy casualties, but thinking they had broken through our defenses, they kept on coming. Each successive wave set off another line of explosives until the waters were a sea of flame. The invasion had failed. But for weeks the sea would give up its dead, and the beaches were awash with bodies.

Receiving a number one standing in the air screw course qualified me to travel to all the other bases to adjust and upgrade all the air screws to the latest design. But I felt sick as I moved from aerodrome to aerodrome, playing the part of a human target, in a bizarre and lethal game. If I had to die, I prayed it would not be out here, alone, away from my buddies.

Desperately needing a rest period, we were sent up to Prestwick, Scotland. The planes still flew there, and maintenance had to be kept up, but it was a respite. Prestwick was only four or five miles from Ayr, where we senior NCOs were billeted. It was from there that I wrote your Mom mischievously, "Am billeted in Ayr with two girls". Later I let her know that one was 76 and one was 78. They were good people and good to us.

Here we were even treated to a hockey game between the English and the Canucks!

Ayr also happens to be the hometown of Robbie Burns, so we had to walk to the 'Three Brigs' and see the hut where he was born. Behind the hut was a graveyard where we entertained ourselves reading the raunchy grave stones on which Robbie Burns had left his mark. One that still sticks out in my mind read: 'Here lies Mary, the slithering bitch'!

On my duty days at Prestwick I was in charge of guarding the aircraft in our dispersal field. There, by a creek, was an old flour mill with a paddlewheel where I spent my nights on a straw mat on the floor. I was in charge of the other guards, and I didn't much care for the job. One night, in the total blackness, without even the light of the stars, a helluva bunch of shooting started. The guys were so antsy that they'd shoot anywhere, everywhere, whenever they'd hear a noise, without even knowing what they were shooting at. It was my responsibility to check out what was going on. Under war conditions I was not allowed to use a flashlight. I strained to see something, anything, inching out cautiously into the utter darkness, wincing as branches reached out for me, slipping on the mossy river bank, paralyzed by the cold fear that my own men would shoot me by mistake. It was one of my worst experiences overseas, but one I could not dodge because duty had to be performed.

Some time, after we left Prestwick, we proceeded to the far north to a place called Thurso. Here we slept in corrugated tin huts placed on hard top so fresh it was still soft. Eight miles out of Thurso was the dispersal point, at a place facing the coast of Norway, where we were informed that the enemy had a train load of gas bombs. There were no hangars there yet, and the snow was four feet deep. It was bitterly and incredibly cold digging the snow away from the aircraft. We would bank the snow up around our empty four gallon gasoline cans, making ourselves a shelter, and burn coke to keep warm. The M.O. was authorized to provide rum rations to keep our blood flowing. He had a glass with tape around it, and the height of the tape was the regulated fill to be given to each man. As he passed it from person to person, each frozen soldier would grasp the treasured glass for warmth, and in so doing would push the tape up a notch higher. By the time he got around to the last person the tape was usually at the top, and the first recipients were howling for justice for themselves. You had to have a sense of humor or you'd have a nervous breakdown. One of the lads did have a nervous breakdown. He managed to dodge the bombs and the close calls, but he was so shell shocked he had to be hospitalized.

Remote as our location was, the Germans still knew we were there. Our gas masks were always handy, and our aircraft and munitions trucks always faced the entrance to the area, ready to scramble. Not far away, a pasture, surrounded by tall trees, was covered with sheep. In case of attack the farmers, at a signal, would send in their sheep dogs and move their sheep, and the pilots knew they could land safely at a point where three lights intersected.

On the way back from the veteran's pub in Thurso, but strictly out of bounds to us, was a stone castle which was owned by one of the big shots of the Air Force over there. The young buggers did a bit of reconnaissance and discovered that the castle employed some presentable young maids. They managed to wangle invitations in and began to spend a lot of time there. Word got to the top brass that the RCAF gang were raising hell up there. But they quieted it down quickly because they didn't want to break the spirit of the men.

One of the guys with a lot of spirit was Alec Laxdal. Alec had salvaged some gun parts from Croydon, which was strictly against the law, but that didn't bother Alec. He built himself a Lewis gun, which he installed in the window of a shack facing a fence. On the fence he placed old gas drums for a bit of target shooting. We named it 'Alec Laxdal's Home Defense'. The gun took four different shells; straight ball, incendiary, tracers and DeWild. When the incendiary hit, there was one hell of a boom as the cans exploded. One day it came close to disaster. Alec told this little scrawny guy to come and shoot the gun. The guy had never shot a Lewis before and Alec thought he needed his education upgraded. But when it kicked back, the muzzle pulled off the windowsill and began spraying ammo everywhere, just missing us. Another time, coming back from the pub, Alec fired his revolver at the cast iron stack of a Nissan hut setting off one hell of a reverberation. They found the guy inside lying flatter than pee on a plate.

At Digby, one day I noticed a small building on the far edge of the field that was the focus of a lot of activity. The aircraft coming out of the shed made a strange noise. Although I could not discern if it had a propeller, the noise was not that of a propeller. Puzzled, I quizzed the visiting Rolls

Royce field engineer that I was working with. He confided to me that I had seen the first experimental jet plane. Later, back in Canada, when I told the fellows that a new plane was coming that did not have a propeller, they thought my brains were scrambled or I had shell shock.

After fourteen months, I had been stationed at nine bases and aerodromes and had seen more of England and Scotland than most natives. The fear, the cold sweat, and the prayer had paid off. We had turned the tide of the war in Britain and written history. One day the news came that some of us were being posted to North Africa, and others would be sent back to man the new Commonwealth Air Training Schools that had been built in Canada in our absence. Thoughts of home swept over me with an aching longing and daydreams teased my mind with bright visions of a long delayed honeymoon.

It was late July, 1941, when we gathered at a seaport named Gouroc where a Dutch ship, the Vollendam, was being refitted after being torpedoed. Days after setting sail we discovered that the repairs had been incomplete, and we were taking on water faster than the pumps could handle it.

"That's alright," quipped a buddy, "We're only a mile from land after all–straight down!"

Despite chilly relations between England and Iceland, we were forced to go to Reykjavik to change ships. Because of the animosity between the two countries, we were strictly ordered to stay on board ship and await orders. But Alec Laxdal had heard the call of his native soil, and with disbelief we watched as he slid down a rope and disappeared into the leaden waters. This time, surely, he had gone too far. But the next day, there he was, wearing a grin bigger than Texas. We could never figure out how he had found his way back to the right ship.

The Battle of Britain was over: we were going home!"

***

After a honeymoon in Banff, Dad continued the nomadic Air Force life. With her ninety pound frame swelling with new life, my mother waited for him to find them a home. She had agreed to stay at her family home in Yorkton until the baby arrived. But she was getting impatient, and with the assurance of her doctor that all was well, she decided to surprise Dad. By the time she arrived at Dad's current station in Lethbridge, after a 500 mile train ride, she was deathly ill. An Air Force nurse quickly turned her over to Dr. Hunt, a skilled but irascible doctor, who did not mince words;

"Who told you that you could have a normal birth? It's a good thing you did not go into labor because neither you nor your baby would have survived."

So it was that I was born by caesarian section into a world torn by conflict and battered by the unrelenting prairie wind.

Somehow it seemed that Providence had intervened so that my mother and I would survive. But to what purpose?

Alfred Adler, the famous psychoanalyst, said that the key to understanding a person's basic processes, the motivations that drive him, and the style of life that characterize him, lies in one's earliest memories.

If so, I was in trouble from the start.

My earliest memory is of walking with my parents, dressed in my best clothes, after a spring rain. As we were skirting a gray concrete block building, a shining puddle caught my eye. It was the apple in my garden of Eden. I did ask my father if I could jump in it. His head moved back three inches on his shoulders in a 'you can't be serious' gesture before delivering his definitive 'No'. But I couldn't bear for opportunity to pass me by. As I watched my puddle recede into the distance I broke away from the custodial hand and made the first big splash of my career. Johanna the rebel.

My other earliest memory also involved an inner conflict. It had come to my attention through the intonations and gesticulations of my elders that there was some sort of difference between the male and the female gender. I decided to research this possibility. Still so small that I could stand beneath a table in the bathroom and be hidden by the table cover, I waited. As the moments passed I grew increasingly apprehensive, feeling I might be violating a taboo, and worse, I might be caught! My father is a formidable man. Finally I decided to rein in my ambitions and darted out of the bathroom.

Adler would say that I am a follower of dreams, a searcher, a headstrong race horse fighting restraint, a gourmet of life, reaching out for meaning, experience, and completion. But still I am dogged by the nemesis of fear.

So where has this taken me? What have I found in the puddle of life?

When I was about four years old Dad left the Air Force and we moved to Ituna, Saskatchewan. Ituna, Dad's boyhood home, remains in my mind as a drab and barren wasteland. It was here I discovered a conflict far more discomfiting and painful than my first scratches of conscience.

My father's feet were sticking out of the end of the bed. My mother was burning the toast in the kitchen. The silence was leaden in my stomach. The two people I loved did not love each other. I ran back and forth frantically trying to get them to speak to each other. When my father spoke it was like thunder. My mother cried softly, desolately. I fled outside into the winter's chill, where great long icicles were hanging from the roof along the descending stairwell, mirroring the chill in my heart. My parents fell from their pedestal that day. With faint guilt I sucked on one of the forbidden icicles, tasting the painful realization that my parents were flawed beings, and I was adrift on an uncertain sea. No more could I lean on them as rocks of stability. I suddenly felt my own separateness, and their separateness, and I was afraid. From that day on there was a hollowness inside of me that could not be filled.

That rift, the first of many, was healed and reopened many times, and flowed like a river of pain through my growing up years.

But if I lived in an embattled world, I did not sit passively on the sidelines. One day my parents and I and another family set off on a jaunt to Regina to see a much touted movie. To my delight the rough earth road nearly bounced me senseless. My parents were less enthused. When we stopped enroute for gas and refreshments at a little country store, my eyes and my heart were immediately captivated by two white balloons that made a rustling noise each time the door admitted a gust of wind. My father was buying cigarettes and my mother was chatting with the other family. I pulled her skirt and tried to get her attention.

"May I have that balloon?" I begged.

"Just a minute, in a minute," my mother said and continued talking.

By now my father was talking animatedly to the other man, and my mother had exited to the washrooms.

To my utter chagrin, the other mother strode over to the balloons and put one in each of her children's hands, as they jumped for joy.

"I wanted one of those!" I sobbed broken heartedly to my mother as she returned.

"There are no more," my mother said with some regret.

In a black mood I returned to the car and sulked the rest of the way to Regina. Perhaps a happy children's movie might have distracted me from my grieving over the white balloon, but this turned out to be an adult movie, circa 1946. Sick at heart, I peered through my fingers as the tension built and a beautiful girl in a pastel toga stood at the edge of a pool about to take her own life. It was too much. Choking back my fear and anger, I flung myself out of my seat and bounded like a wounded rabbit out of the theatre into downtown Regina. I remember how the streets were shiny with rain, and the neon lights bounced red and yellow and green reflections everywhere. And I remember the swish and slosh of the moving vehicles as they moved in and out of the darkness; my darkness.

Across the street from the garage that my Dad built, with our living quarters above, was my grandmother's house. It was a frame house the color of butter, half hidden behind honeysuckle and carigana bushes. My grown up Aunt Mary and Uncle John still lived at home, and one day they told me about Halloween. I was filled with a delicious sense of anticipation. Aunt Mary instructed me that I was to knock on the door and shout as loudly as I could, "Halloween apples". Whoever answered the door would fill my paper pumpkin with candy and treats. Excited, but fearful, I went first to the most familiar house, the home of my only friend, Judy, who lived two doors down across the street in a white frame house behind a picket fence. Through the window in their back door I could see the family still sitting at the supper table, their backs to me, laughing loudly and talking amidst clattering dishes and silverware. I knocked timidly at the door.

"Halloween apples!" I cried, in what I am sure was no more than a hoarse whisper. It was dark and I had never been out by myself in the dark before.

No one replied.

"Halloween apples!" I said and knocked again.

No one turned around. No one heard me. I knocked again weakly and waited, but I had lost heart, and I turned away disconsolately. Next door at Auntie Tillie's house there was no one home.

"Well, at least," I consoled myself, "there is still Aunt Mary. She will give me lots of candy and treats".

I could see Auntie Mary standing by the little shrine in Grandma's living room as I came to the door. It was a lovely little shrine with a statue of Jesus, surrounded by flowers and red and blue vigil lights.

"Halloween apples!" I called with confidence.

Auntie Mary disappeared quickly into the kitchen and came back with a shiny red apple. I stared in disbelief. Frustrated with disappointment I held the apple momentarily in my hands, then threw it at her and ran out of the house.

Among the vivid pictures of those early days was my first birthday invitation from a family my parents knew. My mother and I had shopped together with great care for the present and I had chosen a Little Black Sambo puzzle of which I was very proud. Sure enough, the gift was a hit, and the children jostled and pushed each other to be closest to the table to work on it. I stood on the outside of the group, unable to penetrate the wall of bodies, and too small to see what was going on at the table. Such experiences served only to increase my shyness, bewilderment and isolation.

I did have one companion who loved me unconditionally. My parents had bought me a wiry, nondescript, black and white dog I called Nibsy. My father cautioned me that if I was to have this dog I would have to assume responsibility for him, including the buying of a dog license. He was busy working underneath a big truck, but he tucked the money in my hand and gave me directions. As Ituna is a small village he saw no danger in a five year old going down the block alone to the narrow store front that handled such legalities.

A bespectacled man behind a high counter was talking animatedly to a bearded man, both studying a calendar on the wall as I entered. I waited meekly until they finished talking, then I cleared my throat. As the other man left, I lost sight of the man behind the counter, since the counter was well over my head, but I could hear him walking around and I could smell his pungent cigar. I cleared my throat again. No response. I shuffled from one foot to the other.

"Sir," I said, but there was no reply.

After what seemed like a century, I left the store without being noticed and ran home stinging with shame. Later on my father came back with me, but I cowered behind him as he fulfilled the prescribed duty.

If I loved Nibs with exuberance, my mother's feelings were somewhat more restrained. Although ill with another pregnancy, she was forced into a daily wrestling match with Nibs to get him to take his worm pills. Nibsy fought back doggedly every step of the way, thwarting every attempt. He was a free spirit and intended to remain that way. I found out one day, to my chagrin, that Nibsy was also a freeloader. Mom had let me help her bake a chocolate cake, and then had given me a generous piece to share with all my dolls who sat, I am sure eagerly, in a circle around me, dressed to the nines. I carefully placed a small piece of cake on the pretty glass dishes I had received at Christmas, and put a plate before each doll. When I returned from the kitchen with some milk, a scene of bedlam met my eyes. Dolls were strewn everywhere and there was nary a crumb of cake to be found. An unrepentant Nibs sat licking his chops. I was flabbergasted. I ran downstairs to the garage.

"He ruined my party," I cried to my Dad. "He's bad. I don't want him any more!"

"We'll get rid of him if you really want to," my father said gravely.

"I really want it!" I protested stubbornly.

By the time evening came, I had changed my mind, but Nibs' fate had already been sealed for other reasons. It was the opening my parents had been looking for. Nibs had been threatening and attacking passersby, and people had begun to complain. My Dad explained to me that Nibs would be better off on a farm where he couldn't get into so much trouble.

In no time Dad had found an elderly lady who lived about 14 miles from town and she said she would take him. Three weeks later, however, we were jolted out of our sleep by a clanking up the stairs and a familiar bark. Faithful Nibs had returned home, even though he had to break the chain he had been secured with and drag it for miles. My reawakened hopes were soon dashed when my father found him a new and more humane owner.

As if to heal my anguish over my lost companion, my Uncle Paul showed up at our garage one day with a box full of green branches.

"What is that?" I asked breathlessly.

"Here, put your hand in," said my genial curly haired uncle, carefully guiding my hand along until I felt something very warm and soft. I was ecstatic! A tiny baby bunny! My uncle had found him abandoned on a hunting trip and had thought of another abandoned soul.

My friend, Judy, arrived to find me rearranging the bunny's house, still delirious with excitement. Her joy was more restrained than mine, but we played all afternoon until my Mom called me up for supper. As soon as I finished eating I raced downstairs again. To my consternation and panic the bunny could not be found. I asked everyone's help but no one could find it. Judy said she had not seen it either. I went to bed in sorrow.

Two days later Auntie Tillie told my mother that Judy had come to her house the previous day, flushed and panting with excitement. Clutched tightly to her chest was a tiny baby bunny. As she held her hands out to show it off, Auntie Tillie could see that the guilty child had inadvertently crushed it to death. And so the tattletale photographs in my memory album reveal my first shocking discovery of human treachery.

My mother bandaged my bloodied knees and other bruises of childhood, but who could mend the bruises of my spirit? Who could fill my emptiness? Was there anyone that I could totally depend on? Certainly my own strength was not enough. I remember wandering around, a four year old vagrant in pigtails, looking, looking, looking, aware of a hunger I could not fill. Looking for what? For a flower? For something beautiful in that desolate landscape? For a friend? It seemed life was like sucking on a tin popsicle; a hollow, tasteless experience without sweetness. And at night I was haunted by a dream that I was burning alive, a dream so vivid that its luminous orange flames still crackle in my mind.

I would only learn in later days that the emotional impoverishment of that time was linked to my parents' own struggle for survival: with each other, in business, in the turbulent crosscurrents of our little town, with my paternal grandmother who hung over my mother's head like Damocles sword.

My father's family formed part of the pioneering collage. Our forebears arrived from the Western Ukraine to settle among the rolling hills, the fields, the sloughs, the chokecherries and partridges of Saskatchewan. His maternal grandparents had immigrated to Canada in 1903, after losing five children to a flu epidemic. Given that emotional baggage, my genial great grandfather, Danylo, and his tall handsome wife Ksenia, found the transition to pioneer Canada stressful and unsatisfactory, and returned for a time to the old country. But by the time my grandmother was sixteen, her family was settled for a second time and Maria had gotten a job working at a prairie hotel. She was very content with her first taste of money and independence.

About this time my grandfather showed up on the scene, an eligible older bachelor of some means, who could speak eleven languages and read and write fluently in six. His coming caused quite a stir, and his attentions to Grandma overjoyed her parents. Here was an educated, cultured man, a man of substance, and Maria should marry him. But Maria was not interested in getting married. She was happy with her life as it stood. Although Wasyl could promise her a better life style than most, this was still early in the century when immigrants often lived in soddies dotting the prairies and raising a family was a harrowing, backbreaking affair. She would have none of it. Nevertheless, as recriminations and pressure increased from her family, Maria finally capitulated.

The marriage was a stormy one. The death of their first son, due to what today would probably be termed a crib death, seemed to cause a deeper wedge between them. Wasyl's work as a section foreman for the CPR placed him in Neudorf, a German speaking community. Maria refused to leave Ituna. She wanted to remain among her own people and those who spoke her own language. They saw little of each other. But still this did not generate a greater peace. Maria did not understand her gentle refined husband, nor he her. Having lost one baby, she jealously protected all the others, appropriating all their love for herself alone. Like an anti-pope she set herself up against her husband in everything he said and did. She jealously resented any attachment the children, especially the girls, might feel toward their father, and lost no opportunity to put him down. I remember him as a kindly, noble, melancholy man, quiet and longsuffering. He was a person of deep religious sensitivity, creative and hardworking, who remained dedicated to the family he saw so little. His response to the haranguing attacks of his wife was simply to walk away sadly. He seemed to live in his own Tibetan wilderness, high and lofty.

In retrospect, there was something very strange about Grandpa. He never talked about his past. He never once mentioned his parents. He never told anyone if he had any sisters or brothers or any other relative. He never explained where and how he came to have the education he did, given that education was unavailable to the average person in Russia or Ukraine in the late 1800s. Due to an overheard conversation with a friend we knew that he had held some high position, and that he had had to flee. Other than that he could have simply dropped from the sky. We have his naturalization papers which show that he arrived on this continent in 1904 in New York, and after some time in the States, gravitated to the obscurity and isolation of the Saskatchewan prairies.

My strongest memory of him is the day I begged him to tell me a story. He resisted my entreaties for some time, protesting that he did not know any children's stories. Finally, unable to escape my pleas, we sat on the edge of a bed in a room papered with lines of blue flowers, and he slowly began. He told me of a flight of a family from those who wanted to kill them. Part of the flight was over open water. It was a long and torturous adventure, filled with violence, and I began to cry bitterly:

"Why are you telling me such a sad story?" I asked Grandpa in distress.

"Because that's the way it was," he replied. "Do you want me to stop?" he asked with his kind, sad eyes.

Torn, I answered, "No, go on."

Grandpa did finish the story, and at the time I thought he had told me the story of the flight of the Holy Family to Egypt. In later years I have wondered, if driven by my importunities for a story, he did not tell me the story of his own flight. Nowhere had I ever heard that the Holy Family had to flee over water.

To please Grandma, Grandpa had bought her the general store in Ituna, where she and their large brood could keep busy and make money. From this store Grandma reigned like a queen, dispensing favors and charity with abandon. These were the good times for her. She kept a firm hold on her offspring using a combination of indulgence, guilt and the broomstick. But even in Grandpa's absence there was maelstrom under that roof. Dad, however, managed to live mostly in the eye of the storm. Grandma was proud of his intelligence and depended on him, flaunting his accomplishments to her friends. But it was hard to be oblivious to the fighting, and to the harsh treatment of her two daughters who were forced to flee home in their middle teens, or of the restrictive power she held over the lives of her other children, of the forced homage they had to pay her, of the load of guilt she instilled should they criticize her. After all, did not God Himself command them to honor their mother? Were they allowed to judge her? Her life, she pointed out, was not easy. Was she not their benefactor? A martyr for their sakes? For Dad it became a huge and unassailable conflict, too contradictory to be dealt with. His feelings were filed in file thirteen and buried deeply under duty and respect and honor. But the repressed feelings leaked their acid, nonetheless, into the sinews of everyday life. They created scar tissue, that grew into walls, and that finally compartmentalized life into a safe package for handling. As long as one did not undo the strings, as long as one did not look inside...

Although Dad was well treated, Grandma's favorite son was the eldest, Mike. She granted Mike his every whim and shielded him from all responsibility. At the age of nineteen, Mike became the first person in town to own an automobile, by forging his mother's name on a check. She let the matter pass and entered into his triumph. Mike became a skilled mechanic, but he was erratic, and his constant indulgence with his friends in the good times degenerated into alcoholism.

One night the store burned to the ground. There was no insurance. They lost everything. Gone were the records of all the credit Grandma had extended. It was the beginning of the dirty thirties and the townspeople were happy to forget the debts they owed. Gone was Dad's plan of studying electrical engineering. In 1937, after graduating from high school, Dad instead opted to join the Air Force.

It was while awaiting his discharge that Dad bought a garage business in Ituna. Hoping to help his brother, Mike, who by this time was a mean and dissolute drunk, he made him a deal. Although Mike had no money to invest, Dad offered him a half interest in the business on condition that he stay off the bottle, or at least arrive sober in the morning to do his job. It was a forlorn hope. Not only did Mike run the business into the ground, but in Dad's absence he stole all the money Dad had, and diverted all of the inventory into his own name. It was a bitterly disillusioning and traumatic time for Mom and Dad. When confronted, Mike refused to discuss the matter with them or even to talk to Dad. And when pressed, Mike, as was his wont, became violent. Grandma, ever faithful to Mike, stood on street corners declaiming her other son, and her daughter-in-law, to all passersby. The money was never retrieved, and the town was split into two warring camps. Mom, I suppose because she was not Grandma's own flesh and blood, somehow became her scapegoat. The frustration and injustice continued to grow, and Mom was alarmed to realize that hate was beginning to eat away at her insides and to poison her life. Nothing she tried seemed to help. She found she could not change other people, which was not surprising considering she was having difficulty even changing herself. It was time for a move. Although Dad had managed, by dint of long hours and hard work to rebuild the business, for the sake of his family he decided to sell it and relocate Mom, my new sister, Sandy, and myself to Yorkton.

For me, it was like moving from a desert to an oasis.

For my beleaguered Grandfather, it would not be so easy. Even as he lay dying in the hospital, his wife continued to browbeat him.

He moaned in agony and cried, "Am I to have no peace, even in death?"

As his body lay for viewing in the living room of their little house, Grandma raged in the kitchen, furiously shredding his belongings and stuffing them into the woodstove, along with the little book that was Grandpa's diary and could have answered so many questions.

These, then, were the long shadows that fell upon the ground of my childhood.

CHAPTER 3

"Good memories," my mother reflected, her coal black hair now ashen gray, "are like umbrellas, to give you refuge from the shriveling sun and the driving rain."

But what memories can shield me now? Where can I flee from the horror of today?

Oh yes! There was a sanctuary, a thousand miles and forty years ago. Are the doors still left unlocked to the white two story house with the green shutters? Do dizzying beams of sun, sprinkled with a million glittering specks of dust, still reach through the glass of the veranda, warming Grandpa's bench, along with the geraniums and young tomato plants basking in the window? Just an afternoon's drive, but a galaxy away from the acidic sterility of Ituna, the peaceful brooding presence of my maternal grandparents hangs over all to impart serenity, even amidst the madcap activities of my four young uncles.

I am six years old again and I am swinging on the wrought iron gate, my skin a cascade of freckles cast by the shade of the overhanging trees. I study the scratchy crackling of the cinder path as I drag one shoe, and my breath catches with admiration as my four young uncles bound out of the house and clear the fence with effortless agility, racing to the waiting gravel trucks. I shout to be heard over the rumble of the engines:

"Bring me some Vyko (chocolate milk)!"

They hang out of the windows making faces at me. But I know that as sure as the sun rises, when they come home at lunch there will be chocolate milk and treats for me.

This is a kindly place. Here, for the first time, my heart discovers joy. The billowing clouds are a trampoline for my spirit, and the soft grass is sprinkled with tiny white flowers like fallen stars. Here, at my mother's parents' home in Yorkton, each morning is a gift box to be unwrapped, a fresh delight, rich with untapped possibilities. Even if a wild Saskatchewan electrical storm descends to grip my heart with fear, the sonorous bells of the Church across the field assure me that God's voice is louder than any storm.

I have a number of special places here in my world. There is the store down the road that I visit daily with Grandpa. And, of course, the veranda heavy with the pungency of the rich red geraniums, where I sit with Grandpa to greet all passersby. The boys from St. Joseph's College, across the baseball field, pass our gate on the way to town. Little girls and boys from St. Mary's, the yellow brick school between the College and Church, laugh and chase each other as they go to and fro. On Sundays, the parishioners who worship under the rounded domes of St. Mary's Ukrainian Catholic Church, pass down Darlington Street with friendly waves and pause for a moment of chitchat.

The house and yard are surrounded by carigana bushes and tall murmuring trees that whisper protectively on all sides. One of the largest trees holds a tree house; the only place my uncles and their buddies can escape from me to engage in a little male bonding. They cluck sympathetically as I try to scale their male bastion, but no one offers to help me. The branches are too far apart and I am too small.

So I bounce around to the other side of the house, where wide kitchen windows overlook a mecca of flowers, and greenery, and darting twittering birds. Here peas and sweet peas, carrots, potatoes, celery, currants, strawberries and purple asters grow in wild and delicious profusion. I grab a handful of fresh peas and balance precariously, barefoot, along the broken stone walkway, past a battered watering can and the garden tools that lean against the back of the porch. I look for a place in the shade to eat my peas, drinking in the beauty of yellow snapdragons and velvet hearted blood red poppies that bob willy-nilly here and there, their gracious loveliness like an overflowing of eternity into time.

Next I navigate to the old stone well behind the house, being careful to give a wide berth to the more ferocious of the clucking hens that run frenetically to and fro, pecking at every promising speck on the ground. The well holds all my dreams in its gleaming depths, and I try without success to operate the rough rope and pulley. One day, when I am bigger, I will be able to draw up water and dreams.

The sun is burning hot, so I retreat into the house, where Grandma is making lemon jelly, and I head down to the earthen basement with a bag of sunflower seeds. It takes courage to make my way through the darkness to where my uncles have stashed their comic books, but I revel in the musty smell of the cool damp earth. To my right at the bottom of the stairs is a dim lit pantry full of gleaming jars of preserves. But to the left lies the forbidding coal bin. As I cautiously pick my way past it, I freeze in fright and revulsion as something damp and clammy brushes my cheek.

"It is only Grandpa's long underwear hung to dry," I try to convince my racing heart.

But I waste no time getting around the bin to the other side of the basement, where some diffuse light struggles through a cloudy window and tall heaps of comic books are waiting as my prize. Here the hours pass in peaceful adventure.

Shuffling feet overhead and my Grandpa's voice return me to the present. Grandpa is looking for Uncle Laudie. He was christened Walter, but I nicknamed him Laudie, and the name stuck. I race out back to the barn which is now used for truck maintenance. Usually Uncle Laudie can be found there, lying on his back under a truck, surrounded by a curious gaggle of neighborhood boys who compete in offering their ideas and handing him tools.

My oldest uncle yet at home, Laudie is like the oil he uses to lubricate the truck; the business and household run smoother because of his mild and gentle heart. Garrulous and friendly, he is a simple, approachable man, hard working, without barriers or pretence. His brothers ride him about his interest in patent medicine cures, perceived by them as quackery. They feel he is not too bright, and his lack of schooling makes him overly gullible. But although his ego may take a battering, Laudie sticks doggedly to his own convictions. His only hesitancy is with regard to the opposite sex. He is intrigued by them, no doubt, but has never quite gotten the hang of them, remaining at home by default, the perpetual bachelor.

From somewhere in the barn comes the high-pitched mewing of a new litter of kittens. My rising excitement is tempered by my uncle's warning to leave them be. Unfortunately, what is bounty to me is surplus to my Grandma, and it falls to my Uncle Ernest to be the population control expert. Ernest enjoys playing Machiavelli. On the one hand, he is the most intellectual of my uncles; on the other hand he is a raffish villain and the penultimate tease. Soon I am looking around for those kittens and they are nowhere to be found.

"Hey, Johnson Wax! Get out of here, Johnson Wax!" Ernest taunts me with the pet name he has for me, pulling my braids and squishing me down to the floor as I try to interrogate him.

"Cold blooded murderer!" I shout at him, deciding I will follow him like his shadow until I extract some form of repentance from him.

I could have saved my breath. After dogging his steps and chanting at him the better part of the afternoon, he remains unfazed. In fact, he seems to enjoy the notoriety. So I know I'll have to look for some other means of entertainment. I really don't hate him. With a child's perspicacity I know that his roughness masks an affectionate heart and a deeply spiritual soul.

On the way to the barn I dare myself to look into the murky frothing contents of Grandpa's barrel of sauerkraut. The fermentation in that barrel both fascinates and repels me. Yet it has a status in our household just a little short of an icon. Sauerkraut is on the menu in season and out of season; it is Grandpa's passion, and was the bane of my mother's growing up years. Every fall Grandpa would roll the barrel inside the house for the winter, and my mother recalls ruefully how the whole place would reek of sauerkraut. It was hard enough to pretend to glamour when you were seventeen, only four foot ten, and looked like twelve, but it was positively impossible to create a romantic atmosphere when any perfume you wore was overpowered by the odor of fermented cabbage. So when a young man came calling on Mom she would nervously distract him at the front door while Grandpa, with furrowed brow and dark mutterings, was forced to roll his precious barrel of sauerkraut down to the cellar.

I hear the screen door slam and run to see who has arrived. It seems all of humanity trickled through our back door. Whether to pay a bill or to pass the time of day, people came at all hours, without embarrassment, and were always greeted with warmth. The doors were never locked and no hungry person was ever been sent away without food. I was told about the Great Depression when ragged, unshaven men came daily to our door and Grandma fed them without fear and listened compassionately to their woeful stories. The kitchen was always the scene of an animated conversation. Our house had dual heat sources: coal and politics. Tommy Douglas and his socialist following was an especially good heat source. I can see Grandpa, with his slightly rotund shape in his perennial gray pants and suspenders, pacing back and forth with feverish intensity. The boys make interjections, each anxious to make his point. Grandma sits quietly beside the black wood stove, meanwhile, peeling endless baskets of potatoes, an island of tranquility in a noisy sea. Many nights after I have been sent up to bed, unwilling to let go of the excitement of the day, I lie on the floor with my ear to the brass register which amplifies the sounds of the talking below. Often the discussion is in Ukrainian and I cannot understand what is being said, but I let the sound roll over me, a comforting pulse rising and falling, the rich cadence of voices and rollicking laughter; argumentative, lively, but without rancor or acrimony. In the background the radio drones the music of Al Jolson and the gravelly voice of Louis Armstrong. Suddenly there is an excited hush and the conversation dies in its tracks as Foster Hewitt proclaims: "This is hockey night in Canada!"

On other nights my uncles get a special spring in their step, and the house reeks of Brylecreem, soap and aftershave. Water is heated in the reservoir of the wood stove and is carried carefully to the four legged white tub in the bathroom where there is only cold running water. Then there is whistling and humming and a lot of preening in front of the mirror. I think it takes an extraordinary length of time to arrange a very negligible amount of hair. Scooby and Peko and Metro arrive, wearing their college jackets, and with jaunty grins and twinkling eyes they head off together in their communally owned car known as the Green Hornet. At least they attempt to head off in the Green Hornet. I more often see them pushing it than riding in it.

In the mornings, I am Grandpa's invaluable ally. He stands at the foot of the tall steep stairs, at the end of a long hall hung with a generation of blackened jackets reeking of oil. He is becoming increasingly perturbed:

"Boys! Get up, Boys!"

There is no response. Grandpa mutters agitatedly in Ukrainian. The boys work with him in the family's wood, coal and construction business, and the morning is getting on. I race upstairs and grab the edge of Ernest's gray blanket, pulling with all my might. There is a howl of protest as the cool air rushes over him.

"I'll get you, Johnson Wax!" he threatens, making a lunge for me, but mostly for his blanket.

But I am already at Laudie's bed, threatening him with a glass of water, tickling his nose and the soles of his feet. Lionel sees me coming and makes a dash for it. But Uncle Victor has a death grip on his blanket and has pulled it over his head, piteously pleading for his last moments of sleep. I bounce on top of him.

"No! No! Go away. I'll get up!" he promises. But five minutes later he is sound asleep. Grandpa is yelling again. I use my heaviest artillery on him, bugging him relentlessly until he sits up groggily. Uncle Victor, with his likeable boyish face, black crew cut and school jacket, looks like a typical college boy. He is my special buddy, and I take a great interest in all his concerns, feeling honored to be privy to his deepest feelings, his worries over girls, and the recipient of his earnest warm affection. I love to accompany him to work, bouncing along in the back of the truck and sharing his daily adventures. His exuberant laughter is music to my heart.

Lionel, who I call Linny, is quiet, by contrast, and keeps his feelings under wraps. But my admiration for him borders on the reverential. Breezy, gaunt cheeked, intense, athletic, his engaging, kidding sense of humor steals my heart. Only nine years older than me, he is a crackerjack hockey player and I think he is relentlessly handsome. I spend a lot of time just watching him. Yet there is a shadow of sadness in his eyes and I feel I cannot reach him. Part of the reason for this is because Linny is always getting into trouble with his rowdy friends. I see concern mirrored in the eyes of my elders and I worry. The other, perhaps more basic reason, is that Grandma was never well after Linny was born. My Mom took over as his mother, fussing over him, cooking special things for him because he was so small, reading to him, loving him. Then one day Mom moved away and had me. Lionel had a hard time forgiving me for being born. However, one year he decided to let bygones be bygones and bought me a giant chocolate Easter Rabbit. As he waited for Easter to come, he couldn't resist just eating the tip of one ear. Then, to even it off, he ate the top of the other ear. Soon the rabbit had no ears.

"Are you still going to give it to her?" Grandma asked.

"Sure, there's still lots left," he answered.

But Easter was slow in coming, and all I got was the memory of a chocolate rabbit, and the hooting of my uncles who told the story for years to come.

I didn't mind. I only wanted Lionel to accept me. Although my sister, Sandy, then still a baby, became his favorite, that was okay, because she needed a special pal too.

Anyway, Easter was special to me other ways. That was when Grandma would haul out two galvanized wash tubs and balance them on planks placed between two chairs. In these two tubs grew sweet airy loaves of honey yellow bread which we would decorate with braids and religious symbols. Grandma would cover old grape baskets with brightly colored crepe paper, place sausages, painted eggs, and the wonderful, slightly sweet Paska bread in them, and we would carefully carry the filled baskets to Church for a special blessing. There I would sit waiting in the chapel, in the golden light streaming from the stained glass windows, bathed without and within in a profound and glorious peace.

Grandma was a large woman with salt and pepper hair tied back in a bun. A prominent vein on her right cheek always fascinated me. Grandma was Polish but spoke Ukrainian, and had come from the old country with her rather well to do family, the oldest of three girls. Her mother, my great grandmother, was a cranky woman who always dressed in dark clothes like an old babushka and she, frankly, scared me. But Grandma was considered beautiful and quite a catch and had many suitors. Fortunately for all of us, her sagacity and understanding nature found in Grandpa the perfect match. Grandma and Grandpa always spoke to each other with their eyes; they seemed to have a kind of telepathy. Mom later said that they had the only truly happy marriage of anyone she knew. Their example of loving respect and accord taught me one of the great lessons of my life: that love is possible in this weary aching world. By the time I knew Grandma, her physical beauty had faded. But her inside beauty had no need of physical props.

Grandpa and his brothers had been orphaned at an early age, and at the age of twelve he began to work for his keep on the farm in Germany where he had ended up. The people on the farm were kind to him, and Grandpa often talked about them, but he never did get the chance to go to school, or to learn to read and write. Nevertheless, Grandpa was a good and just man–I can imagine that St. Joseph was something like him. Grandpa successfully ran a livery stable in the early days until a relative defrauded him of all his money. After the man returned from jail Grandpa,

Christian that he was, accepted him back without recriminations. He then turned to farming, but was hit by the dust bowl of the Thirties. Finally, his attempts to support his growing family by selling wood and coal grew into a successful construction business. Until his sons grew old enough to help, Grandpa managed to do all the accounting in his head from memory.

Grandpa dealt with Grandma's sickness with compassion and valor. When Mom would get impatient because so much was left on her young shoulders, Grandpa said to her thoughtfully, "Be careful what you say. You don't know what will happen to you in your future", but he said it with kindness and did not scold her. It was a heavy load for Mom he knew, getting up before school, and sometimes missing school entirely to cook for a whole threshing crew, and he worried about her. The first time Mom killed and cooked a chicken she was only thirteen, a tiny thin girl of hardly eighty pounds. When Grandpa came in, hungry, from the fields, he was silent for a moment until he found the words to tell Mom with patience and diplomacy that one must remove the insides of the chicken before one cooks it. Grandpa always knew instinctively when to speak and when to be silent. He had the sensitivity and wisdom that comes from a true holiness, the battered, sturdy, dusty holiness that grew deep and unobtrusively like the potatoes in his garden.

Grandpa and Grandma shared a silence that was a union of souls. My very happiest memories are of sitting together with them at the kitchen table, hearing the clock tick, studying the harmony of sun and shadow in the garden, being one with each other and with God. It was, I think, my introduction to contemplation.

I wish I could say that I was always loving and generous with Grandma, but it taint so! I was truly ingenious at dodging chores, and I would pester her for hours to take me to the woods around Hopkins Lake to pick hazel nuts. Poor Grandma could hardly raise her arthritic bones from her chair, and she would sit there wearily with her hands on her knees exclaiming, "Oy oy yoy!"

And sometime she would take me.

Only once do I ever remember her getting cross with me. That was the time I decided to run away because she would not let me sleep with the dog. Grandpa's hot button, on the other hand, was my endless, unskilled, tent making in the front yard. I could hear him expostulating with amazement and aggravation to my mother. I guess he could not understand that I wanted a construction business of my own.

In my large extended family in Yorkton my shyness and fearfulness nearly evaporated, and the turbulence of my early life diminished to scattered gusts. At school I made friends and felt accepted. Mind you, I rather liked being the center of attention, and I carefully monitored what others did that won praise and approval. One day, while learning to print, the teacher passed by checking my work with a barely perceptible nod. But at my friend Betty's desk Sister Marcella stopped and praised her lavishly.

"Must be something there I could learn," I said to myself. I navigated up to the pencil sharpener and nearly fell into Betty's lap struggling to see the printing that merited such high praise. The printing was neat, I noted, but it did seem from what I could see that she was printing her 'h's backwards.

"Whatever it takes," I thought to myself.

The next day during printing my page was a masterpiece of tidiness, with every 'h' printed neatly backwards.

I felt like I had been dropped by parachute on the North Pole. The teacher's shocked surprise and icy glare sent me shivering with hypothermia.

So I learned that I must be my own person, and march to the beat of my own drummer.

On my First Communion Day I embodied that principle to the maximum and threw a tremendous tantrum because I was afraid of the flash camera that was to take our class picture. Everyone was painstakingly kind to me, but having taken such a strong stance I felt there was no way I could back down. This stubbornness would remain my nemesis.

Despite the debacle of my First Communion day, I did retain some elements of the religious faith I had been imbued with. I was aware that dolls were not widely touted to have an afterlife. However, with the deeply maternal love I bore my family of dolls I did not want to take any chances. Besides, the ceremony was gripping, the veranda was sunny and warm, and I had a whole afternoon ahead of me. When my Mom came in and found me baptizing my dolls, she was kind but very firm. "No more," she proclaimed with a narrowing of her eyes that precluded argument.

I was in a quandary. I had saved the best for the last. All my dolls were safely baptized but my very favorite, a chocolate colored baby doll with one missing leg. In her minority status, and with the handicap she already had, she, of all my dolls, clearly required baptism. Unfortunately for me, my mother just happened to walk in again as I was pouring the water. It was like landing in the Battle of Normandy.

Betty and I were both competitors and best friends. We shared a boyfriend named Morris with whom I was wildly infatuated. If Morris chased me home, I was euphoric. If he chased Betty home I went around with a face that looked like a torn overshoe. Betty had a habit of beating me out, which was rather trying to our friendship. For Halloween my mother had created a ruffled orange and black costume for me which was sheer fantasy. It was my first costume and I was beside myself with delight. Surely I would win the prize for the best costume! Betty showed up in a blue and white Little Bo Peep outfit with a ruffled parasol and a white shepherd's crook covered with bows and flowers. My eyes bugged out. She was gorgeous! And, of course, she won. At Christmas I did a marathon pout when I was not chosen to wear the angel costume with the satin wings. I did not learn to lose nobly all at once.

During our stay at Grandma's house my Dad and uncles had been busy building us a grocery store just down the block. Mom and Dad then entered into the food business, but soon discovered that to compete with the larger stores they had to stay open for long hours, and especially on weekends. They found themselves working day and night with negligible results. Dad began to look around for another way of making a living. I, in the meantime had become incredibly popular once I discovered I had a philanthropic streak. When my parents discovered where all the candy was disappearing, I was encouraged to find another career choice. It was like the Hindenburg going down.

That spring Dad decided to go to Chicago to learn the refrigeration trade, and soon, to my sorrow, the store was put up for sale. The halcyon days of Yorkton were coming to a close, nor could all my tears change the facts. But somehow the sound of the bells across the field would continue to ring in my heart even as I learned that no joy on earth is permanent.

In the following years we came back to visit at least twice a year, and occasionally my uncles would send me a supply of sunflower seeds and comic books. Each time as we drove away again my sorrow was fresh.

When I was thirteen, my grandmother died. Grandpa had undertaken to be Grandma's nurse and did everything for her. It was touching to see this old man being as tender with her as a young man with his first love. One day, as he held her in his arms bathing her, he suddenly realized that her spirit had quietly, peacefully, fled.

I can still see her lying in her coffin in the Church. Her round face is rosy and she looks just as if she is having a nap before dinner. I watch her still face intently, willing her chest to heave, willing her to sit up, to speak. I hear the deep, sad dirge sung by the men who carry her coffin. It sears my soul with a white heat. I keep turning around, looking up at the doorway, expecting to see her there. But she is gone.

The vacancy this creates in my life, the changes her dying set in motion, give me my first intimations that 'we have not here a lasting city', and my spirit begins to understand that my life is a pilgrimage to a more permanent port of call.

I was twenty-four when I saw my grandfather for the last time. He had had a number of heart attacks, but survived them all to return to dig potatoes in his garden. But without Grandma, it was as if he stood naked against the wind. I was shocked when I saw him last. His once powerful frame was shrunken, and his hair, no longer white, was now yellow with age. He seemed so weak, so vulnerable.

That night, as I tiptoed downstairs to the bathroom, I noticed that Grandpa's thunderous snoring, which usually shook the rafters, was absent. Strangely, his snoring had always been comforting to me and had given me a sense of security. It sounded out like a powerful warning that could ward off all danger and harm. Passing his room I saw that his door was ajar, and there, in the moonlight, I witnessed the most profoundly moving experience of my life. Grandpa was kneeling on the floor in front of an icon of the Trinity that hung on his wall, his arms outstretched, his soul crying out piteously to his God. His words tumbled out with strength and pathos from the very core of his being. What was he saying? I do not know. I think perhaps he was speaking of his utter loneliness and his yearning for heaven. Or perhaps he was praying for his family, for all of us. But it was definitely a dialogue, for at times he would stop and listen, and then he would be pleading and explaining. He seemed to see something that my eyes could not see, and hear something that my ears could not hear. He was completely unaware of my presence. I stood transfixed, shaken to my depths at his passion, a passion that seemed to exceed the strength of his frail body. Then, unwillingly, I forced myself to move, aware that I was an intruder on holy ground.

Grandpa lived a year after that, dying peacefully at last of cancer. But he left this world with undisguised joy and enthusiasm for a world that seemed already more familiar to him than the one he was leaving.

CHAPTER 4

Through coulees, sprinkled with wild flowers or burned brown by the sun, flows the deceptively placid expanse of the Old Man River. Alongside this primary water source, formerly Fort Whoop up, sprang up a grid system of tree lined streets that became the little city of Lethbridge. Lethbridge has the reputation of being the cleanest city in Canada, and justly so, because a funnel formed by the Crows Nest Pass sends nearly constant gale force winds capable of blowing away anything that is not nailed down. In the winter months it sometimes brings the warm chinook winds, the darling of the prairies, which can raise the temperature forty degrees in an hour, suddenly transforming the dead of winter into a spring oasis.

It was here my parents had decided to return, warmed by the memories of the year Dad spent stationed here. He settled the four of us in one of the Bluebird Cabins by Henderson Lake, while he reclaimed a plot of land from gophers and tumbleweed and built us a house. That peach colored house on Twenty First Street would be my home for the next ten years.

My first day of school in the old St. Aloysius School, a ramshackle structure that would soon be torn down, was everything I could have wished it to be. Everyone ran to walk with the "new girl". By day two the novelty had worn off and I felt myself abandoned in a strange land. I understood graphically that I was no longer surrounded by a large supportive extended family and a community in which we were known. The wind blew cold around my ears, and tangled my long braids, and froze my heart.

My reaction was to turn to the world of books. I read voraciously and sometimes eschewed birthday parties and other social occasions to read more. My mother told me I was too selfish to put myself out to make friends. She was right, but I was also afraid of rejection. I had no idea how to go about making friends. Although initially too timid, in Yorkton I had been surrounded by attention and never needed to take that first step towards others. Besides, the world of my dreams was a wonderful and challenging place. I loved fairy tales and horse stories, mysteries and the lives of the saints. I wanted my life to go somewhere. In my dreams it did.

In grade three, I began to discover something about excellence. My teacher, Miss Lacey, could have been an army general. Tall and ascetic, her gray hair pulled back in a bun, no one dared to be out of order in her class. She gave fifteen minutes of math homework every night, and though the students complained about her behind her back, I bore her a grudging admiration. For as tough as she was, she rewarded every semblance of effort. Her all-knowing azure eyes missed nothing that went on, but she was scrupulously fair. A word of praise or recognition from her was a prize indeed. The world, she told us, was like a ship, where everyone played a role. A picture of a ship was pasted on the wall and all the jobs on board were listed. It was up to us to decide what role we wanted to play and to work toward it. I began by scrubbing decks. It was easy, just coasting along, putting in the minimum effort and getting by. Then, one day it occurred to me that I didn't want to spend the year pushing a mop and a pail of dirty water. I wondered, if I gave it some effort, could I improve the situation? The next month I held my breath nervously as I looked up at the postings. I had made First Mate! Before the year's end I was Captain. It was a lesson that stuck.

Around our busy neighborhood I did not lead a totally hermetic existence. In the spring Verna and Rosalind and I, with other neighborhood friends, played hopscotch, skipping, tag and kick the can, and on hot and lazy summer afternoons we laid on the grass and wrote messages on each other's backs. We collected hit parade songs and sang and had sleepovers and told secrets. At the Galt's home across the street, with its large boisterous family, there was a perpetual Monopoly game going which I loved to be a part of, although I was usually bankrupt in the first half hour. I liked the ambience there. Our house seemed so quiet by comparison. I had a recurring dream, or daydream, about a white house I would have some day. It would be two storeys, like the Galts' house, and huge, but it would have white stucco on the outside, many large windows, an area for large tropical plants, as well as a meditation room. I did not know where this house would exist, or when, but I felt that someday I would live in such a house. In my mind I walked through the rooms of this house and wrestled with parts of the details and layout that remained fuzzy. Certainly such a house could never stand on Twenty-First street.

Only a block away, off Mayor Magrath Drive, stood two baseball stadiums, and across from this was Henderson Lake with its lovely lawns, well cared for flowers and busy playgrounds. I spent a lot of time there.

And where the program at the Y had failed to teach me to swim, here it became imperative for two reasons. Firstly, the shallows of the lake were inhabited by blood suckers from hell. Secondly, there was a raft about fifty feet off shore where anybody who was anybody spent the summer days. After a couple of years on the sand keeping company with the blue bottle flies and the younger children, I finally decided that life was no longer tolerable if I could not reach that raft. I remember the fear in my throat, and that lonely solo swim, and the feeling of having arrived as I climbed up that undulating but solid wooden raft.

My warmest, most peaceful memories are of walking or riding my bike downtown on gentle May evenings to sing at Benediction at St. Patrick's Church. The sheltering trees along the streets rustled and breathed with life, and the setting sun through the stain glass windows threw a garment of joyous color that clothed my poor spirit with a quiet intense joy. Although I traveled the route back and forth by myself, I never felt alone. A presence lit my heart that made me feel whole.

I began to consciously realize that I needed more than myself, more than other people, to feel whole. Still, my faith life revolved largely around rules to be followed and ideals to be admired. I was stirred by the impassioned sermons of an old Irish priest, a sort of latter day St. John the Baptist. Adults did not like him much. They would gather in knots in front of St. Patrick's Church murmuring their displeasure.

"But he's right," I would say to myself, studying their discomfort. "What he says is true."

It bothered me that Mom and Dad did not seem to be as strong in the practice of their faith as they had been. Besides his preoccupation with work, Dad and Mom's different backgrounds and expectations were frequently bringing them into conflict. Dad had a lot of his father in him. He was a just man, ostensibly humble and self effacing, devoted. Ever the perfectionist and idealist, Dad lived in a black and white world ruled by moral imperatives and a stern call to duty. He had filed and locked away the ugliness of the past, and the memory of his own wild oats; he angrily refused to acknowledge or discuss that which, by virtue of his years, he determined he had outgrown. He would not let what was past enter into the future he was creating. But even as he denied its existence, the echoes of his upbringing arose unbidden in his relationship with my mother like living fossils from a black lagoon. The emotional blackmail he had undergone from his mother had steeled his perceptions and hardened his temper. The war had eroded his nerves and primed him to expect military precision. Mom had come from softer, kinder stock. She was used to being listened to. She had always expressed her feelings openly and her feelings had been respected. She soon learned that Dad could not easily handle feelings. For him, when his mother had vented her feelings it had always ended up in an acrimonious shouting match. He was not about to suffer a repeat in his own marriage. So he simply side stepped or ignored Mom's feelings–or like Grandpa, in order to keep the peace, walked away. Mom would suffer this for some time, stockpiling her grievances until the measure was full. Then she would blow like a volcano. Dad would be caught off guard, utterly stunned, uncomprehending as to why Mom was behaving so irrationally. She would be hurt and outraged by his insensitivity. He would be incensed and angry about her attack. And so it would go on; a different chapter, and yet the same, every month. I felt like a wounded animal caught in a thorn bush, hurting, always hurting. Our family was being torn apart and I was devoured by fear. I didn't know which was worse, the yelling or the walls of silence. I tried to build bridges between them and to be a peacemaker, but I felt battered by their pain and my own. I can still hear the desperate crying and the hollow echo of our footsteps as we walked the darkened streets and I wondered if I would ever have a home again. I wished I could die and be out of my misery.

I saved my money and went out and bought them a Bible. Mom protested that she couldn't understand the Bible, but I felt that both of them were so locked in their own views, their own self justification, that they needed to find a broader horizon, a purpose bigger and more important than themselves, to bring them back to a common ground. I implored them to forgive each other as Christ had asked us to do and had given us the example. It occurred to me that WE are the living Scripture being written in our times; God's words are dead unless they live in us. This was our challenge as a family: to either be what we believed, or to self-destruct.

But as I read the Old Testament I was perplexed and troubled to read: "The sins of the fathers shall be visited upon their sons for many generations". These are the words of God. Could it be then that God is a vengeful God? How unjust, I thought, that God should punish innocent offspring! Was I the victim of such a curse, as the savage storms of my grandparents' generation continued to blow under the roof of my own home?

Later I came to understand that what God spoke of was not meant as a damning indictment, an unending punishment against His people, but as a straight forward observational statement to warn us. A sad one to be sure! One generation of deformed human beings raising their offspring in their own distorted perceptions and practices. The legacy of sin is sin; the teachers' error recorded over and over again in receptive newly formed brains. We are all teaching. Always.

So what we are is what we teach. But how do we become good teachers? It seemed to me that where men, like oxen, plod around a gristmill in a daily never ending vicious circle, the purpose of redemption is to give us the power to break out of that deadening circle to create life anew.

I clung weakly to that hope. On Sundays I listened to the Hour of St. Francis on radio and the prayer at its conclusion burned into my soul like a beacon:

Lord, make me an instrument of Your peace,
Where there is hatred, let me sow love,
Where there is injury, pardon.
Where there is doubt, faith,
Where there is despair, hope
Where there is darkness, light....

The words of this prayer over the next forty years would continue to give my life direction even when I seemed to forget their meaning. It also made sense to me, and I believed, that in God's Revelation, He, our Manufacturer, had supplied us with operating instructions. If the designers of planes and rocketry had the foresight to build in course correction factors for their craft, surely the Designer of Life itself would leave us a flight plan and a map to find our way. But that was before the hormonal storms of the teens.

At puberty I decided I had to break out of my cocoon and become a butterfly. By this time most of my school mates were well established in cliques, and my laissez faire friendships were not enough. Typically, I went to the library and undertook the study of people. I concluded it was time to exhibit more interest in others, and to spend more time listening. Some of what I heard as a result, at the nightly get-togethers at the baseball stadiums, I did not understand. But there were no lack of volunteers to educate me in the seamier side of life. I listened as my companions talked about the infidelities of their parents in little out of the way motels, and I ached and felt how insecure they were. They were thirteen and fourteen, and they were brittle and callous. What they detested in their parents they seemed bound to emulate. Sex was an adventure but not a source of happiness.

I traveled far a field looking for friendship and excitement, meeting a wide variety of people. My first choices of boyfriends were, by and large, deplorable. Still, I remember the magic of the first day a boy held my hand. I was dazzled. We walked around a lake bedecked in silver, young, unsure of ourselves but caught up in glorious new feelings, sharing, what I was certain, was to be the beginning of a wonderful, enduring relationship. Don seemed as star struck as I. But he rarely spoke to me after that night.

I found my life alternating between giddy heights and soulless depths in a dizzying roller coaster ride. At night I lay in bed, a bundle of yearnings; I wanted so to love and be loved. All my instincts, all my imaginings, led me to dream of that perfect ideal, of understanding and self giving, of being understood and embraced totally in body and in spirit. Like lightning bugs dancing on a darkened field I would spot sparks of this ideal love in someone's eyes—only to have it fade away quickly like a mirage. Among the boys I knew, the ideal was clouded by their humanity, their self-centeredness, their raging hormones. It was difficult to have real friendships as a teenager because of this. Everyone was either too guarded or too reckless. And we were all unfinished, incomplete. One day I cooked and fussed, preparing my best offering for a box social at Church. In hope and anxiety I placed my gourmet meal in a box wrapped with white tissue paper and decorated with red ribbon and roses. An older student whom I had worshipped from afar bid on my box and won. But the prize was bitter. The contents of the box were of more interest to the boy than I was. Besides, my vocal chords were paralyzed, and both of us were stiffer than the cardboard of the box. It was a comedy of awkwardness. Never having experienced the easy give and take of a brother-sister relationship, I had idealized my hapless date into another dimension of reality, far removed from all the shortcomings I felt in myself as a person. But despite this stinging embarrassment, the search for the perfect relationship would go on. Older people, observing our bouts of puppy love, would say condescendingly: "You're just in love with love." Now, as I look back, it seems strangely true. Maybe we were giddy with a Divine spark, with an eternal hope; our sexuality had opened us up to the "other" and we had caught a glimpse of Love Itself. No wonder so many of our early romances floundered on the rocks. The ideal we sought was the ultimate and was far ahead of our youthful immaturity.

My girl friendships also hit patches of turbulence. Always trying to avoid confrontation, I tended to go with the flow. But one day, with my social life on the rocks because of some vicious gossip, I felt my back was to the wall. I held the phone for a long time in my hands, trembling, before I finally dialed with sweaty hands:

"Joanie, this is Johanna. I have heard what you are saying about me. I would like to know why you are saying it, because you know it isn't true. I've always treated you well and liked you—why would you say such things?" I don't recall the rest of the conversation, but somehow out of that honest exchange we became the best of friends. I learned there was confusion in her life and family too. We found a lot to share that summer. Petite, blonde, vivacious and fun, I found things to admire and learn from Joanie. But as the last days of summer holidays came upon us Joanie became glum and quiet.

"What's the matter?" I prodded her.

"I don't want to go back to school…to my school," she said.

"Why not?" I asked, shocked. I'd been to her school dances. They had been fun and Joanie was popular.

She shook her head, mute but determined.

"Where would you like to go?" I asked.

"I'd come to your school if I could."

I looked at my mother. I didn't know if that was possible. I went to St.Joseph's High, a Catholic school—Joanie was not a Catholic. And school began in two days. Mom picked up the phone. The upshot was that Joan joined me at St. Joes that fall, and continued there until her family moved to Calgary. Joanie taught by nuns! What a hoot! She was exempted from religion class, of course, but sometimes she came anyway.

At school I forged ahead, building the "new me". I decided to become a cheerleader and I soon became a part of the squad, cheering for our school team, the neighboring boys' school, as well as for a semi-pro soccer team. I was interested in writing and I became the editor of the school paper and year book. A lot of people thought I was flighty and wild and never had a serious thought in my head. How little they knew! Perhaps I was wild, but other than missing a few curfews, I had a healthy sense of self-preservation. Dad still had a strong streak of the military and the thought of facing him hauled me back from not a few precipices. On one occasion when I ran afoul of his decrees Dad picked me up by the front of my new coat, sending buttons flying in every direction. That experience left a bitterness it took many years to erase.

Sensitive to my needs, Mom tried to aid my burgeoning social life by allowing me to host several parties. The only absolute stricture was a total ban on alcohol. As far as I was concerned personally, this was no big sacrifice, because, having sampled it on occasion, booze promptly fell to the bottom of my list of temptations. Not so, however, for some others among my friends. While I could answer for myself, I could not control them. And so it was that there was a football party at our house after a big game and I was in a state of nervous collapse. I had warned everybody repeatedly: "no bottles!" Mom had been wonderful. She had worked late into the evening preparing chickens and fries and other treats. To my relief, no one brought a bottle, but midway through the evening Terry, the team captain, and Bob, his side kick, arrived, and they were plastered, barely able to stagger. We ushered them quickly and unobtrusively down the steep stairs to the basement, where the party was being held. To the immediate left of the stairs was a tiny bathroom which Bob immediately claimed as his residence. Unfortunately, the latch on the door was broken, and every time Bob's iron grip on the toilet bowl relaxed, he would fall backwards with a thud, his face landing precisely at the bottom of the stairs. We would prop him up, and he would immediately fall over again. We tried to secure the bathroom door, but it would not hold. I surveyed the scenario with horror, terrified that my mother, or worse, my father, would come down with another tray of food and find his vacant eyes staring up at them.

What were we to do with him? Would the stench of his vomiting or his moaning give us away? Would Terry play the fool and get me into trouble while I was busy with Bob? That night was a lesson in misery never to be forgotten.

At long last we ushered out the last football hero and said a prayer of thanks that Mom and Dad were none the wiser. The girls stayed on for a slumber party and we were all weak with relief.

The next morning was Sunday and we sleepily trudged off to Church. On our return I thought I was having a hallucination. I hoped it was a hallucination. Sitting across from the house was Bob's car, known as the Black Moriah.

"What are you doing here?" I hissed at him in panic. "You didn't spend the whole night here, did you?"

"Nah," Terry disclaimed.

"Well, what ARE you doing here?"

I noticed Bob's face and his mouth looked strangely sunken.

"I came back to ask your Dad if he had seen my teeth," Bob moaned.

The bottom fell out of my stomach. I did not want to go into that house. My feet felt like they were encased in blocks of concrete. Although I knew there was no avoiding it, I snuck in the back door, quieter, I hoped, than a shadow.

"Johanna!" It was not a voice. It was thunder.

"What?" I answered weakly.

"What went on here last night? Some imbecile just came to the door and asked me for his teeth!"

That I survived is a tribute to the foresight of God Who handed down a commandment forbidding murder.

In a quixotic footnote, some weeks later I answered the door to find a grinning middle-aged man standing there.

"Is Wild Bill home?" he asked with enthusiasm.

"Wild Bill?" I asked incredulously, "Who do you mean? My Dad?"

"Hell, yes!" he laughed. "Just passing through–haven't seen him for years–but Wild Bill was known from coast to coast. Damn, we had fun!"

CHAPTER 5

My mother's story is also a part of who I am.

I was twelve when she went into the hospital for the first time. It was nothing serious but it exposed me to responsibility I had not had before. I did not carry it well. Mom did her housekeeping according to a rigid schedule, and she was meticulous. She began to give me more chores, but she usually redid what I had done. I wanted to see dirt before I cleaned. Mom preferred to anticipate dirt. I felt I could do the chores around my school and social schedule. Mom felt that vacuuming could only be done on Thursday, even if this was the day there was school bowling. I alternated between passive resistance and verbal resentment. She would begin the story: "When I was your age.... " an oft repeated saga I particularly hated to hear. I felt she was a fanatic. She felt I was incorrigible. We were probably both right.

Dad would go to Mom's defense and add a few chores of his own.

"Please plant these roses for me," he said one day, lugging in five roses, their roots tightly bound in several layers of burlap, "I don't have time."

"But I don't know how to plant roses," I rushed to say.

"You put them in the ground." he glowered at me. "That can't be too difficult".

"Okay," I thought to myself churlishly, "I'll do just that. I'll put them in the ground just as they are".

Which I did.

They died.

Later on, my mother recorded her memoirs of the days to come:

***

"December, 1955.

The winds tore down from the Crow's Nest Pass that day, careening through the streets of Lethbridge like comets, whirling the old snow into ivory tusks and jagged dunes. Trees whined in protest and old boots and garbage can lids formed low projectiles, bounding off gutters and buildings. But I was warm and secure in my bath, listening to the sounds of chatter from my two daughters down the hall. Mechanically I soaped and rinsed, enjoying the steaming hot water. Johanna says I have asbestos skin. She can't even handle the hot rinse water I use on my dishes. It's always a point of contention.

But suddenly I froze in all that hot water. *Was that a lump on my right breast? Surely not!* Always the radio and newspapers keep talking about the dark menace of cancer invading our society. Always they warn: examine your breasts, see your doctor regularly. But that is someone else's reality, not mine. *This could not be happening to me!* I got out of the bath carefully, deliberately, fighting panic, willing myself back into an ordinary day in my ordinary world. I almost succeeded, except for a tiny raw spot of uncertainty that kept on popping up, unbidden.

By February I went to see the doctor, complaining of two weeks of tiredness and edginess. He examined me with quick skilled hands.

"Do you know you have a lump on your right breast?" he asked carefully.

"Yes, I thought I did."

"When did you first notice it?"

"In December."

"Why didn't you come to see me right away?" his voice was displeased and incredulous.

"Because I didn't believe (didn't want to believe!) it was really there."

His eyebrows twitched up and down in agitation. I could see he was annoyed and disturbed by my attitude. Dr. Hunt was a big studious buffalo of a man, the prototype of a dedicated doctor, but not given to niceties. Still, beneath his brusqueness was a caring that had followed us through the years, a sentinel on the alert.

He left an appointment slip for the cancer clinic in my hand. I was angry. Something was wrong, but I knew it wasn't cancer. Surely not cancer!

The real reason for my tiredness and agitation became evident two days later. In his preoccupation with my lump Doctor Hunt had neglected my presenting symptoms, or at least had misinterpreted them. He failed to notice that I was pregnant! It had never occurred to me either. I was, after all, thirty-nine years old, my family half grown, and pregnancy was the farthest thing from my mind. But I began to hemorrhage badly and ended up in the hospital. It turned out that my miscarriage actually saved my life, because it was the symptoms of this that had finally brought me in to see the doctor.

Within days thereafter I could no longer deny I had a lump. In fact, I no longer had just one lump, but many, and my whole breast was rapidly becoming hard.

I returned to the hospital, scheduled for a biopsy.

As outlined to me it was a simple procedure. I was optimistic that my lumps were benign and paid scant attention to Dr. Hunt's attempts to inform me and prepare me should it happen that they were malignant.

I woke up with shock after the operation to find that I had had a radical mastectomy. My breast, underarm muscles, lymph nodes–all gone!

I still couldn't believe it.

"Why," I asked Dr. Hunt, "why did you do this? Why did you remove so much?"

"Pauline," he said, stopping me in my flight to unreality, "you do have cancer. There is absolutely no doubt about it. One look in the microscope confirmed it, even before the pathologist's report. Not only that, but you have the fastest growing strain. But I have to say that you are very lucky you came in when you did, because I feel confident that we've got it all."

It was only then that the truth finally began to filter in and I knew I must deal with this new path destiny had placed me on. I decided then I would fight my way back to health.

But I did feel sorry for myself, shut away alone in that muted pastel hospital room; mutilated, weak, disfigured. I tried to sleep but could not. Every noise, every shadow irked and tormented me. In the next room a man was moaning and carrying on at length.

"Just like a man," I complained to the nurse. "Can't take a bit of pain."

"That man," the nurse said gently, "just had his legs amputated."

At the beginning of April I began going five days a week for a series of twenty-six deep x-ray treatments. I looked at my hollow-eyed, transparent skinned brothers and sisters standing in line, and I said to myself, *I'm not like them. I'm not ever going to let myself become that sick!*

But I soon was. The nausea was different from the morning sickness of pregnancy. It was worse. A burning suffused me from within, dark and unquenchable. Halfway through the treatments I no longer wanted to live.

Dr. Hunt assured me, "If I build up your blood it will be a little easier."

And it was.

But still, from April to July, my spirit was pilloried in a dark hole from which it seemed impossible to emerge. Which only goes to show how myopic is our human vision. Eventually, however, the sun did begin to shine again and crowded into my hole of misery. One day I looked in the mirror at my sunken face and saw a new alertness in my eyes.

It's over, I said with relief. *It's all behind me now. I am a survivor.*

And yet...two weeks passed, with summer bringing back to me the ever fresh surprise of life. I decided to recondition those of my depleted muscles that remained by painting our new garden fence. It was a 'do or die' proposition. I nearly died. It was far more difficult than I had imagined. And as I felt the gentle breezes of summer caressing my neck, and bringing healing, I also became aware of an edginess, a tension in myself. My nerves jumped like cold drops of water hitting a hot pan. *Had my cancer returned?* A radio program put some of my fears in this regard to rest. It informed me that in the next fifteen to twenty-five years I would lose only a small fraction of the total radiation broadcast into my body. How could any cancer return to the site of this deadly radiation? *But, if not cancer, what?*

It took me two months to return to the doctor's office, with symptoms that increasingly aped those of my two previous miscarriages. Dr. Hunt looked at me thoughtfully and prescribed a pregnancy test.

It was two weeks before I heard from him again, which puzzled me a lot. When he finally called he said, "Do you know that your test is positive?"

"How wonderful," I reacted with relief. "I was so afraid it was cancer. At least," I joked, "I know pregnancy is not a fatal disease."

But Dr. Hunt did not laugh. He ordered me to his office at once.

His face and voice made me nervous.

"I've spent the last two weeks reading and covering everything I could find on cancer," he stated. "None of the specialists here with whom I've consulted have had a case like yours. The statistics I've turned up, however, indicate that 18 out of 25 women experience a reoccurrence of cancer during pregnancy. Pregnancy, as you know, releases powerful hormones which stimulate growth. In light of this, the safest course is to book you into the Municipal Hospital for a D and C."

"The Municipal Hospital?" I stuttered uncomprehendingly. All my previous surgery had been done at St. Michael's. "You know I've always gone to St. Michael's."

Dr. Hunt looked uneasily at his brother, and fellow physician, who had just entered the room in time, it seemed, to bolster his argument. "Well, you know, they won't allow this procedure at St. Michael's."

My antenna was up, but I was confused and in shock. Questions bounced helter-skelter through my mind, unformed, disjointed.

"You really have no alternative," the other Dr. Hunt was saying.

I faced the formidable duo and wondered how I could second-guess them. They had stood by me so faithfully, so tenderly, through so many terrible days. Now they were telling me that I had to have this thing done—but not at my own hospital! Could I question their judgment? But the questions came. In spite of myself the questions came.

The phone rang as I arrived home. It was my friend, Rose. But there was such a lump in my throat that all I could manage in greeting was a strangled squeak. She, with intuition and concern, promptly sent over our parish priest. Stumbling and incoherent, I somehow told him about the D and C. He didn't say anything. He just listened and looked at me gently. Then he patted a little book into my hand and asked me to read it. He explained that St. Michael's would not permit primary abortions for the destruction of a fetus, but only secondarily if it happened as a result of other treatment, such as the removal of a tumor in the uterus.

By myself later my mind was still in disarray, seemingly unable to focus on the issue at hand. Abortion, Father Thompson called it, not merely a D and C. Aimlessly, I picked up the book he had given me and a page fell open randomly in my hands. As if charged with electricity the words seemed to leap alive off the page: "Thou shalt not kill."

Suddenly the tension was gone and the roadway ahead was clear. By a wonderful mercy I was able to fall into a deep and peaceful sleep. The next morning my husband, Bill, asked me anxiously, "Are you going ahead with it?"

"No, I'm not," I said, floating on my cloud of serenity.

"I'm so glad," he said, eyes shining, coming over to enclose me in his arms.

Dr. Hunt's reaction was not so ecstatic. He was angry.

"Do you know what you are doing?" he asked. "Don't you want to live for your two girls? Is this what your Pope wants?"

"The Pope has nothing to do with it," I replied evenly. "It's a law of God."

He stepped back as if he had been slapped. I felt bad because I knew him to be a good and conscientious doctor.

"If that's the way you feel about it...." he said, and fell silent.

The months dragged by grudgingly through a long and deadly winter. As the doctor had warned, it was not an easy pregnancy. I developed complications requiring blood transfusions, and a worrying kidney condition. Nevertheless, I somehow did carry the baby to full term. Because my two girls had been born by caesarian section, Dr. Hunt began to plan for my third caesarian.

"Do you want your surgery on Friday the 13th?" he asked quizzically, "or are you superstitious?"

"I don't care," I laughed.

He pushed it ahead to Monday anyway.

"You know, while I am at it I should do a tubal ligation," he said. "You shouldn't push your luck. With your poor health you would never survive a fourth caesarian."

"Oh," I laughed it off, "I'm forty years old. I don't think there's much chance of that."

"On the contrary, I've just had a fifty year old woman who had a miscarriage."

"Still, I just don't feel good about it," I shrugged.

Dr. Hunt shook his head in wonder and let the subject drop.

Thursday night I began to feel pain and to pass blood.

"What are labor pains like?" I asked my nurse casually.

Dr. Hunt bounded into the room.

"What about those pains?" he demanded abruptly.

The pains followed me through that mild April night, and the next morning I was wheeled into surgery.

It was mid-afternoon before I began to return to consciousness. It had taken the doctors two and a half hours to clear out all my adhesions as well as deliver the baby, so it was an impatient husband who sat fidgeting by my side. As he saw me reaching through my grogginess, he said softly but triumphantly, "Do you know we have a son?"

A son! Long awaited, long desired! My heart skipped and sang.

"Now we have everything! A good marriage, two beautiful daughters, and now, at last, a son."

Both of us had come from large families of boys, and I had always assumed I would have sons as well to carry on the family pranks and the family business. Now we did have one of our own!

I drifted back contentedly to my sedated sleep. Gradually I became aware through the haze that Sister Cordis was trying to talk to me. It was awhile before her words broke through.

"The baby is not well, Pauline, but we are fighting for him. We are doing everything that is possible."

I managed to ask, "If he survives the night, will he be alright?"

"Yes, he will, if he survives the night."

And the waves of sleep overpowered me again.

The chaplain's voice was the next to nudge my foggy brain.

"We may have to baptize the baby," he was saying.

But the words never really registered. I felt like I was just having a dream.

But we awake from all dreams, and I was suddenly, chillingly aware that I was awake and alone in my room. Where was my husband? Home feeding the girls? But if the baby needed baptizing wouldn't he be here? It was so confusing...

Suddenly I saw Sister Mary Peter standing in the door of the room, a ruddy faced colossus of a woman, with tears streaming down her face.

"To think I would have to be the one to tell you," she cried.

When I saw her face I knew our son had died. It was not a dream.

"Where's Bill? Does he know?" I asked.

"He's been in the hospital all the time, but he's been too broken up to come and face you. Father Thompson and the doctor have been with him."

Her red rimmed eyes told me more than her words had. It was bad. Bill had survived the Battle of Britain with negligible scars. He had stood by his buddies as they fell like wheat, their life's blood mingling into a single river of death called war. But to lose his son?

"Please, Sister Mary Peter, please tell him to come and see me. I want to see him."

It was midnight when I looked up to see his clouded eyes, and I said, "It's all right. IT WAS NEVER MEANT TO BE. That kind of happiness was not intended for this world. Perhaps it is only a foretaste, a prelude, a promise...."

I could see the weight perceptibly rolling from his back. Could it be that it was my reaction that he most feared? As the more emotional of the two of us, did he fear that I could not field this latest blow? My words fell on him like balm, like quiet cleansing rain when the storm has passed.

Sorrow mingled with relief as I looked at him. *I have accepted this well, realistically,*, I congratulated myself. I was little prepared for the tidal wave of bitterness that flowed over me the following day. It was precipitated and unleashed by a magazine article. Thinking I would be wise to keep my mind healthily diverted, I purposefully picked up a magazine to read. The words of a title jolted me: "40,000 UNWANTED BABIES". In Japan, in a country that had no room for children of mixed parentage, there were 40,000 unwanted G.I. babies. It struck bone. I wanted my baby more than anything–but I didn't have a choice. Somewhere there were 40,000 children that no one wanted. How could it be? It was like Satan's cruel finger taunting me, rubbing salt into my open wound. It seemed my heart would collapse as our baby's lungs had collapsed.

Why, God, why? I cried over and over again. *Why our son? Why us? How could you do it? How cruel,* I accused God. *You knew... You know all things... I risked my life.... You know how much we wanted that baby!*

The questions kept pounding through my head and heart like unremitting hammers, while I crawled into my private crevasse of despair. I guess it was exhaustion that downed me at last. In any event, out of that dark death of my hopes and dreams I began to see a new road emerging.

When my husband visited me the following day I said to him, "I hope we can adopt a boy, if my health improves. I want to adopt a boy who would be the same age as our son would have been."

Little could I have foreseen how God would answer this prayer long after I had forgotten making it myself.

This fledgling hope and prayer gave me the incentive and motivation to help myself, and to try to get better as soon as possible. I beat a path to the bathroom rather than face the dreaded catheter, and the kidney condition that had haunted me began to abate. I felt buoyed up, almost tangibly, on the prayers of others, especially those of the Sisters at the hospital. When Sister Mary Peter wanted to put some extra punch in her prayers, she would give up her favorite weakness, marachino chocolates. Only God knows how many marachino chocolates she gave up on my account!

Soon I was caught up in the whirl of life, the foibles of my teenager and the growing pains of Sandy, and life returned to a sense of normalcy that I had almost forgotten. Fifteen months later I began to have an odd familiar feeling. It felt like pregnancy.

Oh, oh! I thought in alarm, how *am I going to tell the doctor?* Somehow the fear of a pregnancy at 41, after everything I had been through, was overshadowed by the fear of facing him. It took me three months to work up the courage to make an appointment.

Dr. Hunt was amazingly calm. Perhaps he had given up on me and become resigned to his headstrong patient. Maybe he was just having a good day. It was a big relief to me; no more dire predictions, no heated encounters.

For my part, I thought to myself, *God took our son because He knew he could never be well, but now He intends to send us another son.*

It was a blissful pregnancy. I had no problems at all. My kidneys held out, I did not accumulate a lot of fluid, and this time I carried my baby comfortably without stress or strain. Dewdrops glistened expectantly on our tulips and daffodils as I entered the hospital to have my fourth caesarian, almost two years to the day of the birth and death of our little son. My husband joked as I went into surgery that this time I should just have them install a zipper.

My calm was shattered on the operating table. Under the influence of the spinal I was numb, but conscious, and heard with alarm the sharp intake of breath as they opened me up.

"Oh my God, what a hell of a mess!" one of the doctors exclaimed.

Cancer, I thought, *I'm full of cancer!*

Just before I was put under I heard: "Here's a leg. It's a girl."

Baby June dazzled me. She was perfect and looked up into my eyes with such a vivid recognition that I was startled. Never had I had a baby so aware as a newborn.

There is some reason she had to be a girl, I thought.

But there was still a knot sitting in my stomach waiting to be untied. I waited anxiously for the doctor's visit. He couldn't understand what I was alarmed about. Obviously he was unaware of what I had heard on the operating table. As I repeated the words to him he looked at me soberly.

"I hope I never have to do another operation like that. It was like fighting for time trying to cut through a dense jungle. All your internal organs were entirely buried and overgrown with adhesions. I have never seen anything like that before. But no, there is no cancer."

So often I have tried to figure out the Mind of God and His plan for me and have failed miserably. But I don't doubt now that there is a plan. Perhaps I am the heroine of my own novel! As a life-long reader, how often I have escaped into the adventures of others, experiencing vicariously the trials and challenges of others, watching as some hero, great or small, duels with and rises above adversity. There would be no story without conflict, no growth without challenge. I think I am better because of everything that has happened to me. And now, I wonder what the Author of Life has to say in the chapters that still have to be written?"

***

During my Mom's travails I was often numb, wishing neither to see the future, nor to live in the present. I threw myself into my successes at school and kept my other feelings closely under wraps. How well I succeeded at my camouflage was brought home to me with bitter irony one day when a boy sitting in front of me in class turned and said to me in annoyance, "What's the matter with you? You're always smiling."

But I did little smiling inside. Life was tense. Mom and Dad and I continued our dance like unmatched partners, stepping on each other's feet. When Mom arrived home from the hospital three days early she found the house in disarray and I came home to find her in tears. My life seemed to be a comedy of errors.

I do remember with warmth and appreciation the food and the special words of comfort that our neighbors extended. I was especially touched by Mrs. Lev, my friend Rosalind's mother. She was a nervous mother who suffered constant head-aches, worried that Rosalind would get into trouble, worried about her husband's unemployment, worried about everything. I can still see the day Mrs. Lev was mixing up some of her marvelous poppyseed cookies and Rosalind came home with a poor report card.

"What do you have to say about this? How do you explain this?" she shook the offending paper in dismay at Rosalind.

"Heredity!" yelled Rosalind, heading out of the door with her mother in hot pursuit waving her wooden spoon.

But for all her worries she found time to send over food and to reach out to us in our worries.

My sister, Sandy, seemed invulnerable to most of the things that gave me pain. Because she was so much younger she could leave the heavies to me. We got along like most siblings; our relationship swung between affection and fury. Sandy, a scrawny, scrappy bundle of action, preferred to ignore the differences in our ages and aped everything I did. This became hugely annoying in my teens when I would bring home a boyfriend and she would stick to him like crazy glue. She would bat her eyelashes furiously and coach the embarrassed boy, "Why don't you give her a kiss?" And then her pet rabbit, whether because he was jealous or because he wanted to place a claim on him too, would circle the stunned boy and spray him. Not many relationships survived that kind of initiation!

But Sandy's teachers, and just about everyone else, thought the world of Sandy. When she had to miss a piano lesson, Mr. Barrows would mourn, "Oh, how can I get through the day without her? She's my sunshine, my bright spot!"

This certainly came as a shocker to my mother. With her boundless energy Sandy more frequently had Mom in tears then in stitches.

"Sandy," she asked her one day, puzzled, "how is it that everyone says such good things about you, yet I seldom see that side of you at home?"

Sandy looked at her with that special look of patience that is reserved for someone who does not understand a very elementary fact.

"Mom," she explained, "I have a good side and a bad side, and the good side gets all used up when I'm out."

It was the truth.

When Baby June arrived, just before I turned sixteen, she found three mothers, as it were, to dote over her; Mom, Sandy and I. Responding to all the attention, full of the joy of life, she toddled through life like an innocent, animated cartoon, doling out love and affection inexhaustibly. She was her own unique self. Not for her the swings and slides at the playground; she was hooked on the water fountain. In chagrin we would spend an afternoon standing in line fourteen times. She was also hooked on music. Sandy became her special teacher, singing to her and pulling her highchair next to the piano while she played. For this we would pay the price. Come Saturday morning, when we wanted to sleep in, June would descend upon us, with the imperative enthusiasm of new life, demanding, "Mucus (meaning music)! Dance!" and everyone would have to tumble out of bed to dance.

Dancing was Sandy's passion too. She had always begged Mom to take ballet, but there was no qualified ballet school in town at the time. To her delight, however, she made friends with a girl named Sue who had recently moved from Regina, and Sue already had five years of ballet. The two girls became fast friends, and Sue set out to teach Sandy everything she knew.

During Sandy's eleventh summer she was required to get a routine medical done for summer camp. She had gone to camp the summer before and had found her element there. Athletic and outgoing, she excelled in swimming and skits, and her exploits became part of the camp lore. But when she came out of the doctor's office that day she was pale and shaking with anger. Doctor Hunt had found a bladder infection and said she was not well enough to go to camp that year. Sandy could neither understand nor accept this, and life was pretty difficult around our house when Sandy's friends all left for camp without her. But gradually her anger ebbed, if for no other reason than she no longer had the energy to be angry. For her birthday on August 25, I tried to help make it up to her by planning the biggest birthday party of her life. Sandy reacted wanly, and after a brief appearance at her party she wandered off and spent the afternoon in bed. Then I knew that Sandy was really ill.

Her infection had proved difficult to treat, and after further testing Dr. Hunt had determined that she also had infected kidneys. Aggressive treatment did not produce the desired effect. The doctors were puzzled. In

October we had an appointment for our first ever family portrait. Sandy and Mom were late in arriving at the studio because of an appointment with a specialist. When they finally showed up, Mom's face registered strain. In tow, like a rag of a person, was my sister, her eyes tortured and bleak.

Sandy had gone in for the appointment sassy and bold. The doctor told her that she had nephritis, a chronic condition for which there was no cure. However, he hoped to control it and make it manageable by a strict curtailment of all her activities and diet. No more sports, no more dancing.

Rebelliously Sandy burst forth, "And what will happen if I don't follow all these rules?"

The answer was direct and unexpected: "You will die."

Every time I look at that picture I relive that day. Gaunt and taut, Sandy's face looks like a hunted wolf.

The doctor said that the nephritis had been caused by a strep infection that had become chronic and gone underground. In such cases the strep will either attack the heart, causing rheumatic fever, or the kidneys, as was Sandy's case. I thought back to the strep throat that Sandy had had that spring, after a winter of swimming lessons, and waiting for the bus on those frigid January and February days. She had been given an antibiotic, and in time we thought she had recovered. Then I remembered back to the previous Halloween. Had I unwittingly set this whole thing in motion? I had volunteered to set up for the party at school and had to be there early. Dad had dropped us off, but it turned out the janitor was very late. It was a howling, bitter night and the wind reached through our jackets to chill our bones. We gasped and huddled together as the cold air cut into our lungs. It seemed the janitor would never come. But Sandy was worse off than I was. I had dressed in the big floppy clothes of a hobo, but under her jacket Sandy wore only the flimsy Tinkerbell costume I had made for her. She came down with a strep throat right after that.

Unbeknownst to us, with this simple night of fun, Sandy crossed a bridge and turned a corner from which there would be no turning back.

CHAPTER 6

As I headed down Twentieth Street toward Seventh Avenue, my well worn route from school, the sun felt sweet on my neck and I wondered what Mom had cooking for dinner. Mom was a superb cook, and except for French Canadian pea soup which I detested, she daily filled our home with aromas to die for. Our relationship had improved over the past year, perhaps because now Mom talked to me more like an ally, sharing her worries and vulnerabilities as well as her happy thoughts. I'm not sure how, or why, or through what soul searching, this change had come to be, but its effect was like magic. Perhaps she realized I was no longer a child, or even a recalcitrant teen, but now I was a person in my own right, with something to offer. It made me feel more responsible for her happiness, and more willing to go the extra mile.

As I turned the corner my street came into view and I froze into a statue. Another accident! The third in as many months! Why suddenly had my corner become the focus for car accidents? Last month it was our Student Council president and his sweetheart. Now again there was glass everywhere. A baby had been thrown through the front window and landed on the boulevard. A woman paced back and forth, back and forth, talking frenetically to herself, seeing no one. A knife had sliced through this ordinary spring day, uncovering the stark reality of death. The atmosphere was charged with electricity. The hunks of twisted metal that were cars lay abandoned, and ambulance attendants scooped up the remains of the bodies.

My stomach felt sick and sore. This was no longer an ordinary day. The fabric of the day had been ripped apart. What did it really matter what my mother had cooking on the stove? Is there really any such thing as ordinary? Does ordinary even exist?

I walked home in a daze, past the wreckage, powerless. The haunting words of a psalm wrapped themselves around my consciousness and echoed in the wind:

"Man's days are like grass;
Like a flower of the field he blooms;
The wind sweeps over him and he is gone,

59

And his place knows him no more.
But the kindness of the Lord is from eternity to
eternity...." (Psalm 103:15-17)

In the night I took a walk beneath the stars to mull and think. Here I found reality again. But it was a different reality than the world of my school, my play, my work. Here the walls of everyday retreated and my spirit expanded to touch infinity. I sensed a benign, awesome and reassuring Presence.

What do You want me to do, Lord? I cried.

I longed to be independent, and I feared it too. The time was coming to take charge of my life, and I grieved for the irrevocable passing of the years. My father was worried about me, convinced from my outward demeanor that I was losing my faith. One day in anger and frustration he shouted at me:

"I would rather see you dead than lose your faith!"

He could not understand that I was on my own journey (and I was not about to tell him!). My relationship with God had to come from within me.

In those halcyon days of the late fifties, the mad race for materialism was on. The post war prosperity had brought comfort and ease. Science promised answers for every human need. There seemed little motivation to follow old rules and restrictions. Headlines would soon proclaim "God is Dead!" Heroes would be replaced with the unkempt face of the anti-hero. We were at the dawn of the 'Me' generation. It wasn't sex that was the big taboo, it was any discussion of spirituality, of our inner lives. Reality was only to be thought of as that which we could see and quantify. 'Me' was just a surface thing. While Moses had disappeared up the mountain to commune with the unseen God, our people had built a golden calf of the here and now. From the Catholic school I attended I had acquired the necessary guidelines and knowledge, but there was a gap between me and the God of glorious hope I had been introduced to. I watched my peers wrestle with guilt over their sexuality. They felt they had two choices: either to repudiate the Church as they knew it, or to repudiate themselves. Many repudiated the Church, or step by step walked away until the Voice of God was only a dim memory. I myself had not blazed any glorious new trails of morality.

Still, when the moonlight poured into my basement window, there were many nights I could not sleep. I would fall onto my knees and wrestle in tears and secrecy like a Jacob of today's world with that ancient angel. Sure I was having fun—or was I? The excitement of living for the next big party, falling in and out of love.... How tawdry it seemed at times. How blank in between. How could I forsake the Christ Who had walked with me over bumpy and lonely roads? I had too many bruises from life to think I could do it myself. I knew, ultimately, that every party would end. I had come into this world alone and I would exit it the same way. There had been constant reminders, like the accidents, reminding me that life was more than just having a good time. I realized with awful finality that my life is the only investment I have, to gain or to lose.

"What does it profit a man to gain the whole world and suffer the loss of his own soul?" Christ had asked.

The question burned inside. *What was I doing?* I deplored the evil and lack of real love, the corruption and imperfections of my world. But I saw this same weakness, this same corruption in myself. I saw that I was being sucked up into the very vortex of the evil I hated. I was no better, no stronger than anyone else. How I longed for the warmth of a lover's arms, someone to bring me comfort and peace and take me away from it all—but more, I feared for the loss of my own soul.

How could I make right what was wrong in my life?

"Though your sins are as scarlet, they will be made whiter than snow," Christ had said. How many times I had pulled myself to Confession with dry mouth and sweaty palms and come out renewed, light, free and dancing. My experience told me that Christ had given us the gift of new beginnings. If I botched up my painting He would lean down in love and give me a new canvas to work on. The nuns at school had told us that there were two ways we might experience sorrow and rebirth: the first, a less perfect way, by regretting our behavior because it might cost us our soul. I had certainly experienced that. But the second, perfect contrition, perfect repentance, is being sorry for sin because it offends God, Who is all Good. I had trouble with that. I wasn't at all sure I knew what perfect Good was. It certainly lay outside my experience. I wanted to do things right. The Presence I had sensed in my life was certainly comforting and protective, but Perfect Goodness? What was that? What did it mean? The myopia in my eyes existed also in my soul. The world I could see at close range offered me no perfect models that I could clutch with my hands and with which I could educate my heart.

Yet because I had seen beauty, I knew that Beauty existed. Because I had caught a glimpse of truth, I knew Truth existed. Because I had been touched by love, I knew Love existed.

I knew instinctively that I would never be happy until I had reached that Perfect Love. I had hungered for it since I was a five year old girl wandering around desolately in Ituna. This is the real lottery, I knew. This is the jackpot. But, how far off I was.

If Miss Lacey, my formidable but fair grade three teacher, had rewarded our every good striving, I felt He would too. Could He be less loving, less accepting, than His creatures?

What would I have to give for His Joy? *Everything that I am....*

But how? I needed solid guidance, a sure and proven way. Christ said that He was the Way, the Truth and the Life. I felt my best bet was in tagging along with those who were giving their lives to follow Him. Neither the nuns at school nor at the hospital struck a resonant chord in me. But one night, at a dance, a group of us ran into an old acquaintance who used to hang around the ballpark.

"Pat, where have you been? We haven't seen you for ages!"

"Well, actually, I'm on the run," she said, looking around furtively. "I was placed in the Good Shepherd Home in Edmonton, but I ran away."

"No kidding! What was it like there? I've heard the nuns there have dungeons and they make you wear a ball and chain," one girl burst out eagerly.

"No, no, it's actually not bad. There's school, sports, TV...its okay. But I missed my friends."

I was intrigued. Was this something for me? I did not feel cut out to teach or to nurse, but dealing with people's psychological agonies–that I could identify with. I'd been there. I would look into this.

Self-consciously I phoned our parish priest. The name Pat had given us was inexact–it was actually a nickname. However, he got me the correct address.

Weeks later I arrived in Edmonton by Greyhound and gave the address to a young cabbie.

"Are you one of the girls there?" the cabbie asked.

"No," I hesitated awkwardly, "I'm going to become a nun."

The cabbie nearly hit a tree. He looked back in alarm.

"Why would you want to do that? Can't you get a boyfriend?" He switched off the meter. "You're good looking. How old are you?"

"Seventeen," I answered.

"That's much too young to make up your mind!"

I wondered nervously why he had turned off the meter. But I soon saw that he had found himself a mission: to turn me away from this wild idea. My mother had tried too. Only after I assured him that this was only a visit did he switch the meter back on and drive me to the address.

"Well then, you'll see for yourself," he said.

The Sisters were exquisitely kind to me, feeding me, talking to me and asking me questions. A cloistered monastic Order, they had been founded four hundred years before by St. John Eudes to care for those girls who were society's cast offs. In addition to the three vows of poverty, chastity and obedience, they took a fourth vow to dedicate their lives to the care of these girls. They wore long graceful creamy white habits, with a full length panel that swung free front and back and this was called a scapular. Professed nuns wore back veils and a silver embossed heart. The Novices I saw walking around wore white veils.

In order to enter a Roman Catholic Order, I also had to get a dispensation from the Ukrainian Metropolitan, since I was born into the Byzantine rite.

"Why is that?" I asked.

"The day will come when communism will fall and we will be called upon to help our oppressed people. We must preserve our language and faith culture so we can be there for them on that day."

The iron curtain did not seem in eminent danger of collapse to me.

"I don't even speak Ukrainian," I said, "and I have been raised mostly in the Roman Catholic rite," I explained.

I got my dispensation.

November 11, 1959, was a morning remarkable for its utter cold. On that day I had the last breakfast I would ever have in my home on Twenty First Street. Like a metronome, the moments, the days, the weeks had ticked off, and I was keenly aware that everything was for the last time. It seemed like dying. Dad was going to accompany me. Baby June cried a lot as we fought the merciless wind toward the train station. My sister, Sandy, was in the hospital. My throat was tight, conversation impossible, the wind slashing my tears into trickles of ice. I lowered my head as I entered the railway car, hoping that no one would recognize me, that no one would ask me a question. Resolutely I sat down and faced the window. Within moments we were going over the High Level Bridge, the highest bridge for its length in the world. Below, the tiny, snowy outlines of bushes and trees passed by, and the odd building, and the slow river choked with ice, so dwarfed and inconsequential. I saw the snowy ropes above the river where I had risked my life swinging. All the sorrows and joys of my life passed by. That small world below that I had been so immersed in, so bewildered by, so hurt by, so familiar with, was, after all, so small, like a cardboard village that could be forgotten in a corner.

Soon we were traveling over a wide open plain of crisp unremitting cold, the clickety-clack of the train rushing me relentlessly toward my destination. Fittingly, somehow, the heat went off in the cars for several hours as if to snuff out the last of the old life that remained to me.

We rang the doorbell, staring at the stern curtainless windows, and at the world of snow around us, a howling desert as removed from time and space as the landscape of a foreign planet. Dad left me there in the visitor's room with an older Sister, whose bulky ankles protruded out of a patchy yellowed habit, once white. This turned out to be my Superior, Mother Immaculate Heart, who I grew to esteem as one of the great women of the Church. In my hands Dad awkwardly left a box of chocolates. Though ordinarily I have an enthusiastic sweet tooth, these chocolates somehow seemed like an intrusion from another world.

I was next introduced to Sister Divine Heart, the new Directoress of the Novitiate, whom I had met in the blur of my visit. One of the first questions she asked me was, "Do you like to pray?"

I hesitated a second, then decided I should be truthful. Despite the evenings in my room on my knees, despite my church attendance, praying was not the first thing that came into my mind when I thought of having a good time. So I answered "no". I remember how I dreaded saying the rosary with my family when I was little. I always lost track of where we were and I would get into trouble for daydreaming. In actual fact, what did

I know about prayer? Pious was never a word that was used to describe me. I could imagine the shock waves in Lethbridge when the word got out that I had entered a monastery.

Sister Divine Heart promptly handed me a little book which she asked me to read, and when some thought in it grabbed me, I was to sit and soak in it like a tea bag. So there I sat in the dark chapel, lit only by a single light over my pew, while the other Sisters, I am sure, were planning what to do with this strange duck. Recognition hit me like a bolt of lightning as I looked at the title of the book: 'The Imitation of Christ'—it was the same book an aunt, who was a nun, had sent me a year or two before. I had looked at it apathetically then, thought 'Borrring!' and thrown it to the back of my closet, never even opening the cover. How ironic! God, have you a sense of humor, or are you trying to tell me something? Well, perhaps now I should listen and give it a try. In any event, if I am turning over a new leaf, I must be open to the guidance of God. And as I slipped effortlessly through the pages, to my shock and amazement, I found that the author, who had lived a thousand years ago, was reading my heart today. I was exposed, exhorted, lifted up!

There were several stages to go through before becoming a full fledged nun. The first stage is postulancy. For this period of six months or more I was outfitted in a mid-calf length black dress with a black cape, the most gawdawful thing I had ever laid eyes on. I gulped as I put it on, and cringed even further when I was adorned with a short black veil with a white rim, which was held uncertainly in place by an elastic band. I had always been a little self conscious about my looks, feeling I was a tad short of Elizabeth Taylor. With this outfit I was afraid my vanity was dying by lethal injection.

After this, with the approval of the whole community of professed nuns, at a ceremony that was my betrothal to Christ, I would be adorned in a wedding dress and given the white Habit of the Order, including the white veil that identified me as a Novice in training. I liked the Habit; unlike the garb of postulancy, it was flowing and graceful, even flattering. The canonical year then stood before me. It was the first of the two years of the Novitiate, and was devoted to prayer and reflection, to study and discernment, to determine if one is suited for religious life. During the second year the candidate is exposed to the work of the Order, and to more study. At the end of two years the community again votes, and if the candidate wishes, with the permission of the community, she is invited to take her first temporary vows. These usually last for three years, but can be extended, before final vows are taken.

It turned out not to be the solemn world I had supposed, peopled by driven saints with an ascetic agenda. I learned that the joy of heaven must begin on earth, and to laugh at one's self is a very fine sort of asceticism. My ideas of religious life, so clear to me, were very funny to the other Sisters. I had based all my 'knowledge' on such dubious books as 'I Jumped Over the Wall', and it stretched their diplomacy to the snapping point when I sent all my bras home. They very kindly informed me that the basic trust we were counseled to have in heavenly support, did not extend to this basic undergarment.

At the confluence of two halls, beside some stairs, was a large gong, much like the one in the old J. Arthur Rank movies. This was struck by a wooden mallet, and this bell called us to the different functions of our lives. In short order I was assigned the duty of ringing this bell, an honor which was bestowed on me, I suspect, for the purpose of getting me to think in terms of punctuality. Easily distracted from my task, the Sisters in the Novitiate would play the Lone Ranger theme from the William Tell Overture as I sprinted madly down the hall, hoping the Superior had not looked at her watch.

Our daily schedule began with this bell at 5:30 a.m. By 6:00 a.m. we were to be in the chapel to chant Matins and Lauds, the official morning prayer of the Church. A double row of choir stalls faced each other on each side of the chapel, and Sisters were assigned by turn to go to the center of the chapel to lead the prayers. I loved chanting the Office, which was composed mostly of psalms from the book of Psalms from the Old Testament. We marked the hours of the day five times a day, as the voice of all mankind, bringing to God the sorrow and needs and praise of His people. Whether in the predawn darkness or the golden glow of dusk, we prayed for all who did not pray, but who yearned to be filled. I felt I was a part of the gigantic plan of God, lending my voice to the great communion of saints in heaven and on earth. Although this was a solemn event, and maybe because it was such a solemn event, on occasion something funny would happen, and in the attempt to stifle our laughter, we would end up exploding. Ripples of shaking would move along the lines of Sisters until the Superior would give up on us and say;

"Alright, Sisters, go say your Office in particular," which meant we would say it privately that day.

I really think God was in on the joke most times. After all, who but the Almighty would allow that Sister Gertrude, our resident mathematician, and the absolute epitomy of primness and propriety, would lose her skirt as she officiated in choir. Had it happened to one of us, we would have laughed. That it happened to Sister Gertrude sent us into spasms of hysteria.

After the morning Office we would meditate for a half hour, followed by Mass and breakfast time. Breakfast was held downstairs in the Sisters' dining room, called the 'refectory', and would consist of a buffet of toast, cereal, porridge or eggs, depending on the day. Before we got down to the chores of the day we would return to chapel to chant the 'little hours': Tierce, Sext and None. In the early days my chores brought me back down to look after the Sister's refectory. The Sisters' quarters were strictly cloistered and no one else was allowed to enter, and so was the Sisters' refectory–with one exception. Gladys had come to live with the Sisters thirty years before. One of a set of twins, she had been brain damaged during a difficult birth, and was abandoned to the Sisters. Gladys never let that hold her back. She was a loveable, irascible, wiry old lady with a head covered with what looked like an SOS pad. She moved down the hall with the alacrity of a storm trooper, and was accorded more privileges than a Cardinal. Although she could not read or write, her brain functioned well enough on an everyday level to do small tasks, and thus she was my 'helper' in the refectory. This suited her fine because her main aim in life was to get in the thick of everything going on. When she loved, she loved faithfully and ferociously, and we would all hear about it. Whoever did her a good turn won her enduring and outspoken friendship. Her various preferences among the Sisters were a source of great amusement and teasing, and the Sisters would bicker in front of Gladys just to get her ire up, until she was provoked enough to straighten them all out. Her favorite and eternal saying was "Big deal!" It was her pronouncement and her judgment on all the 'affairs of state' in the convent. She loved to be teased and her eyes were quick and merry. When she found you out she would grab your arm with both bony hands and exclaim, "Oh Mudder!" chuckling and laughing. The most outlandish thing we ever pulled on her was at the election for a new Superior. The convent had a German shepherd named Chief, and we convinced her that since Sister Immaculate Heart had worked so hard all these years, she deserved a rest, but none of the other Sisters wanted all that responsibility either. Since Gladys said "no way" to being Superior, we had elected the dog, Chief. Gladys believed us–almost. In any case, she was beside herself with curiosity. The only time she was not allowed in the refectory was when the Sisters were assembled there. But she desperately wanted to see who was sitting in the Superior's chair. The votes were hardly tallied when the doors swung wide open and there stood Gladys indignantly, uttering a resounding "Big deal!"

After lunch we had 'obedience', a little ceremony in which charges (jobs) were assigned or changed, and this was followed by a short period of recreation. Classes or work took up the rest of the afternoon, with the exception of a half hour of spiritual reading. Vespers were said at five, followed by a half hour of meditation. During supper we generally had someone read aloud, except when the Superior uttered the welcome words "Blessed be God". This was the signal to talk, and general pandemonium broke forth. From supper to 8:15 we had recreation. We would play games, walk, roller-skate, play badminton, work on sewing, art or handicrafts. During this time, once or twice, the Sisters would take turns reminding each other of the presence of God. This took two forms; either a simple reminder, or a short quote from scripture. This simple exercise was invaluable to me. Soon I felt that God was with me in all aspects of my day. I no longer had to look for Him; He was there. The study of our Rule of life also assured me that when I was doing what was required of me I was doing the Will of God. After the isolation and some of the questionable turns my life had taken, there was a tremendous freedom and joy in feeling I was in the right place at the right time, blending my being with Universal Harmony. This belief made all of us feel light hearted and carefree, and was, I think, responsible for a lot of the spontaneous fun we had. Even the nightly reminders sometimes took a silly turn. One day mischievous Sr. Michael took her turn, solemnly intoning the words from Scripture: "He stinketh." As we did a double take, she tossed her head and defended her choice: "Lazarus—after three days in the tomb. Martha." Or occasionally on a hot day there was a plaintive, "I thirst!", and the Directoress of the Novitiate would smile and treat us to a bottle of pop.

As an exercise in the Novitiate to train us in the spirit of obedience we asked for small permissions. Because of the totally routine nature of these permissions, it was our theory that Sister Divine Heart never heard a word we said. So to test this out one day Sr. Nicholas asked casually:

"Mother, may I go out and sit on the incinerator?"

"Yes, Sister," came the unwavering reply.

At 8:15 we had Compline, a short night Office, and from then till morning it was the Grand Silence, which was to be broken only for needs of charity. Of course, those Sisters directly employed with the girls were dispensed while they were with them.

Except for the news from home, these were serene days. How different from the situation I now find myself in!

CHAPTER 7

The seasons were measured in changes of medication. The pulse of the family was telescoped into the sound of spraying gravel as the car left the driveway to the soft roll of Sandy's wheelchair down the hospital corridors.

The chronicles of these wheelchair voyages reached me in the monastery in a series of letters:

***

At Home
Lethbridge, Alberta

January 27, 1960

Dear Unfunny Sister,

I'm glad you miss me cause then you'll appreciate me when I come down. Now be prepared cause I'm going to flatter you so that no dog will eat me up when I go down there. I don't exactly mustard (or do I mean relish?) the idea of being eaten alive. Now you'd better not show this letter to the other Sisters cause they are liable to get some weird idea that I'm some sort of monster with a disastrous streak in me. When I get off the train in Edmonton they'll probably have a cage sitting and waiting for me.

Brian's sister is too at the hospital.

I hope my blood goes down because a few days ago I got to go downstairs and I played tag with Holly (one of two foster children Mom was looking after) and June. Talking about June, I asked her who was nice and she said, "Dandah" (translated means Johanna). June is getting very fond of walking around without her clothes. And when you ask her sometimes who wet her pants, she answers, "Dandah". Now, why did you wet her pants?

By the way, you said you were a religious. A religious what?

You'd better quit bragging about those popcorn balls and candy you make or I'll make you send me some. (I wouldn't mind if you sent some anyway though).

I'm trying to be a little more prompt so I hope you appreciate it. You act like I wrote every century or something. Well, you must realize that I have only all day to write but I just can't find the time.

Honey just got home from school and June and Mom just woke up so things will start rolling so I'd better go now.

Bye for now,
Signed,
Your goofy sister,
SANDRA

***

St. Michael's hospital

February 16

Dear Johanna,

What's the big idea! I did write you a letter but maybe the lady at the hospital didn't mail it. Do you know I could have gone ahead to grade eight if I hadn't gotten sick, and I still might because I'm so smart?

No, I'm not giving the nurses a hard time. I'm a pleasure to have around I'll have you know. Tomorrow the doctor might let me go home, and then he might not. It all depends on my blood test which he is going to look at this afternoon. Today everyone had to get needles for Jondis, or Jontis, or whatever you call it, that makes you turn yellow, and I got one right in the place that holds me up. I've been in already two weeks this time, and only Pat and Mary have come up to see me and they brought their report cards.

Pat rose from 17th place in the class to 6th. I wonder what my standing would be.

The little girl, Barbie, that's in with me has to go to Calgary for an operation on her kidneys.

Oh yes, sister dear, I can't eat those candies, etc. that you sent. No candies, pop, popcorn, chips or anything except 42,358 eggnocks. Mom and Dad brought me some wheat and rice crackers that are good though.

Mom says you don't look too funny but I'll have to decide that for myself. When I get better I'll be coming down there, so you better tell the Sisters to get a medical to make sure they can manage me. But I can imagine what it takes to put up with you, so they'll probably be prepared. Now don't get killed on that toboggan cause I want to go up there and see if you look funny.

'bye for now,
Signed
Your cute sister,
Sandy

P.S. How do they ever get you up in the morning?

***

St. Michael's Hospital
Just before dinner
Tuesday (April)

Dear Sister Mary Etc. Etc. (Johanna)

Have you broken into your new collection of names yet? I mean did they hit you with a bottle of champagne and paint your name on you? Or do they only do that with boats?

I am very sorry for neglecting my writing but I am so very unbusy I just couldn't get around to it. I'm putting on weight something awful and I now have such a big seat I don't know where to put it. A couple of days ago Mom was in the trunk and got out the brown photo album and in it I found several pictures of you and some male having a goof of a time, so naturally I pasted them in the album so everyone could get a roar out of them.

June is so cute. Pretty soon it is going to be her birthday and then yours and mine. Just imagine, me a teenager! I told Mom that it's a good thing that I'm in here sick, because if I wasn't I'd be wanting to do everything that Honey is doing. And believe me, she's getting away with a lot. More than you ever could.

By the way, we're phoning you at Easter, and you may make a collect call whenever you want. If I can get June to write you a "wetter" as she always says she is doing, then I will enclose it. Goom bye for now.

Your goofy sister
Sandy

***

St. Michael's Hospital
Wednesday, June 29th

Dear Sis,

Velly solly for not writing for so long. Yup, I'm back in the hospital with another flare-up. Mom doesn't think I am going to be in here too long but the doctor does, and I am quite worried. I haven't seen June for more than two weeks now, and I am extremely lonesome for her. Tomorrow the kids get out of school and next week the fair starts. Mom is going to take June and Holly I think. I guess June will get more of a kick out of it than she did last year. I wish I could have taken her. Mary was in to see me and she is going to Gull Lake with her parents for two weeks. Nice sandy beaches, swimming and living in a cabin. Linda is leaving for camp on July 5th. I wish I had something to look forward to besides doctors and nurses as I have had to the past year.

Right now I have a cold and cough. It started one morning when I couldn't talk, and I have a steamer in here now. My blood was 110 when I came in, but since I've got this cold it's probably gone higher. I will sure miss taking June to the fair. I wish I could get well. After all, I've only been sick for a year.

Love,
Sandy

P.S. I have prayed but as you can see it hasn't done much good.

***

My heart cried when I saw her writing, shaky with weakness and tears, and I worried about her, locked in the bleak reality of her sickness. From the sound of her shadowed spirit I knew that her battle was "not against flesh and blood but against the powers and principalities of darkness." I put her in the hands of God, praying that this darkness would not overcome her. In a searing moment of pain I begged God, if she was to die–a hypothesis not yet entertained by the family–if she were to die–please, God, let me know if she overcomes the darkness she is battling? Please let it be a sign of her victory that she die of an illness other than her present affliction of Bright's disease.

***

Her next letter sounded better:

Dear President Eisenhower,

I am sorry but pretty soon you won't be able to sign your letters that way cause pretty soon he won't be president anymore. My goofy self is exceptionally fine–I don't know why–but I don't feel at all like biting anyone. As for me running the hospital–well–that's putting it mildly. I have more privaledges than all the other patients put together. Every night Mom brings June up to the waiting room at the end of the hall and I go down there–bed and all. After all the kids are settled down for the night, the nurses take me down to the kitchen to have something to eat. This something usually consists of pop, coffee with ice cream in it, jelly sandwiches and watermelon. I get to watch TV till all hours–my record so far is 11:15 P.M. But these are only a mere sample of what I get away with. I am in the same room I was in when you left. I like it best here cause it's so easy to bother the nurses, as the office is right next door. There aren't any kids even near my age so I like to be alone best, because if they do put someone in here, it's some two year old with the strongest pair of vocal chords in North America.

Tonight Mom, Dad, and June came up and brought me an orange milkshake. June also gave me three pieces of 'buggle gum' (translated means bubble gum). Father Thompson came along then and June naturally pipes up, "Hi, Father Thompson"–about forty times. They have had nine Masses said for me, my name broadcast in Church, prayers by various people in the parish, and all the Sisters over at the residence praying for me. I also received Extreme Unction (the Sacrament of the Sick), but that doesn't mean I'm getting ready to conk out or anything. And the doctor hasn't been sitting around either. They've put me on cortisone, antibiotics, and every morning just about, I get an intravenous. The intravenous is the protein I'm losing from my blood. And it only costs $21.00 a bottle. But Mom and Dad don't have to pay for it. I sure was shocked when Father McClellan asked me if I wanted to receive Extreme Unction, and so was Mom. But he said it had nothing to do with dying, but just that I had been sick for quite awhile so I had the qualifications. I had it this morning.

Oh! I must tell you before I forget. A couple of days ago someone mistook (???) the ashtray in the elevator for a bedpan. The scent finally got so bad that it was called to the attention of a nurse who promptly disposed of it in a more suitable place. But the stink still remained so they had to air out the elevator. I think the person responsible for this shouldn't be wandering around loose, but should be sent someplace to either be examined for bladder weakness or shown the difference between a bedpan and an ashtray.

I'm sending you a bee-u-ti-full picture of what I drew, so appreciate it. I am on a salt free diet, but it isn't very salt free, especially when they send a shaker of it up on my tray all the time. (Naturally I never use it.)

Yours,
The Monster

***

Mom wrote in her memoirs:

"Sandy had been sick a year when the doctor called one hot sticky July day to tell us that the latest culture done indicated that Sandy was in grave condition. I began to pray urgently, desperately for a miracle.

Ironically, the day of the doctor's call had been a bad day at work for my husband. Overloaded with a big contract, his top apprentice had quit suddenly, out of the blue, leaving him critically shorthanded. He was in a black mood when he walked in the door that night. As I listened to him rave and rant as if it was the end of the world, I thought to myself: *Oh, wow! How can I tell you? I have the worst news of all!*

Disaster has a way of rearranging priorities."

***

I was sitting on my bed on August 19th, the feast of St. John Eudes, the founder of our Order, when the phone rang. The sun was setting, and the sun of Sandy's life was touching its horizon. Sandy's body, severely overwrought for a week with the undischarged poisons from her malfunctioning kidneys, had gone into convulsions. Now her kidneys had stopped functioning altogether, and her body was so swollen from the restrained fluid that she was unrecognizable as a human being. For ten continuous hours the convulsions raged, and the doctor warned that should she, by some inconceivable chance, survive, she would be a vegetable. He had been with her through the long hours and he knew that her brain would have been unalterably damaged by its long starvation of oxygen.

***

Mom wrote: "I looked down at the unrecognizable shape of my daughter that black Saturday and again I found myself crying, *Why, God, why?* It was the one prayer I remembered saying to God as a young mother:

Whatever you do, God, don't ever let one of my children die. Don't ever let it happen to me. I couldn't take it.

And here it was happening to me again, not once, but twice."

***

For two and a half days Sandy laid in a coma, out of contact with the world. Sunday afternoon Sister Cordis, just back from Rome, joined the weary waiting group.

"I have a feeling she can hear us," she said as she stood by the bedside. She removed the crucifix from her neck and held it close to Sandy's enormously swollen lips. "Kiss the crucifix, Sandy," she whispered by her ear.

Sandy kissed the crucifix.

And she sat, bolt upright in bed, wide-eyed and alert, and said, "Can I have a popsicle?"

Simultaneously, the vast amount of fluid in her body began to pour out of her in great gushes, to Sandy's great embarrassment, and her kidneys ended their vacation. Incredibly, she was the Sandy of old, bright, clear eyed and merry.

Three days later when Sandy celebrated her birthday it was like Mardi Gras.

***

Dear President,

I've got just piles to tell you. I'll start by telling you that while I'm writing this I'm hatching some shrimp eggs. You see, for my birthday, along with all kinds of things, I got a microscope (60 power). The doctor says that some of his are only that strong. It cost $15.00, but Mom got it cheaper. In this set, along with the microscope, was a set of shrimp eggs. So, I'm hatching them, it's as simple as that. But the guy at the radio station got all confused, because when the nurse called him he explained it over the air like I was sitting on them to keep them warm.... I had them in the water since yesterday and they split open today. I didn't have much hope of them living, and I was so surprised when I looked this morning that I had the nurse phone home... I got scads of stuff for my birthday, even a nylon bed-jacket from the staff. I guess they like me, aye! My eggs will be full grown within two days and I'll be able to keep them for two weeks, but that's all.

I'm all better now, but I was pretty sick a week ago. When I was sick Sister Cordis gave me a cross blessed by the Pope and told me to kiss it, which I did. I don't think you would have recognized me I was so swollen.

I have to eat dinner now.

Goofily yours,
Louis Pasteur

***

Sandy came home in September. The Lord of Life had leaned His ear compassionately to our plea. The x-rays showed her kidneys were extensively damaged, but inexplicably they continued to work. She came off her strict diet, but she was weak sometimes, and occasionally nauseous. Twice she experienced a momentary paralysis of her right side. Meanwhile the remainder of the excess fluid continued to seep out of her tissues. She explained to me brightly that her ankles were crying! Joyfully she entered into the excitement of the family in building a new house, going over to inspect the pink bathtub she had specially chosen.

But somehow I suspected that this recovery might only be a temporary reprieve, an act of the gallantry of God, Who Himself had His Face wiped by one of us along His highway of pain.

On October 24 I stood on a wide open plain with the rest of my milieu, and I, as always, stood ahead of Sandy because, after all, I was older, more experienced. And suddenly, like a deer, she sprinted ahead of us all, and with her trembling childish hands she jousted with the Infinite, the Perfect, the True. And with a Love greater than we can conceive.

When supper came that evening, Sandy was experiencing difficulty in breathing. Mom went to her bedroom, concerned, unable to reach either doctor or priest, and she heard Sandy repeat in a tone of amazement:

"I'm going to die! I'm going to die! I'm going to die!"

Mom sat by her side and asked her quietly, helplessly, desperately, "Sandy, are you really going to die? Do you feel this?"

And Sandy tried to wipe away the pain her words had caused, "No, Mom, I'm not going to die... I love you all so very much".

The ambulance came. June began to cry a strange piercing cry that would suffer no consolation; and Sandy was beyond the help of any oxygen tent on earth.

***

Of this night my Mom said:

"I looked down at the body of my daughter, her spirit fled to the arms of God. My eldest daughter and son were gone from me too. Then, in a moment of stunning clarity, I understood what God had done. It was one of those rare moments of insight, a panoramic vision of a larger reality. It was like my spirit had been taken to a high mountain and I could look down at all that had been. And I saw! And I saw!

Now I knew why I had to have another girl, why June was given to us.

I suddenly became aware that Dr. Carter was still standing at the other side of the bed.

"Doctor," I said, and the sheer forcefulness of my tone startled him. "Doctor, don't ever tell anyone to have an abortion. At this moment, if I had had that abortion, I would be the most violent patient in the mental hospital."

His look was haunted, inscrutable. I often wonder if he recalls these words of mine, spoken at the culmination of so momentous a journey.

Strangely, I found I neither cried nor grieved at this moment. Too many things had happened. I was glad to see Sandy beyond all suffering now. But more than that, our lives had been touched by the Hand of God and His kindness, and we had seen some flickerings of His purposes for us. And we had June.

Sandy was buried, not at a funeral Mass, but at a Mass of the Angels, dressed in white, her hair garlanded with flowers. Her classmates were her pallbearers. One young boy, confounded by his first glimpse of our mortality, announced plaintively, "But she was my best girlfriend!"

Father Thompson said of her: "Sometimes it takes an artist many years to create a picture, and sometimes a masterpiece is created in the shortest of time."

People overwhelmed us with their kindness, gifts of food and sympathy. I reached out for their comfort, and their caring amazed me. We are all such everyday, hum drum sort of people. None of us are leaders of nations. We have never talked in parliament, written a hit song, nor will we ever get one iota of mention in any book of history. But each of us is an integral note in a universal harmony. Every life is truly extraordinary because it is written into time with the pencil of God's Love."

***

Mother Superior put her arm around me. "Sweetheart, I have something to tell you," she whispered in the mornings dim light. "Your Sister died last night, dear Sister."

"Dead?" I echoed to my soul's pit. "Of what did she die?"

"Of pneumonia," her voice said.

And I could have shouted for joy. Through the years it has remained with me, and I think it will resound in me until the moment of my own death; a single, immutable, serene communication of joy. I had my answer. God had answered me. Sandy was dead, but she had died rich in a tested and proven love.

***

On her bedside table, among all her books and possessions, Sandy had left us a parting gift, a letter written, probably in early July, to her dear friend, Sue, and never mailed:

***

Dear Sue,

I am back in the hospital. It was one of the hardest things to do, but I went back. I'm trying to take it better than I did before, but there are times when this is nearly impossible. Once, when I was feeling particularly 'blue', I wrote a letter to Johanna, and anytime I start feeling sorry for myself I read the letter she sent back to me. It was beautiful. This past month that I have spent in here so far has changed me a lot. Inwardly I knew I'd have to come back, but I was fighting it. I'll probably be in here for the rest of the summer, but I find this hard to admit. In one part of the letter she, Johanna, writes: "Like most things in life, we don't know WHY He put you in the hospital, but we can only pray and trust Him. By being where you are, you are more pleasing to Him than all your friends put together." And Sue, I know now that this is a gift from God—not a punishment. God only knows what I've gone through this past year. The disappointments—I don't think I could bear them again, but, who knows, maybe I have even more to come. And, too, it hurts to see my Mother and Father suffering along with me. Johanna says: "There is some special purpose and some special grace you are receiving, or will receive, if only you ask, by being sick, which no one else in the world will receive. In the eyes of God you are set apart". This must be true, Sue, for it makes me heartbroken to see all my friends off to camp, holidays and what not. It really hurts. And yet, I'm beginning to realize that these hurts are blessings, because someday, if I offer these hurts up right I'll be rewarded for them in heaven. Right now I'd give just about anything to go on holidays. To Banff. To get a tan. To be out in the fresh air and smell the pine trees. TO GO SWIMMING. But I can't, but as Johanna says, someday this will pay off. I am learning to say "Thy Will, not mine, be done, O Lord". This is so hard. The nights are so lonely—I want to see June so bad. Imagine yourself separated from Tommy! I had to give up my family and leave them, and the thing that keeps me going through all this is the thought that someday, just as sure as I'm lying here in this bed, someday I'll get rewarded for it, a hundred times as much as I've ever had to suffer. It seems a long way off—but who knows—I may not be alive tomorrow. Then—all days I do not feel like this. Some days I feel that everybody hates me and I hate everybody. Some days I feel close to God and other days I feel like screaming at Him. Sometimes I feel that I have a cut or a sore deep down inside and that He just wants to hurt me. Just as sure as if He was rubbing salt or vinegar in it. It's so hard, Sue, it really is. Sometimes I feel so lost, and I know that Mom and Dad realize what I'm going through, and that in turn makes it worse. Then when Johanna wrote this it picked me up quite a bit. She says: "The Little Flower says, "It is love alone that counts!" She did not do anything extraordinary, but she saw Christ in all her companions, and tried to act the way Christ would act. She didn't do big things–only little things (which are harder because there are only a few big things to do, but many little things). She didn't always succeed, but she never stopped trying. The way she writes and sounds you would think she had very great feelings of devotion–but on the contrary, the devil tempted her very severely against her faith. She felt like you," writes Johanna, "that praying doesn't do much good. St. Therese was so dry, so empty of devotion, that she slept through many prayers and meditations." I've grown up in mind quite a bit, Sue, and I don't want to sound preachy, but I realize if I offer this up I can become a saint, and I pray that someday I will. Life is so short and yet so long. I don't have to do big things and I don't want to. But I hope that someday you too are as lucky (?) as I.

Yours,
Sandra

***

Sandy's "someday" had come.

Her chaplain later wrote: "In the last stages she became almost ethereal. She seemed to be half in another world, in the constant presence of God."

Now, through the plunging whirl of snow, on a hilltop, like the world's most haunting advertisement, is a grave, where all the seeds of time are buried and cold and waiting. But like vagrant dandelion seeds, insouciant, fertile, undefeated by the snow, the seeds of her summer fall into the seasons of our lives, reminding us always of a springtime that is yet to come.

Ever and always I will love her–who was younger than I, yet taught me so much; who I guided, who has guided me.

One strange thing that struck Mom was that she never dreamt of Sandy in the long months after her death. Of everything else she dreamed, and she longed to see Sandy's face again, at least in a dream.

Then, one day when the spring came, my mother found herself working at the kitchen sink, doing her usual chores. She became gradually conscious of skipping and singing. As she had so often done, she walked to the front door and found Sandy dancing up and down the front steps. But then, from habit, she found herself scolding Sandy:

"No, Sandy, you can't dance! You're sick!"

And then the realization fully seeped in…. "You are dead…. " And her voice trailed off in puzzlement and fear.

Sandy, her hair flying, turned and looked at her mother, and there was tenderness and ecstasy in her face.

"No, Mom," she said, "Now I can dance forever!"

CHAPTER 8

Through the many months of sharing Sandy's struggle I encountered my own mortality. My nerves and sinews and flesh relived her dying. In the surrender of her health, her youth, her will, I recognized the reality that would also face me. I cringed as I thought of her poor body lying beneath the ground in the frozen days of January. And yet, in her, I too was set free. In her, I had faced death, and survived.

The Sisters wanted to know what name I would like to take. As Abram had become Abraham, as Simon had become Peter, as Saul had become Paul, a new name signified the death of the old man and the beginning of new life and responsibilities. I fumbled around in my mind. I liked John, the young Apostle, who was a poetic dreamer like me, and who was beloved by Jesus for his innocent heart.

"John," I said resolutely–I had a mental block; the word evangelist skipped my mind. "You know, John–of the cross." In my mind that was the indelible picture of John, the teen age apostle, the only one with the guts to accompany Jesus to Calvary.

"Very good," Mother Superior said. "John of the Cross was a mystic, a contemporary of St. Theresa of Avila, who was responsible along with her for the renewal of religious life. He, like Theresa, is a doctor of the Church, and has taught us much about contemplative prayer."

"Oh," I said weakly. I had never heard of him. Still, I decided this was perhaps a manifestation of the Divine Will for me. Sister John of the Cross I became.

The flowing white Habit I received on my Clothing Day was like a baptismal garment, a return to innocence, and I wore it with trepidation and joy. I discovered a new life, far removed from the cold observance of rules and obligations. In some ways I saw my faith for the first time. I was introduced to wonderful books and unimagined springs of inspiration. I felt warm and lighthearted. I understood St. Augustine's feeling when he wrote: "You have made us for Yourself, O God, and our hearts are restless until they rest in You."

So, on this twenty-five acre oasis overlooking the North Saskatchewan River, I thrust down my roots. I reveled in my association with the Sisters, and found that each had her unique personality and spirituality–and also a rich vein of silliness.

Sister Vincent was a tiny, bubbly, happy Dominican Sister who had come to stay with us while she learned English. Two young Sisters, Sister Michael and Sister Aloysius, were immediately on her case. They dogged her steps, with the excuse that they were teaching her English, frenched her bed and pulled all sorts of practical jokes on her. Sister Vincent lived in a constant state of embarrassment over her hilarious blunders in English, aided and abetted by the cheerful misguidance of her two tormentors. Every time I saw Sister Vincent, her chipmunk cheeks were red and she was laughing. Finally, after three months, her Superior was coming to evaluate what kind of progress she was making. Sister Vincent was in a perfect dither.

"What shall I say, what shall I say?" the little nun foolishly asked Sister Michael. "My English is not so good," she wailed in her thick French accent.

"Well." Sister Michael volunteered, "Your Superior will no doubt ask you if you are having a good time."

"And what I say to her, what I say," Sister Vincent asked breathlessly.

Sister Michael had a fit of coughing behind her hand. "When she asks if you are having a good time you say: "Yes, Sister, I am having a helluva good time."

Gullible Sr. Vincent wandered down the hall, her brows furrowed in concentration as she memorized the phrase.

The next day the two culprits hung around outside the visiting room as the Superior arrived. Suddenly there was a burst of laughter from the hall and Sister Vincent, realizing she had been had, ran out into the hall after them, shaking her fist.

The loveable gullibility of Sr. Vincent also provided entertainment for the special ungraded class she began to teach as her English improved–in spite of Sr. Michael and Sister Aloysius. These girls, who had never been able to function in a school setting, loved Sister Vincent, but they could also be incorrigible. One day, casting about for something to say to deal with some miscreants, she finally translated directly from the French:

"Take the door!" she ordered the two misbehaving girls, and her face, seldom without a smile, was stern.

The two girls blinked, chuckled, and waltzed out of the room.

The next morning there was a ruckus down the school hall, and Sister Vincent, her face flushed, her hands waving, and totally inarticulate with excitement, directed us to her class room. The door was missing.

Sports were taken nearly as seriously in the monastery as a papal election. Although there was only one television available to the Sisters, and that behind a locked cupboard in the girls' gym, there were a few radios here and there. I discovered this one night when I came across our Directoress of Novices with her head stuck in a Novitiate cupboard. The only light in the room was from the full moon and the red glow of an exit light above the door. There she stood, frozen into immobility with her head in the cupboard, unaware of my presence. My curiosity was going into overdrive until suddenly I heard the faint roar of a crowd, and I knew she was into a game. But the game I'll always remember was the year the Ottawa Roughriders went against the Edmonton Eskimos for the Grey Cup. This, we decided, was cause for a great celebration, and in the days leading up to the game, Sister Nicholas, loyal Alberta fan that she was, began, in a small way, her own corsage manufacturing company. Wielding spools of gold and green ribbon she soon had us sporting colorful bows on our Habits. The only self proclaimed deviant who would not wear a bow was Sister Monica, who, having lived at one time in Toronto, retained some perverse loyalty to the East. Risking martyrdom, she appeared one day in a red and white corsage. For weeks she was harassed and browbeaten, but managed to flit around smiling with her dignity unruffled. Never mind that her underwear came back from the laundry dyed yellow and green. Never mind that a letter arrived for her, ostensibly from the coach of the Edmonton Eskimos, begging her prayerful support. She never flinched, never abandoned her loyalty to Ottawa. The only person not wearing a corsage was our Superior, Sister Immaculate Heart. We offered to make her one, but she seemed busy and distracted with all her administrative work, and we couldn't get her interested. Perhaps she wanted to maintain a more serious aspect with the social workers and the public who were always coming to our door. In any case, our devotion was known to the Eskimos, and one player even donated a uniform so Sister Nicholas could wear it on Halloween.

On the day of the game we lined up our chairs in front of the gym cupboard, and the monastery was virtually shut down. The only person absent was our Superior. Downstairs, the girls and the supervising Sisters were having a loud celebration of their own. Cheering resounded through the monastery, but became more subdued, and finally broke into lamentations as Ottawa stole the final touchdown. We were just turning our attention to Sister Monica, who was smirking and looking exceptionally pleased with herself, when Sister Immaculate Heart appeared. She marched around the gym with the high stepping finesse of a drum majorette, her chin held high, flashing a red and white corsage that was bigger than a dinner plate! Gym chairs were knocked over in surprise as thirty-five flabbergasted nuns fell over themselves to turn around and see our Superior's march of triumph.

Sister Immaculate Heart was an amazing woman. We young Sisters in the Novitiate looked for any opportunity we could to invite her to the Novitiate for a special meal or event, all so that we could have her to ourselves and grill her. She was a superb story teller. But perhaps that was because her story was so unusual.

She was born on a farm in Minnesota, on the plains south of Lake Superior, early in the twentieth century, part of a large family. One day, on a calm afternoon that was suddenly overtaken by thunderheads, her father was crossing a field and was separating the wires of a barb wire fence to climb through when he was struck by lightning. He had a hole blown through his hat, his hair was singed, and his skin jaundiced, but he was otherwise alive and well. Later, he survived being struck by lightning a second time! Her young, healthy brother shocked the family in another way, by predicting his own death. Two years later he was found, parked along the side of the road, in the place he had predicted, sitting behind his steering wheel, dead of a heart attack. Their trials were many. By the time Sister Immaculate Heart was a young teenager her family home had burned down twice!

One windy morning she went out to buy a hat. She had concluded her purchase, but was still standing in the millinery shop, located on the second floor of the building, when pandemonium broke out. Someone burst into the shop yelling,

"Run for your lives! Get to the train! A fire is coming!"

Down on the street a stiff wind lifted her skirt like a sail, and she heard an ominous rushing sound, deep and low like advancing thunder. The whole skyline was ablaze and flames hurtled and catapulted like fiery tumbleweeds across the fields of dry grass, reaching out for her town. The air was thick with smoke and it seared her throat. Swept along in a surging tide of people, she was half shoved and half carried down the two blocks to where two trains stood on parallel tracks. All around her people were coughing and in panic. Some people had managed to grab a few belongings, but they were ordered to abandon them or they would not be allowed on the train. Scuffles broke out. But someone grabbed her, still clutching her hat box, and boosted her onto a cattle car where people were crammed together like toothpicks. There was already a red hue in the air as the train lurched to life, its engine drowned by a crackling roar. The heat was intense. Suddenly a terrific din arose, and looking back fearfully, Sister beheld a cataclysm of horror. The train that had stood beside them had been slower to leave. The terrible flames had pursued and overtaken it, enveloping it and its human cargo. She could see people moving in the midst of the sea of flames, in a scene straight from hell. The screams and cries of the dying echoed and reechoed in her head as in a sound chamber long after they left the stricken land. Crushed in her hands in a vise like grip, she found herself still holding her new hat, the sole remnant of a normal world that had been destroyed. The train took them to a distant city where they were given shelter. It was eighty days before they were able to locate the rest of her family for her. Five towns of the American Midwest had been wiped off the map that day.

With these extraordinary beginnings, it is perhaps not surprising that her life would not follow the beaten track. At fifteen she opted to join a missionary Order which was headed up to Canada. Troubles beset the little missionary group, and soon after it arrived in Edmonton, it disbanded. Sister found herself alone, at fifteen, in a pioneer country, a thousand miles from home. A kindly bishop told her about another Order of Sisters, the Sisters of Our Lady of Charity of Refuge, who had recently taken up residence in Edmonton. R. B. Chadwick, Superintendent of Dependent and Delinquent Children for the Province of Alberta, had invited these Sisters up from Pittsburg to help deal with the abandoned and delinquent children who were byproducts of the rapid growth and urbanization of the

West. He had toured the United States, and was impressed by these Sisters who dedicated their lives to helping girls with problems. With them Sister Immaculate Heart made a fresh start.

Times were hard for those early Sisters. They were poor, and yet helped the poor, subsisting themselves mainly on a diet of corn meal mush. The girls they took in were themselves destitute, so the Sisters went begging to businesses and mining and construction camps to support them. They endured frenzied religious bigotry, inadequate housing, crowded conditions and overwork. The Providence of God came to their rescue in a magnificent and surprising manner. A Protestant philanthropist named O'Connell, who had heard of their work, bequeathed a fifty acre estate to them. It stood on a bluff looking across to the MacDonald Hotel in downtown Edmonton, and boasted a large palatial home. This was not the end of the Sister's struggles, however, but at least now they had a home. They became farmers to support themselves, grew vegetables and potatoes, and regaled each other with hilarious escapades trying to round up their wayward cattle. Sister Annunciation slept in the chicken coop to keep the fires stoked during the bitter Edmonton winters, so that they would not lose the chickens and eggs they depended on. And although the special apostolate of the Sisters was to troubled and wayward girls, Edmonton was too young and too rough to be able to specialize. The Sisters ended up caring for anyone and everyone who was considered undesirable: abandoned babies, children from poor and broken homes, the mentally deficient, epileptics and even the criminally insane. In later years a first, and then a second addition, was built on to the original mansion, and housed one hundred and fifty girls who were either orphaned or in temporary care. At the other end of the property a second large building came to be. This housed the bulk of the Sisters, a school, medical facility, and accommodation for a hundred and fifty girls who had been committed by the courts, social service agencies, and occasionally by parents who could not cope.

In 1952 Sister Immaculate Heart was elected Superior. The young girl from Minnesota had become the head of a multimillion dollar institution and the mother figure to thousands of girls. She proved to be a formidable administrator, and a strong, just and inspired leader. Her human qualities, irradiated by her great faith, gave her a piercing directness and a boundless tenderness. A large homely woman with a round face and rimless glasses, her unprepossessing physical attributes were only underscored more by her propensity to wear the oldest, most patched Habits. She was hardly the image of success by worldly standards. And yet she was the most well balanced person I ever met. My Directoress in the Novitiate used to say to us: "The supernatural builds on the natural. If you are a neurotic, you are going to love God neurotically...." Sister Immaculate Heart was anything but neurotic in the way she loved. She met the criteria laid down in the second century by St. Irenaeus when he said: "The glory of God is man fully alive...." If there is a criticism to be levied against her, it is that she tended to carry the load alone, rarely sharing her burdens with her Sisters. As a woman she held as much power as a woman can hold in the Church. Being an older Order of the Church, as opposed to a congregation, each monastery was independent, and while the Superior worked in cooperation with the local bishop, she was answerable only to God and the Holy Father. Happily for us, Sister Immaculate Heart was gifted with humor, prudence and love. She was also, as I discovered, a woman of humility.

Older Sisters commonly delegated some of the more onerous and menial tasks to the youngest Sisters. They felt that they had paid their dues, and that it was for the young to be tested and grow to maturity. One day I was coming down the back stairs and saw Margaret sitting on a chair in the hall. She was looking disconsolate as she often did. Margaret was a woman in late middle age, one of the derelicts who had been abandoned to the Sisters. Margaret was dull and obese, a misshapen, repulsive creature with a mild flat personality. Sister Immaculate Heart was hurrying past me down the stairs when Margaret's plaintive wail stopped her in her tracks.

"What is the matter, Margaret?" Sister asked her kindly, caressing her grey head.

I couldn't hear Margaret's mumbled reply, but Sister Immaculate Heart understood.

"Its okay, Margaret, I will help you," she said.

With that, Sister Immaculate Heart knelt on the floor in front of Margaret, helped her remove her shoes and socks, and clipped the old woman's toe nails for her. I was stunned and touched. Sister Immaculate Heart had been in a rush. Another Sister might have called for help. But Sister Immaculate Heart completed the job cheerfully and gave Margaret a warm pat on the back.

One of the secret expectations I had harbored about religious life was that it would be dull and boring. This turned out not to be the case. There was always something to learn and do, and even during my first year in Novitiate, the canonical year which is given to study and prayer, there was always something to laugh about or some physical activity to enjoy. It happened that there was a long winding service road flanking our property and running down almost to the North Saskatchewan River. It began at one corner of the property and ended down under the bluff where the O'Connell Institute sat. It was totally private, and we soon discovered it was an awesome toboggan hill. An additional bonus was a wide strip of tall trees on the river side of the road, providing us a quiet retreat by the water. In the summer this became our wilderness where we could picnic and read and talk. In the winter we would tuck up our Habits, don long gingham aprons, and enjoy some thrills and spills on the hill. One time a lone hydro worker was startled to meet up with several toboggans of laughing nuns barreling around the curve at top speed. It must have been a sight worth seeing, because the next day as we were sliding, and in some cases somersaulting, a whole line of men's heads suddenly bobbed up simultaneously out of the gully, just like gophers out of their holes. I wonder if the hydro worker had sold tickets?

Several times each winter we would take the orphans down the hill on special outings. We would toboggan with them, and then we would build a giant bonfire and roast wieners, sing, and play games. On one particularly cold day the flu had been making the rounds, and Sister Helen, one of the regulars, was stricken down and unable to go. To cancel the outing would have been a huge disappointment to the children, so we set out to corral another Sister. Sister Monica, who was about fifty we guessed, was still energetic and vivacious, and we thought, daring.

"Not so," Sister Monica protested, "I have never been on a toboggan in my life and I'm not about to start now!"

"Now, Sister," Sister Immaculate Heart cajoled her, "be a little humble."

"But I'll get hurt. I just know I'll get hurt!" Sister Monica wailed.

"Come on, Sister," we pleaded. "No one has ever been hurt on that hill! It is not at all steep. And we need you! Think of the children!"

"Anyway, I have nothing to wear," Sister Monica excused herself.

"You'll be warm just like we are in jackets and extra aprons."

"Forget it! It is 18 degrees below zero! I'm very sensitive to the cold."

"Hmmm," said one of the older Sisters thoughtfully, "I think we have just the answer for you."

"What?" asked Sister Monica suspiciously.

"Remember that old army trunk that was left here when Father Dan died?"

"Oh no! If you think I am going to wear some of Father Dan's long underwear, you're crazy! What if I had an accident? What if I landed up in the hospital? I'd die of embarrassment, I'd just die! How could I explain why I am wearing a pair of man's long underwear?"

"Sister, it will never happen. The hill is not icy now and it's not even very fast."

The indomitable Sister Monica grinned in defeat, crawled on the toboggan, made it to the first turn, fell off, and broke her leg.

I'm sure Father Dan was laughing in heaven with us over this. Father Dan had been sent to us by the Bishop to spend his last days with us. He was suffering from some sort of a degenerative heart disease, and the Bishop asked if we would look after him. He felt that good food, quiet, and loving care, would help Father Dan to conserve his little remaining physical strength and allow him to die in peace. Father Dan had other ideas. Whenever he could, in defiance of doctor's orders, he was out skipping with the children. When a passing nun would chide him about his health he would blow up his chest and roar and chase after her at a full gallop like a mean old ogre, much to the delight of the children. He loved to hear them squeal and did whatever he could to get them all worked up.

At last, as he lay dying in the hospital, Archbishop Jordan came to the hospital to give him a pep talk. Father Dan listened quietly as the Archbishop waxed eloquent about the beauties and joys of heaven. Finally, when he was finished, Father Dan said, deadpan, "But your Excellency, I *like* Edmonton."

Among the Sisters of the community, the two that emerged like lead horses in a team, were Sister Francis and Sister Divine Heart, the Directoress of the Novitiate. They were the Peter and Paul of the monastery; two antithetical personalities. Sister Francis was a tiny, gaunt, physically fragile Sister, with rock hard determination. She was the ultimate ascetic, but genuinely spiritual and not, I thought, unkind. She had been the previous Sister in charge of the Novitiate. When Sister Divine Heart took the position over, her personality and convictions changed the atmosphere of the Novitiate. Sister Divine Heart felt that Sister Francis had stressed surface obedience to the Rule to the detriment of understanding and growth of the heart. Sister Divine Heart sought to be a loving guide, who stressed faithfulness without rigidity. Being the most junior of the Sisters, I felt in no position to judge these differences and merely liked both Sisters immensely. Like different flowers in a garden each seemed to have her own beauty.

In due time Sister Francis succeeded Sister Immaculate Heart as Superior, and we felt the influence of the Poverello of Assisi himself. Nary a curtain graced a window, and in the Sisters' quarters hard straight back chairs were the rule. Habits were worn until they resembled lace curtains, so thin they were. But Sister Francis had a grace, a charm, a smile that was irresistible. After five months in office we began to prepare for the feast of Saint Francis of Assisi, her feast day. Despite her "tut-tuts" we had decorated the refectory in blue and white streamers, and had prepared a real celebration. The night before the feast day Sister Francis and several other Sisters had gone out to take a special social work course. As they came in the door, Sister Francis grasped the railing of the stairs saying she felt woozy and nauseous, and with Sister Immaculate Heart's assistance, went straight to her room. My room was directly across the hall from hers, and I could hear Sister Immaculate Heart saying with concern,

"What's the matter, dear Sister?"

I heard sharp moaning, and then silence. This year Sister Francis was to celebrate her feast day in heaven. It gave me a strange feeling, a sense of awe, that I, the youngest of the Sisters, had heard my Superior die.

After Sister Francis' death, Sister Divine Heart was elected Superior. As if by magic, curtains appeared at the windows and a few soft chairs were provided for the elderly Sisters. Meals improved, and we were even allowed an occasional sleep in. Gentleness tempered the austerity of the Rule.

Here, as in marriage, the constant interplay of different personalities can grate and provide sources of penance. The only difference is that in marriage it is presupposed that a mutual attraction has drawn two people together. In religious life it is not necessarily so. And in our Order we are never transferred; we have the same companions for life. Christ said, "If you only love those who love you, what merit is it to you? Even the pagans do that...." But the Rule and customs do try to make allowance and give guidance for times of friction. In an exercise called the Chapter of Faults Sisters are called on a regular basis to forgive each other. There can be no 'divorces' among those who have vowed their lives to serve Love.

To discourage the forming of cliques, seating at table is assigned yearly by lot to encourage the Sisters to be friendly to all, and not merely to those more to one's taste. Although in close quarters small differences can seem large, our calling is to give God the first place in our lives, and the test of this is to serve Him in all of His people. We can never have peace on earth until we rise above differences in background, temperament and understanding. Still, one Sister would come into the room and open the window. Another would complain of the cold and close the window. Sometimes the dominant would grate on the less dominant, the meticulous on the disorganized.

Some nights I would go out and sit on the bluff overlooking the city. Each of the minute twinkling lights I saw below me on the flats represented the sum total of the life and problems of a family. But, up here, the conflicts and dramas being enacted below seemed so tiny, so far away, so inconsequential. They were swallowed up by the night, and all that would remain of importance is that light which each of these lives would cast upon the earth.

There was an older Sister who I particularly admired, and I was pleased that she seemed to like me too. I loved it when she would join us on jaunts down the hill. She was gung ho for anything, tall, funny and interesting. Then suddenly she grew cold toward me, and started avoiding me. I was troubled and racked my brain to discover if I had offended her in some way. I was never able to come up with a plausible answer. The only thing I could come up with, and it seemed to be too petty to be true, was that I got a higher mark in a correspondence course we were both taking. When I made my Profession and was admitted to the full community, the problem became more acute because I was around her more by necessity. Whenever I would enter a room Sister Clare would make fun of me, mimic my laugh or turn away from me coldly. She unlocked all my insecurities, all my self doubts and I felt awkward and misshapen around her. If I tried to talk to her, to question her, she refused to talk. I never found out the reason for her behavior, but it caused a profound sadness in my life. I had heard that there was something different, something painful in her background that she did not want to discuss. I could only conclude that despite her apparent strength, that strength was called up in the service of defending a wounded ego. Although I prayed about it and tried to distance myself from it, it remained a thorn in my heart.

Except for this, my years in the monastery were a time of healing. It was Christ the Healer, Christ the Lover, Who made this so. I had wondered as a teenager what perfect goodness, perfect love was. I had often felt unloved, alienated from this very earth I was called to walk upon. But, then, I certainly was no paragon of virtue myself. My faith was cerebral; beautiful, but cerebral. Then one day while I was still a Novice, we were having our daily lesson in the Novitiate. The topic for this day revolved around the chapters from the Gospel of Luke in which Jesus says:

"Behold the lilies of the field; they neither toil nor spin, yet not even Solomon in all of his glory was arrayed like one of these. If God so clothes in splendor the grass of the field which grows today and tomorrow is thrown into the fire, how much more will he provide for you, O you of little faith...."

And: "Are not five sparrows sold for a few pennies? Yet not one of them is neglected by God. I tell you, the very hairs of your head are numbered. Do not be afraid; you are of more value than many sparrows."

Sister Divine Heart used these passages to illustrate God's love for us. She reminded us that if no sparrow would fall from the sky, nor would a hair fall from our head without our Father's permission, God is not a far off God watching us swim around in the fish bowl of life. He is an intimate God Who is involved and interested in the tiniest aspects of our lives, in our every whim. She went on to say that, in fact, love is often proved, not by doing big things–even a stranger may save a person drowning in a lake–but often it is by doing the small, inconsequential things that show we are tuned in to one another. It is often these little "hairs on our head" that count the most in everyday life, and are at once the greatest and the most difficult proofs of love. This is the way God loves us. This is the way we are called to love each other.

This was an almost constant theme of Sister Divine Heart. A smile would crease her serene face and her eyes would embrace us. "How is every little thing?" was her customary greeting.

It was nice, of course, but I had heard it all before. My head was assenting, but it was my heart that had been wounded and was often non-functional. Mine was often a routine, dry faith.

The lesson ended and Sister Divine Heart remained sitting, fiddling absent mindedly in the drawer at the end of the long table where we had been sitting. Finding a calendar there, she said to Sister Maureen, a postulant who was standing in front of me, "Sister, would you like this calendar?"

"Oh, yes, thank you," Sister Maureen replied.

Suddenly it occurred to me that I would like a calendar too. A small thing. Not a matter of importance. But, my periods were irregular. Might help me to keep tabs on them.

"May I have a calendar too?" I asked.

"I'm sorry, Sister," Sister Divine Heart smiled. "I only had that one."

"No big deal," I shrugged to myself, grabbing a sweater to ward off a late spring gale and setting off for the O'Connell. The road there was single lane and ran along the bluff for about a block's distance, with a breathtaking view of the city. About half way there, by a clump of three large evergreens, a huge white semi pulled up beside me. There was no identifying name written on the truck that I could see. *What was he doing on our private land? Surely he must be lost.* The huge truck looked out of place on our tiny road.

The driver rolled down his window, leaned out and asked, "Sister, do you want a calendar?"

I felt like I had been struck by lightning.

"Yes!" I managed to murmur before the tears started to gush like the runoff of spring.

Then the gigantic truck backed out carefully along the curved road, and out around the corner to the private road that fronted the monastery; no mean feat for a big rig. Finally, he was able to right himself as he turned to leave through the quiet residential area to which he had inexplicably come.

It was a simple calendar, without advertising, having a picture of a dark haired girl and a black and white dog.

The experience of that day caused a paradigm shift in my life. One moment I was straitjacketed in my cerebral, cardboard, caricature of love, the tattered debris of a lost Eden. In the next, Heaven had reached down and hugged me, touched me, recognized me, a mere nothing on planet earth. I would never be alone again.

Many times, in being careful not to be deceived, I have questioned my faith experiences. Are they real, or are they merely subjective flights of my imagination, projections of my wishes, comfort mechanisms of my psyche? But even my imagination could not have conjured up that huge, solid, three dimensional semi, and the pretty calendar that sat squarely in my hand.

Finally, I felt the love of my God, palpably, existentially, intimately. As the North Saskatchewan River flowed down below me, powering the city, so I found in my heart a boundless river of light and joy. That light has lived in me through the years to illumine a million darknesses, and its reality shines within me still.

Can it save my sanity tonight?

CHAPTER 9

The summer sun poured over my white veil like hot syrup as I headed over to the O'Connell to look after eighteen preschoolers for the afternoon. It would be my first time to relieve one of the Sisters, and I was determined to dazzle them with my competency and enthusiasm.

The playground was in a fenced in area shaded, thankfully, by two large trees. Copious lilac bushes and a wilderness of shrubs obscured the chain link fence, creating a lovely natural enclave for the children to play in. As I scrambled to learn the youngsters' names, I was first taken by a pair of curly headed blonde sisters, radiant in lovely sundresses, whose names were Melody and Harmony. They were three and four years old, and though they were in care, they had a mother somewhere who must have worked for a fashion magazine. Dogging their steps faithfully was a dark skinned buddy with a cherubic face named Penny. The three comprised an amazing, non-stop whirlwind. I wondered what had happened to the parents of such lovely children? But my wondering was cut short as shrill little voices clamored for attention, swinging on my skirts, begging for a push on the merry-go-round, pushing against me for a cuddle. Suddenly I noted that the Melody, Harmony, Penny trio were sans socks and underwear.

"Where did you put them?" I asked in chagrin, looking around fruitlessly for the missing clothes.

They looked up at me with large blank eyes as if I was speaking a foreign language.

"Come, show me where you put them?" I cajoled them. But they knew they had a neophyte here.

"They put them in the bushes," a playmate volunteered.

I interrupted their play to make them walk around the bushes. But if we were playing hide and seek, I was losing. The three of them had apparently come from another planet and were unacquainted with underwear.

By suppertime I had to admit that I had been outwitted by three preschoolers. Surely a prestigious beginning! It was some consolation that no one else could locate the missing underwear either. It was two years later, when deep autumn had denuded the landscape, that one day I noticed a dot of color, like summer's signature, caught in the clutches of some dark branches.

Although I spent most of my time at the main house, the children at the O'Connell would always watch like hawks for any young Sisters out for a walk, and descend on us like clouds of grasshoppers. They seemed to have divided us up among themselves so that each of us 'belonged' to a certain group. Three little Metis girls, one of them blonde, had claimed me. From me they sought that one-on-one attention that the over burdened Sisters in charge had little time for. Two additions had already been made to the original mansion and still the children kept coming. In the Fifties their numbers swelled to one hundred and fifty children, and yet there were only four able bodied and two elderly nuns at the O'Connell to look after that mob. That meant long days and no time off. Sister Monica was often up with the babies at night, and then still had to be up at dawn to begin a day that would stretch into the evening darkness. It was not an ideal situation and her voice would get shrill and her eyes bloodshot. Service clubs in the community did help with parties and entertainment, and donated pets for the children. Art and crafts, ballet, tap and square dancing were taught weekly and the girls had their own school. Those who grew up at O'Connell were prepared to meet the world by being sent to nursing school, secretarial college, or wherever their talents led them. But O'Connell remained their home and a refuge for their hearts. The life sized crucifix overlooking the entrance to the O'Connell was the gift one girl made with her first pay check. Not all the children were orphans though. Some came for a time when marriages collapsed or because of sickness in the family, neglect, or desertion. There were two children with Downs Syndrome, and a large child with heavy leg braces who I often saw waiting on the roadside for the parental visit that rarely happened. Her parents were busy professionals who had no place in their lives for a handicapped daughter. The Sisters received no financial remuneration for most of the children.

I chafed under the restrictions that we were forced to place on the children. There was a tree in the yard with low sweeping branches that begged to be climbed. But we had learned the hard way that our children could not afford that kind of freedom. As indifferent as some of the parents were, when it came to broken bones or scraped knees the parents could turn into avenging angels. Of course, nobody wants these things to happen, but in the rough and tumble of ordinary life, amidst the learning and exploration of childhood, scraped knees and bruises happen. The saddest example of this happened to the finest of Sisters. Sister Nativity hailed from Newfoundland and she was the gentlest soul I ever met. Her large sensitive eyes and motherliness brought calm and security to hundreds of young lives stressed out by life's events. She seemed to have an imperturbable peace. Like most everybody, Sister Nativity's life fell into a set routine that would enable her to satisfy everyone's basic needs. Every morning promptly at ten o'clock she bathed the tiniest children. Gloria, one of the Down's Syndrome children, always hung around, eager to assist her. Like most Down's Syndrome children she craved and doled out boundless affection, along with occasional displays of dogged stubbornness. One day a long distance call came in for Sister Nativity just at ten A.M. When Gloria saw no sign of Sister Nativity she took it into her head to begin without her. She went to the nursery and got the baby and ran just the right amount of water in the tub. But Gloria did not know enough to check the temperature of the water, which was very hot. The baby's cries brought Sister on the run, but criminal charges were brought against Sister Nativity.

In the early Sixties the government mounted a campaign to find homes for all the children in orphanages. It was felt that institutions, no matter how good, were not equipped to give the individualized and personalized care of a family home. Already experienced in foster care, and feeling Sandy's absence keenly, Mom met my three little tagalongs and promptly fell in love with them. The quandary was: who could she take home with her? Because two of them were sisters and our house was not large, she finally opted to take home Edie. June was thrilled to get a new sister to go along with the new brother that Mom and Dad had adopted. But I worried about the other two. Caught in the crosscurrents of two cultures they were considered difficult to place. I can still see the disappointment on their faces. I pray that they found homes where love was waiting.

Edie was like a gopher on the prairies, standing at the edge of her hole, surveying the world warily, always poised to escape. For a whole year she said not one word to my Dad. Unused to men, I am sure she found his loud voice and strong manner intimidating. But with June and John, the newly adopted son, she relaxed. Mom coached Edie in her schoolwork until her marks soared. She gained confidence, and made friends. Too many friends. Edie roared into her teens like an unbridled horse. Soon Edie's wishes for unfettered independence created a showdown. On the bitterest day of the winter while a storm slashed the house with knife edge winds, Edie insisted she must go out to meet her friends. Mom forbade it. Cars were sputtering in driveways and the intense cold had virtually shut down the city. Edie was adamant. Mom warned her that if she wanted to be a part of this family she would have to accept family guidelines, and in this case, it meant a 'no'. Undaunted, Edie disappeared outside into the storm. Mom realized she had lost control. Edie was contrite when she returned much later, but Mom had already contacted Edie's social worker, and Edie was reassigned to a farming family where it was felt she could not run wild. Although Edie maintained contact for some time, Mom worried about her and missed her. She wondered if she had been too inflexible, if there had been some other better way she could have handled the situation. We heard, eventually, that Edith became a hair dresser, married, had a son, divorced. Somewhere in this world is a grown woman now, named Edith, who left a lasting mark on my mother's heart.

The white lattice window coverings of the main house are cross stitched in my mind. Behind their ornamental appearance is the reality of Mapleridge. What appears as decorative lattice is made of iron: Mapleridge is a closed institution for delinquent teenagers. It is a huge E shaped building, with the monastery taking up the upper floor of one arm of the E, the school the other, with the chapel, gym and visiting rooms comprising the back spine of the E. Two different groups of girls inhabit the two outside wings of the bottom floor, with the dining rooms, the Sister's refectory, the kitchen and the laundry for both institutions located between them. There are also offices and receiving rooms for girls brought by in during the night by the police, where they are held until such time as they can be medically examined and assigned to the appropriate group. One group is mostly younger girls who are first offenders, runaways, or considered out of control by their parents. The second group is composed of more serious offenders who are committed by the courts. What most of the girls have in common is a dysfunctional family and a background of alcoholism, abuse, and neglect. The girls represent every racial, economic and religious background, or lack thereof, and usually are behind in school. Some of the girls just need mothering; others bring the simmering hostilities and gang vendettas of the streets with them. The year before I entered a riot had erupted between the two groups of girls, who were usually kept separated. But for the most part, the Sisters, by staying tuned in, managed to defuse fights before they started. I only remember one other episode of violence. The girls liked hanging out and helping around the kitchen because they were expert samplers and always willing to donate their services. But one evening after everyone had left, as Sister Immaculate Conception was bent over the counter planning the menu for the next day, three girls came up behind her and beat her unconscious with a coke bottle. They grabbed her keys, got into the locked cooler and made off with two institutional sized containers of vanilla and lemon extract, escaping then through the delivery door behind the kitchen. By the time the police found them they were very sick and one of the girls may have sustained permanent kidney damage.

I felt I could read the heart of this generation—it was my generation. I spoke its language. I knew its rootlessness, its bravado, its pain. I was attuned to its nerves, its sinews and the tremors of its life. My shoes were muddy with its despair, giddy with its excitement, sick with its anomie. If I had suffered through a foolish, agonizing, aching adolescence, it had to be for a purpose. Perhaps the rope of my experience could be thrown to someone else.

Because I was so young, in years and monastic life, I had little responsibility for the girls, other than putting on skits and plays with them. This turned out to be responsibility enough. I thought it would be exciting for the girls, and enhance their self esteem, to achieve something as a group, something that would be good enough to present to the outside world. I soon discovered what I had let myself in for. Most nights I went to rehearsal with my stomach in knots. During our first play one of my actresses attempted suicide. The night of another dress rehearsal a thirteen-year old red head, who had seemed as cool as a cucumber, went around the gym smashing her fists into the rough concrete wall until she had broken all the veins in her hands. It wasn't the play, as such; that day she had given her baby up for adoption. If one of my main characters was not sick, then she had run away. It was a gut wrenching challenge for me, but not less for the girls, who needed to learn how to believe in themselves, to work as a team and be accountable, to stick with a job, to memorize lines and come in on cue. With wonderful costumes and the generous help of Edmonton's theatre society we staged a successful three act version of Little Women, and the girls were magnificent. It gave them a great deal of pride in themselves and helped them to deal with a whole lot of emotions that had been bottled up. Yet it was the back stage dramas that I most remember.

In order to rehabilitate the girls and reintroduce them to society the nuns realized they needed to play the role of Henry Higgins in 'My Fair Lady'. Our girls could dress to the nines, but the moment they opened their mouths you knew where they were coming from. We were fortunate to have the help of professional models in the community who helped us to stage a major fashion show every year. These good women provided the girls with practical and social skills to help lift them up from the streets and prepare them to get jobs. They taught them how to talk, how to walk, basic personal hygiene, make-up and how to handle a job interview. The Fashion Show itself was a glittery and glamorous evening, always well attended by the public. The girls modeled dresses they had made themselves, which really added to their sense of accomplishment.

With varied success we attempted to put on dances for the girls. We felt we had to teach them how to behave, and give them the opportunity to have ordinary teen age fun associating with boys who would treat them with respect. We hand picked and prepped the boys and did manage to have a number of successful dances. But on more than one occasion dances were cancelled at the last minute because of nervous parents who did not want their sons associating, even under strict supervision, with 'that kind of girl'.

In later years a swimming pool, tennis courts and five cottages, each with room for twelve girls and two nuns, were built to ease the girls into a more home like setting. The school was outfitted with home economics labs and all the latest bells and whistles. It gave the girls the opportunity to catch up to their peers academically and thus avoid the stigma of failure. Once the girls had caught up and gained privileges they would be allowed to attend regular outside schools. School, however, was a struggle for most of them. Their emotional problems tended to overshadow and impair their concentration, and most, frankly, were not overly interested in learning. Therefore, it puzzled Sister Aloysius that a steady stream of books began disappearing from the library. She wondered if it indicated a growing interest in reading. Then, one day a Sister brought her the binding of a book she had found dumped in the trash can in the dorm. Inside the covers a ragged, stubbly edge of paper was left. It looked like it had been chewed! In the following weeks other books in the same condition began to turn up under beds and in the garbage. It appeared that one of the girls was suffering from parorexia, which took the form of an abnormal craving for the printed word. The finger of suspicion pointed to a diminutive girl named Christina.

"Who can tell me the meaning of the word 'environment'?" Sister Aloysius quizzed her class.

No one raised a hand.

"Alright, Ellen, please look up environment in the big dictionary in the back and report to the class what it means?"

Ellen trotted obediently to the back of the room.

"It ain't here, Mother! The dictionary's gone."

Sister Aloysius hesitated a moment in frustration, "What do you mean its not there?" Then her eyes narrowed and she stared into a pair of wide brown eyes in the front row:

"Christina," she ordered, "Open your mouth!"

***

Girls' faces parade through my mind, and through my heart. Barbara: a lovely, graceful girl who should have been a model, not a delinquent. Lorraine: who got a job in a pizza place after she left, and brought me my first pizza. Sharon: who ran away and now comes back to visit us in an iron lung. She was hitch hiking west of Calgary when a truck picked her up. The driver was drunk and he demolished the truck. Sharon's spinal cord was crushed and she ended up in an iron lung. She was such a pretty girl, with fine delicate features. I remember her fine mind and her soul full of beautiful poetry. But sad...and filled with so many questions...

And there is Beth, who at sixteen contracted some deadly form of emphysema, and asked if she could come back so that she could die among us. We fixed her up a special room where she held court among all the girls. She died among gentleness and laughter, and the girls learned something about death and about life.

I remember Camille. She was twelve, pensive, intense, her jet dark eyes patrolling the halls, seeking attention. She was the victim of incest. No wonder she acted out. Her father and four brothers were all having sexual relations with her. She didn't have a clue what a normal relationship was like.

And there was June, a pretty girl with blond hair curling up at her ears, and guarded sober blue eyes. Hers was an adoption gone awry, and June ran away repeatedly until she was sent to us. In the more than a year that she was with us she had never spoken more than a dozen words. Yet she behaved well and seemed almost content with us. Since she had shown no inclination to run away from us, she was given outside privileges. She would attach herself to some Sister she liked, and as the Sister sat saying her Office or reading, she would come and sit quietly on the grass at her feet, seeming just to enjoy the sense of companionship. Her eyes, alert like a deer, never missed anything. She belonged to no groups, seeking neither the approbation of her peers nor their blame. Actually, she seemed to have gained a sort of respect from the girls, either because of her strange silence or because she felt no need to be a part of their pecking order.

Or there was Ruth, who seemed oddly detached, lost in her own world of mysteries, wrestling with her own demons. She talked, but rarely communicated. She was a normal looking girl, an attractive brunette, with dark wistful eyes. We struggled to reach her but seemed always to be chasing shadows, her reality ever evading discovery. Then the Sisters commented one day on an apparent thawing, a warming up. Sister Clare took Ruth out to pick flowers that night. It was a gentle summer evening; the sunset painted the sky with glory and twittering birds everywhere prepared for the hush of the night. Ruth seemed responsive, serene, almost normal. Then, when Sister Clare went in the shed to get a pail of water for the flowers, Ruth was gone. Later her broken body was found on the cement at the bottom of the high level bridge. A picture was found fluttering in the breeze at the place where Ruth had plunged forever into her darkness; a picture of her mother and father.

I found the Habits we wore were an advantage to us. The lives of our girls were so scarred with negative and destructive relationships that they came to us angry, devious, and manipulative. But the girls were fascinated by us. Our Habits set us apart from everything they knew, and though they tested us, they felt able to trust us when they could trust no one else. We were there for them not because it was a job, or even because it was a duty. We were there because we had chosen to leave the world they knew to be with them. Our fourth vow to serve them was a proclamation of their value; to the Father Who had given them being, and to us. It helped them to believe in themselves, in their own potential.

"Don't give me that shit!" a girl was screaming at her social worker as I came down the hall, "Don't pretend you care for us. It's a job for you. You think I don't know you get paid to talk to me? You leave here at five and go home to your life. You don't care! The Sisters, they care! They are here for us always!"

For a lot of the girls what began as a custodial institution, a punishment, ended up becoming a home. The visiting rooms were always full of girls; coming back to show us their children and husbands, to share successes, to get the courage to work through failures, to be affirmed, warmed and to feel loved. Or just to share funny stories and to see faces that had become part of the landscape of their lives. It was an odd celebration, this kinship between the women in the long flowing robes and the children of the streets.

A priest at a retreat put things in perspective:

"Don't ever imagine that you are somehow better, superior, more valued by God than these children of the streets. Most of you have come from good homes, stable homes, loving homes, but these children carry the cross of Christ. A prostitute from 97th street who shows kindness for a sister in need may be more pleasing to God than you with all your prayers, because she is giving her widow's mite from her heart. She is widowed of support, of help, of love, and what she gives she gives out of her extreme poverty."

The year after my first Profession of Vows I was sent along to help supervise a group of twenty-seven girls at summer camp. The Sisters had rented a camp facility by a small shimmering lake. It was in a secluded area, surrounded by lovely woods teeming with life. Behind the long spacious building that housed us all was a hill topped by a plateau just big enough for a baseball diamond. It was a place filled with a special stillness, broken only by the lapping of the water against the beach, the croaking of frogs and the crying of loons.

The girls that had come with us for this week of camping had had to earn the privilege. Still, as I looked around me, I could see it would be a challenging group, I was relieved that Sister Immaculate Heart had come along. Her presence and experience, as well as her caring heart, somehow influenced the girls and commanded their respect. I knew there would be no unsolvable problems while she was around.

She was not around for long. By day two, whether from an insect bite or some severe allergy, she broke out in a terrible rash and was having trouble breathing. We had to get her to a hospital immediately, and she remained there for the rest of the camp!

That left Sister Nicholas, Sister Magdalene and me, all of us more or less neophytes. Sister Magdalene was busy full time with the cooking and other physical needs of the camp. Sister Nicholas and I were left with the running of the camp.

Alarm bells were going off in my head. I assessed the situation. Little June was along. She would do her own thing. I didn't expect any problems from her. Tracy and Sherry would be going home in a couple of weeks, as soon as social workers could complete arrangements with their parents. I knew them quite well; they were easy going and they liked me and seemed quite stable. Pat was another matter. She was schizophrenic and withdrawn and had no social skills. She did alarming things to get personal attention. I would have to be on guard that she did nothing to harm herself, and I could count on her to try running away.

Running away proved to be one of our big problems. But God sent us a special angel on wheels. Despite the remote location, girls were constantly going missing. They would manage to find their way to the highway and hitchhike. Every time Father Ben left the rectory for any reason, he would meet up with a couple of them on the highway. Some girls he brought back several times. We saw lot of Father Ben!

But my worst problem at that camp was a girl named Vicki. She was a leader among the girls and I knew I would have to get her on side if this camp were to succeed at all. Vicki was an air head, an agitator, a manipulator. It always amazed me which girls arose to assume leadership among their peers. It was never the brighter or better girls. It was always the most brash, the loudest and most brazen. Although Vicki could feign sweetness she was often unpleasant, even to those who followed her. I guess they were afraid of her. With the dark roots of her bleached hair showing, she faced the world—and me—with defiance. I chose to overlook the defiance, and the fawning subservience, and the whispering behind my back, and I treated her like my first lieutenant. I asked her to organize the baseball games, the scavenger hunts, and the frog races. Pleased that I accepted her leadership among the girls, she did cooperate with me part time. But Vicki craved excitement. She spent her time masterminding cruel pranks on the girls, and kept the gossip mills churning at full tilt. Some of the girls ran away just to get away from her. But I felt helpless to do anything about it. In a forced confrontation I feared I would lose and a riot could break out. She had a henchman, Josie, a big, dull girl built like a fullback, and she was always at Vicki's side, doing her bidding and glorying in the status it gave her. I felt like I was dancing on hot coals always trying to keep abreast of their constant audacious scheming. Still, I felt some satisfaction that by keeping the peace at all costs, that I wouldn't be reading about this camp in the newspapers, and that most of the girls would succeed in having a good time. The activities had been well planned, and we had good long talks on the beach at night. We sang and grew closer. No one dared to ask why I gave in to Vicki so much. I guess they knew. The last night we had a scavenger hunt, the most difficult yet and it called for real ingenuity. The other team made our list and they thought they would get us good. We worked our way around most of the items but we were really stumped over 'mistletoe'. The other team was already savoring their victory under the leadership of Sister Nicholas when I came into the cabin towing a Sunday Missal on a string. It brought down the house!

Two hours before we were due to leave for home on the chartered bus that final morning, Vicki and Josie disappeared from camp along with Tracy and Sherry. Not even Father Ben, who had succeeded in picking up all our other runaways, could find them. I was livid with frustration and anxiety. How could Vicki persuade the two best kids in camp to go with her? They were due to go home. They had everything to lose. But that was Vicki's craft, her power. I recognized, too, that Vicki had deliberately chosen those two because they were compliant, and they liked to hang around me rather than her. It was crass and vindictive, Vicki's specialty.

Meanwhile, the bus sat and waited. We searched the camp area thoroughly but we could go no further because the situation had the girls agitated and tense and we could not leave them alone. I did not want to leave without Tracy and Sherry but what could I do? We waited. Suddenly we heard a rustling in the underbrush and out marched Vicki and Josie, flushed and feverish with victory. Behind them, heads hung low, followed Tracy and Sherry meekly. Little knots of girls stood waiting uneasily, looking at Vicki, looking at me. The air was electric with tension.

What should I do? How should I handle this? The answer was not coming. The love and acceptance and patience–so much patience–I had extended to her so freely had been trampled underfoot in disdain!

Vicki headed straight for me. She tramped up to me brazenly, audaciously, smirking as she looked me straight in the eye. Instinct took over. I lifted my hand and slapped her across the face.

What have I done? I wailed inside myself. I shocked myself. We were never to raise our hands against a girl. My fingers had barely grazed her cheek but...

Everyone on the beach was frozen in shock. It was like a game of statues. No one moved. Endlessly. For a long, long moment no one seemed to breathe. After a few startled seconds Vicki regained her composure and immediately began to agitate.

June, as silent as usual, broke away unnoticed from the group she stood with and headed purposefully toward me.

"Now what?" I wondered.

But her eyes formed a silent salute as she reached out toward me and shook my hand.

Suddenly it seemed like a radio was turned on all over the beach. Girls were moving and talking and laughing. Only Vicki stood still now, her bubble burst, bewildered, deflated, dethroned.

CHAPTER 10

There is only blackness. And silence. Even the owls in the woods have been sucked into the vortex of the night. A misty rain tiptoes across my shoulders and cools my feverish cheeks. If only it could quell the fire in my gut and unclench the fist of fear that holds my life in bondage.

Kindly darkness rests on me. It is a darkness that is not dark. It is the dawn I fear. But in my memory there is a different light. I possess this light. It is mine. My consciousness is stained with the vestigial dye of the colors of ten thousand days. Memories are the postcards I send back to myself on the edge of this abyss. I have captured time, bottled it, given it definition even as it has defined me. Like a child filling a vessel by a stream I stop and drink, but the river flows on, powerful, inexorable.

Like the highway.

The Greyhound bus gobbles up the miles, efficient servant of the twentieth century that it is. The flat golden plains stretch as far as the eye can see, bleached under the spell of late July. The grain ripples beneath the eye of the scorching wind. Puny wire fences mark off man's domain, and telephone poles flick by with hypnotic frequency.

Then, suddenly, without warning, the fields are interrupted by a valley. But what a valley! Like Divine energy gone wild with a carving knife, the unsuspecting tableland ends abruptly in sheer jagged serrated cliffs falling to the flat plain below. There, in the middle of the forbidding badlands, an oasis of green, the city of Drumheller, sits ensconced amid the eerie fortress walls of a million years of erosion. The old playground of the dinosaurs is the setting for a two week drama workshop put on by the National Theatre. Here to hone my talents, I am accompanied by Sister Good Counsel, a sage and gung ho elementary school teacher. We bed down in a vacant convent and head out in the morning to a high school that sizzles at the base of barren hills, the domain of gophers and rattlesnakes.

Our Religious Habits form a sharp contrast with the other casually dressed participants who are milling around in the quadrangle in front of the school. We wait curiously for the notables from the theatre world who will be our instructors. A young man in a blue shirt and khaki pants is standing close to the flagpole and he turns around. Our eyes intersect, and there is sudden recognition and warmth flowing although we have never met. I am conscious immediately that I feel drawn to him, and I know instinctively that his perception is the same.

Madame Springfield arrives along with Freda De Branscoville, bright lights from the theatre of Eastern Canada. Thomas Kerr, a born in Alberta talent, joins them, followed by others.

Madame Springfield is small, slim, graceful, animated, with rapier eyes. She is forthright, provocative, encouraging, vital. She will encourage me to keep a daily diary, for which I have neither time nor self discipline. She is a purveyor of drama, and she is fascinated by the different world from which I come.

Freda introduces herself. She has a rich, resonating contralto voice and a shock of auburn hair. We are divided into groups. I shuffle off with my group for a class in improvisation with Freda. Soon we are immersed in the Stanislavski Method. We cease being who we are. (It was so easy then....) We are assigned a rapid succession of new personae. We are three years old. We are seniors. We are Spanish migrant workers. We are angry. We are giddy. We sweat. Our psyches are pulled in all directions. Our emotional resources are taxed.

Freda stands before us and intones:

"Break! Break! Break!
at the foot of thy crags, O Sea!
O would that my heart could utter
the thoughts that arise in me...."

Her deep voice sears us and draws us into a well of the human spirit. I cannot eradicate her voice from my head; her fury, her pathos, her heartbreak. This is not drama. This is where drama comes from: the reality we share.

She tells us about her young love. The good life. Traveling. A marvelous husband, wealthy, urbane. Strange unexplained silences. Distance. The shock of discovering her husband's homosexuality. Her grief, her questions, words said and words unsaid. The final silence of an airplane crash and death beside his lover. Freda is the voice of the human condition. Hurting, fighting, hoping, despairing.

"I want you to share something with us now," she said, "Each of us has unresolved conflicts, moments of pain, of growth. I want you to take such a moment and face it now. You will do it in mime. You will use no words, no props. You will make us see it as you see it."

There is a gasping and a shuffling in the group. Then concentration.

"What shall I do?" I ask myself in consternation.

I remember that due to the laws of enclosure of the cloister that I could not attend my sister's funeral. Today I will attend that funeral. I will lay my hand on her cold flesh and say my goodbyes. I do not begrudge her her leave taking. I am, instead, in awe of the adventure she has undertaken before me, and I am grateful for the hand of God in her life. But today I will take my parting from her mortal remains.

I see her casket and I touch her pale skin with the tips of my fingers for the last time. I see the crown of flowers in her hair and remember the summers of our lives. Thirteen years of togetherness pour out my eyes in silent cleansing rivers. Now it is done. It is over until I meet her again when time for me stops.

I lift my eyes from behind their cloud and the silence in the room is palpable. It goes on and on. I look through blurry eyes at human forms frozen into my grief. They do not move. They do not speak.

Finally Freda breaks the silence. "Okay," she says gently, "What did you see? What happened?"

"She seemed to be saying goodbye," one voice answers.

"Someone has died," another pipes up.

"Is this right?" Freda asks me.

"Yes. My sister. I wasn't at her funeral."

"Very good," Freda said, her eyes meeting mine in the sisterhood of the flesh. "Thank you, Sister."

The class spills out into the quadrangle. Sadly, the young man in the blue shirt had not been in my group. But I seek out his finely chiseled features in the crowd, and find his pale blue sensitive eyes smiling at me nearby. He introduces himself. Bob. From Calgary. He is Catholic. We trade stories and laugh. I feel bubbly and warm with a heat that has nothing to do with the July sun.

We have a section of the play "The Dark at the Top of the Stairs" to do with Tom Kerr. I am not entranced with the play or my part. I just can't relate to it. But the other sessions are fun. We sing and are silly and enjoy each other. Madame Springfield's room is by our social area, and our hullabaloo soon drives her scurrying out of her quarters to seek peace and quiet elsewhere. Bob's presence is a constant joy. I cannot believe how I am drawn to him. We are like kindred spirits, thinking as one, magnetized to each other. I see respect in his eyes so I know he would never overstep the boundaries of friendship, but there is incredible feeling there too, a gentle and intense loving light. One day he is grabbed by a young group and invited to go climbing. I remain behind and feel forlorn. I wonder about my own feelings.

What is happening? I ask myself. *Can these feelings be reconciled with my vocation as a nun?*

But the days tumble over one another and soon there is a wrenching sorrow to know we must say good bye. Bob hovers around, and when the cab comes to take us back to the convent to pick up our things, he impulsively asks Sister Good Counsel if he can tag along with us for the ride. Sister's eyebrow flickers briefly, but she agrees. He takes my address and promises to visit me. I go home with a rainbow in my sky.

Three weeks later I am summoned to the visiting rooms. As he had requested and promised, there he was. I reach the doorway and see Bob's tall slim form standing a trifle apprehensively beside the window. As he turns around I look again at those eyes which have spoken so eloquently, which possess such an extraordinary light. But to my surprise his eyes are like anyone else's eyes today. There is eagerness and friendliness in them. But the light is gone. Suddenly, inexplicably, we have nothing in common but our common shell of humanity and our hunger for something more. We talk of nothing in particular, and I am puzzled and somewhat relieved as Bob walks out of my life.

What is the meaning of this? I question myself in the chapel in the lengthening twilight. I am shaken that the mystical attraction I felt for him has evaporated like smoke. I am no longer captivated by his charm. Where is that special person I experienced? My rainbow has returned to the mystery of the heavens from where it came. My mind takes me back to another relationship of my early youth when my heart was first startled by the magical touch of love. I had been overwhelmed, my expectations so vast that the entire sky of my existence rang with joy and anticipation. But it too had disappeared like a mirage in the desert.

Why? I ask.

In the stillness Christ speaks to my understanding.

"Love Me with passion," He says to me. "In the enervating routine of daily life, in the constant drill of duty, don't become like a machine. Don't give me less than you would give a human love."

Someone flicks on the chapel light and its white beam falls across the blue eyes and finely chiseled features of the Christ figure over the altar.

"I will be a storm in your heart until you love Me with passion!" He says to me.

I remember a day when Sister Nicholas and I were sitting in the gym with the girls watching the movie 'The Student Prince'. Sister Nicholas had noticed how enthralled I was by the wonderful love relationship between the prince and a barmaid. She leaned over to me and whispered, "If human love is so beautiful, what is Divine love?"

Have I, my God, fallen asleep at the great bonfire of Your love, that fire that has ignited a billion suns? And did You drop a spark on my drowsy eyes to wake me from my torpor?

I suddenly understand that God is not the stage manager of planet earth–He is the Romantic Lead! He is Passion itself and the source of all self giving love. He gives us the light of our minds that we might choose to love. He is the Prince of creation and we are the poor barmaids who He calls into relationship with Himself.

Again I remember the words of the early writer, St. Irenaeus: "The glory of God is man fully alive...." No life is fully alive unless it burns with passion.

Thank you, Lord, for reminding me that You are Love.

But where is Your Love tonight?

CHAPTER 11

All the great thoughts of the greatest minds of history were at my disposal! The year after my temporary profession of vows I was sent to the University of Alberta, majoring in psychology and minoring in philosophy. I was in my element.

The registration forms required us to register under our family surnames. Hardly had the ink dried on my application when I received a phone call from a friendly, bubbling, imploring female voice:

"We have just heard that you will be attending our university, and we would be very honored to have you become a member of our sorority."

I gulped. "I will be at the university, but I don't think you understand...." I began.

"I assure you, we have a lot to offer. We have taken a vote already and you have been unanimously chosen. Please don't disappoint us. We will be waiting for you at four on Thursday in front of Student Services?" she gushed. "You will recognize us by the sorority pins on our blue scarves."

"But you don't know me," I protested.

"Don't worry, Mary Tudor," she reassured me. "We feel we have made a good choice, and I think you will find you have made a good choice...."

Mary Tudor?! I began to laugh. Now I understand. But surely my handwriting is not THAT bad!

"Actually," I said, "I am a nun."

Dead silence. My contact appeared to have a speech impediment. After several garbled noises there came some rapid backpedaling followed by a click.

"Terrible down draft around here," I giggled to Sr. Monica, who stared at me uncomprehendingly.

I discovered the campus to be an eclectic mix of efficient boxy buildings, gracious ivy covered halls, a splash of the modern in brick and glass, and, during my second year, in some sort of an architectural rebellion, a new library sprang up which was most aptly nicknamed 'the Golden Pagoda'.

One of the oldest buildings, St. Joseph's College, decorated in the dark wood of its time, and pregnant with the musty smell of old books, was a busy concourse for those taking Christian studies, or just seeking a quiet place to study, pray, or hang out. It was there Father Dore, a tall, white haired, austere man of awesome intellect presided over Thomistic philosophy, while Father James Daley led us through Apologetics. Father Daley was a middle aged man who kept his sensitivity hidden under a crusty exterior. He quickly nicknamed me 'St. John'. He would barrel down the hallways, head down, apparently lost to everything but his own thoughts, but would always grunt: "St. John!" as he passed me by. Only the closest of scrutiny would reveal the twinkle in his eye.

I was stimulated and intoxicated by philosophy. In it I found the map of my mind and the deepest understanding of history. Had I been given the chance, I would have jumped at the opportunity of doing nothing else but burying myself in philosophy for a couple of years. But statistics, geography and English divided my days, plus a plethora of psychology courses that held a varying degree of interest for me. A psychologist was needed to work with the girls under our care, and if I was to be a helper and a healer, I would have to know man in all his humanity and the aberrations thereof.

In the waning sun of autumn I took to wearing running shoes to get to my classes, which usually managed to be at opposite ends of the campus. I became known as 'the nun on the run' and it felt good to be me.

The psychology department was located in the two lower floors of the old Arts and Science Building and was peopled by a variety of fascinating individuals. The Boltons, a married couple, both psychologists, had come up from Berkely in California. Catholic, like myself, they were strong and vibrant people who had been tried in the furnace of dissent and anarchy that was Berkley. By contrast, there was Dr. Willy Runquist, a jock, an ex hockey star, who looked the antithesis of an intellectual. Although I took no courses from him he knew exactly who I was, thanks, it seemed to some information being passed among the faculty. Willy was always on the go, and with his easy manner and his crew cut, he reminded me of my uncles. He had nicknamed me 'Babe', and took great delight in startling people down the hallways by greeting me at the top of his voice with a lusty, "Hey, Babe!" Dr. Jack Hunter, assistant dean, looked like an aging teen idol with his shiny black hair. But his face was puffy and bore the marks of a man who has lived too well. Some of the students said that his glazed eyes were due to drugs. My practicum at the Royal Alexandra hospital was directed by a dear jovial old soul named Dr. Steinmetz, who always referred to himself as my "uncle".

I noticed that my Habit gave me an edge in relationships. People either trusted me at once and were able to relate to me without masks or barriers, or they crossed to the other side of the street to avoid meeting me. These latter were a challenge to me and I went out of my way to destroy their stereotypes and prejudices.

Nowhere was there more hostility than in my Honors Seminar in Psychology. Every Thursday night we would meet, nineteen of us who were considered to be the brightest young lights among the thousands registered in psychology classes. Several of the students were openly aghast to have to share a table with a nun, and Professor Bill Somers, our mentor, was bemused, but intrigued. A lot of the students there were in a direct flight from all forms of religion and hoped in the scientific approach of psychology to excoriate from their souls any vestige of theological tampering. In fact, some of these seemed to turn to psychology as a substitute religion. My appearance there was greeted as an anachronistic hallucination.

"I want you to feel you can speak freely here, as equals," Dr. Somers welcomed us, as we seated ourselves around a large dark wood table. "Dr. Hunter and I feel you have something to contribute and we are not here to pull rank. We encourage an interdisciplinary approach to learning and we feel that the future of psychology will be enriched by such an approach."

Dr. Somers was a handsome man in his mid thirties, with wavy brown hair and a beard. He impressed me with his calm openness and by the sincerity of his pursuit of truth.

"Each of you has a reason why you are here tonight. Why have you chosen psychology?" he asked of each of us.

"I don't know. I'm just checking it out," a tall leggy brunette called Donna said seductively, checking out Dr. Somers with her large liquid green eyes.

Somers stiffened in irritation at her cloying dependent manner.

"My father is a doctor; I decided to try something else. Frankly, I don't want to march in his shadow," came a voice from the end of the table.

"I want to study something factual, something empirical, that will sound the death knell on all the old superstitions and creeds that have messed up my family and the world." A tall thin young man in glasses turned and glared at me bitterly, with a suggestion of triumph: "I don't accept your creed, your gospel," Allen proclaimed with acid superiority.

"You don't have to accept my truth," I retorted with a smile, hoping to thaw him a little. "But I hope you will find a truth to resonate in you that is worth living for, and that will be 'good news' for the world."

"Nice try, Sister," Claude interjected churlishly, "but the truth is that religion has been used to control people. If you're honest you'll have to admit that religious people run around with their hatchets, holding them over other peoples' heads."

I began to fumble energetically in my book bag under the table. I lifted my head and everyone was looking at me with askance.

"Sorry," I said mischievously, "I was just looking for my hatchet. I must have misplaced it."

There were a couple of groans and some laughter. The atmosphere lightened a little.

I smiled at Allan and Claude. "It would be foolish to totally deny what you've said," I conceded. "Many people do distort religion or use it for their own selfish ends. But some doctors and other professionals also play God, make mistakes, and some even abuse their patients. But this does not invalidate all of medicine."

Dr. Somers sat back in his chair, puffing on his ever present brier pipe. "Excuse me," he said, "It seems to me that the word 'truth' is being bandied about here rather loosely. I have my personal reservations about whether, in the last analysis, we are even capable of finding or knowing 'truth'. I guess you would call me an agnostic, Sister. I would like to know God. He may even exist. But at this time in my life, I've had to conclude that we cannot know anything with certainty."

"But then," I looked at him quizzically, "by what knowledge do you know that you cannot know? You have just proclaimed a certainty that sounds a lot like the proclamation of a truth."

Dr. Somers drew heartily on his pipe, studying me steadily with a gleam in his eye. Then he stared reflectively at the table.

"You have a good point there. Yes." He looked at me keenly and with respect.

"Yes, that sounds all fine and dandy," Claude protested after a moment of silence. The faces around the table looked alert, except for Donna who was looking disinterested and crossing and re-crossing her legs. "But," he carried on, "science is built on the observation of physical phenomena. That is what I like. God is not an empirical phenomenon that can be seen and measured. By definition He can't be put in a little box."

"But in fact, we often do try to put Him in a little box, and then we wonder why we don't find Him worthy of our belief," I said ruefully, "and a lot of our problems which we ascribe to religion come from just this fact."

"I've got to add a codicil to what Claude just said," Clem interjected thoughtfully. "Sometimes in science we infer from the theoretical framework we have constructed more than we can actually see. In calculating the periodic table we knew that there had to be more elements than we had physical knowledge of. And this proved to be true. The same in astronomy. The existence of certain celestial phenomena and physical laws sometimes leads us to posit the existence of other celestial bodies or occurrences that we have not yet perceived in a telescope."

"Similarly," I added, "although the nature of God must mostly be the stuff of revelation and faith, for my own part, I believe the existence of God can be inferred from reason."

"Can't buy it," Allan snapped.

"Okay," I said, "One of the basic assumptions in science is that physical laws are interdependent, and that things in this world are in relationship to other things. Because of this, the studying of cause and effect becomes the primary tool to accumulate our knowledge. Everything we see has been caused by something else. We get into these long progressions of one thing leading back to the thing before it. By this means we can go back from the observation of everything we see, everything that is the effect of something else, until finally we must posit the existence of a Primary Cause Who we call God. Similarly, we see that motion is a fact. And we know that a thing cannot be reduced from potency to act except by that which is already in act. Every atom that exists is an explosion of motion! If everything that is moved is moved by another, this must sooner or later lead us back to an unmoved Mover Who is God."

"Yes, but everything we see is finite. How can we go back to something that is infinite?" Allan sneers.

"I think we must. Everything that we see comes into existence and perishes. Any particular thing we look at is contingent and cannot explain

119

its own existence. That is, it is not necessary in itself; it could either be or not be. If it was necessary it would always have existed and could not pass away. Reason tells us that there must be one necessary Being by which all contingent beings came into existence."

"But this Being hardly sounds like your personal God of Christianity," someone objects.

"True," I agree, "but you realize, that if none of these contingent beings possess their own being of themselves, then neither can they possess their own beauty, their own truth, their own goodness of themselves. There must be one Who is perfection, Who is ultimate Beauty, Goodness and Truth. We see beauty in the world, so we know Beauty exists. We see goodness in the world, and although only a partial goodness, we know that Goodness exists. I like to think that all that is beautiful, true and good in this world—nature, music, human love–these are all love letters from our Creator, written for our spirits to know His Reality. The art reflects the heart of the artist."

"Yes", Clem added, "and I cannot believe that some Intelligence does not direct our universe. After all, how do bees communicate with each other, and what about all the incredible animal instincts, not to mention the complexity of our bodies and minds? Then look at all the inorganic components of our world and universe. They have no volition or knowledge of themselves, but we see them, too, behaving in a universal ordered harmony. Obviously, since they have no ability to direct themselves we must infer a Designer, a Creator of all this."

Our discussions were far ranging and intense. We went on to discuss perception and the mechanics of learning, with me bringing in the difference between Aristotle and Thomas Aquinas' understanding of psychology and the process of knowing. Dr. Somers invited me to stay and discuss it with him in greater depth.

The next day in a large amphitheatre class of more than five hundred students, Dr. Somers paused in his prepared text on knowledge and learning and added the codicil: "Some of these ideas I will have to rethink after my discussion with Sister last night."

I was stunned–that a professor of his stature would make such a public declaration–by his humility in allowing a young student to challenge his whole approach to the subject he taught. I grew to admire this man more and more for his intellectual honesty, his fairness, his simple forthrightness. *What a marvelous creature the Lord of Creation has fashioned,* I thought!

I was no less awestruck by the greatness I saw in some of my fellow students who I got to know so well through the Seminar. They shared so much with me—their worries and doubts, their aspirations, their affection; and I found a profound honesty in them, a concern for the value of their own lives and decisions, and a caring for others. Wherever they are planted in life today they will have enriched the garden of the earth. Although some of my fellow students, like Donna, whose agenda revolved around her own emotional needs, remained indifferent or averse to me, I was particularly pleased to win a grudging respect from the more hostile elements of the class like Allan. He and Claude continued to challenge me, but their barbs were blunted, and they no longer avoided me. I understood that the history of their hurts and disillusion and prejudice was buried deep in their psyches below the level of reason. When reason gained ascendance in an argument, stormy emotions often drowned out the result. But Claude especially had warmed up. Wiry and quick, with eyes like two black bullets, witty and inquisitive, he became the spice in my days. Someday, I prayed, let them find the faith that will bring their hearts home.

I knew, by then, that to find God with your reason was not the same thing as to find Him in your heart. I had watched my girlfriend Joanie play around for years with thoughts about God, but for her, when faith finally came, it struck like a lightning bolt.

I was never really sure why she had wanted to attend my Catholic high school. She drifted in and out of religion class as the spirit moved her; she certainly hadn't come for that. She had been exposed to some elements of faith, and later, when I entered the monastery she had asked some questions. But even when she agreed with my answers she never saw any need to make a personal commitment of her own. Then, one weekend when she was up to visit me in the monastery, she accompanied me to Mass.

Father Champagne was a strange sort of priest. Living in a monastery one might expect to receive frequent and inspired homilies. But Father Champagne's mastery of English was poor, and he was a bashful man. In all the time he came to serve as our chaplain he had never given a single sermon. So it was with some shock and fascination that I saw him leave the altar abruptly that day and march toward the front pews where a dozen or so of our girls had been cutting up—not by any means an unusual occurrence. In a blistering tone he berated them for their noisy and disrespectful behavior. He spoke to them of the real presence of Jesus Christ, the Son of God Himself, in the consecrated Hosts on the altar. He went back in history and asked them why God would have asked that a mere dumb lamb be sacrificed by the Jewish people for the Passover? And why were they commanded to eat this lamb that had been sacrificed? He told them that this was to prepare our understanding for what was right now happening on this altar; the eternal Sacrifice of Him whom the Father called the Lamb of God. He explained that the manna of the Old Testament also prefigured this Bread of Life Who comes to us now. God, he said, is offering us a share in His own Life! He is our Divine blood transfusion, bringing health back to our bodies and spirits. And He laid down His life in a frightful agony so that we might be united to Him.

Although surprised by his vehemence, I didn't find Father's explanation anything out of the ordinary. His unskilled and awkward wording with his thick accent did not qualify him as a great orator, which probably explained why he so seldom spoke. I doubted that his speech would have much impact on the girls.

I turned to look at Joanie as we left the chapel and was shocked to see that she was deathly pale.

"I believe what he said!" she blurted out in amazement. "I have to enter the Church."

I was dumfounded. While I had sat there so nonchalantly, something tender and terrible had happened within my friend's spirit. The mystery of God had embraced her and called her home. She could talk of nothing else for the duration of the visit, and I advised her to go to see a priest at the Church nearest her home.

Soon she was writing me back. Her parents absolutely forbade her to enter the Church as long as she lived under their roof. They cajoled her; what if she should fall in love with someone of a different faith and choose to marry him. Joanie agreed to wait.

But God had His own plan for my friend. Soon she met her soul mate, a young man named Pat, who happened to be a fervent Catholic.

The phone rang. It was Joanie: "Johanna," she sang out in excitement, "I've bought Pat a rosary as my gift to him for our engagement. But what do I do with it? I mean, how do I get it blessed or what?"

I smiled. Prayers from the heart are certainly valid with or without a blessed rosary. "Take it to Mass," I suggested, and simply approach the priest later on the way out and ask for the blessing."

But Joanie wanted more. She wanted to make an appointment with the priest. I chuckled at her solemn formality and gave her the name of a priest I knew at the cathedral in Calgary. Things moved quickly from there; after the rocky road she had experienced with her own family, it was an enriching experience to become a part of Pat's large loving family. For me, it was my joy to share what was most precious in my life, a living relationship with God.

I was not so lucky with my dearly loved mentor, Dr. Somers. At the end of my third year at the University of Alberta, the need at the monastery for a psychologist had become critical. Although I was not qualified for the position yet, I offered to cut a year from my studies in Edmonton and proceed directly to graduate school. I was able to do this because I already had all the courses I needed for my degree, but I was touched and surprised when the Dean of Arts, Dr. Smith, personally summoned me to his office and tried to convince me to stay. It was hard to go. I felt blessed in the years I had spent at the University of Alberta, and I was grateful that I had been able to make some small difference. I felt a stab of regret at the thought of leaving the many good friends I had made, but leave I must.

As the year ended, I returned to pick up some papers and to say good bye to Dr. Somers. When I entered his smoky, cluttered office, Donna was sitting there. I immediately knew I had interrupted something, and by the electricity in the air and the preoccupied sidelong glances passing back and forth I sensed that my much admired mentor, a married man with young sons, was having an affair with his student. My mouth felt like chalk and my stomach felt sick. It was the sensation of standing at the foot of a great mountain and seeing it crumble; the sadness of seeing a wonderful monument being defaced.

How can a man measure truth with a soul that is false?

CHAPTER 12

May 2, 1965

Dear Most Reverend (?) Niece (Johnson Wax),

Upon checking unanswered correspondence with my private secretary—who incidentally occupies so much of my generous time—I find that our incoming mail exceeds our output by approximately 4 to 1. I guess this is to be expected when one adopts the policy of pleasure before business. However, rest assured that you are remembered in our annual prayers (long may we live!). As yet we cannot say that we have felt the effect of your prayers—I think you need more practice. By this method one can achieve perfection.

Your card announcing the great day in your life—your Final Profession—was met with great joy and a desire to attend such a function. I am yet uncertain whether I shall obtain sufficient time off, but will know by midweek. If things work out as I hope they will, then you might just be lucky enough to see your handsome uncle (kind-hearted, warm-blooded, etc.). However, should circumstances not permit, we shall make every effort to be there in spirit (but not in spirits). My interfering partner here has just requested that if we do not show up, the least we should receive from you is a wall-to-wall picture (not necessarily with halo).

Your requests for a picture of our ample brood presents a rather difficult task as the present day cameras can only encompass so many figures, and to take individual photos would require more than one roll of film, which brings up the question of cost. (However, we live in hope that perhaps some day the world may get to know us.) Tonight I will be babysitting Bratinella and the hordes. Perhaps you have a little extra room at the orphanage? I hope you don't think I'm in the habit of exaggerating: actions speak louder than words, and believe me there's plenty of action around here.

Dad is in the hospital again after another mild heart attack but is making favorable progress. Unless my eyes deceive me, I should be an uncle again—#3 for Victor. Don't know when though. Afraid to ask.

By the way, I believe the Yorkton nuisance grounds are looking for a good rat exterminator; if I remember correctly a little girl I used to know was pretty good at it... But I hear the place you are in has big high walls and doors that are kept locked continuously so Johnson Wax can't polish her way out.

I suppose I ought to end this chapter or I might find myself making nasty remarks—no matter how true they may be.

May the Lord bless you and all the good Sisters in your wonderful work.

Sincerely,
Ernest and Co.

***

Ha! Typical Ernest! He thinks he is a knight in King Arthur's Court; our relationship is an ongoing jousting match. I love hearing from him, and it will be good recreation answering him in kind. If I don't see him on my Profession Day I will have a go at it.

***

Final Profession Day...

I have had goose bumps over this for months. Some days I wish I could hold back the clock, but the day rushes toward me like a tumbleweed driven by a prairie wind. Of course, if I am not ready, I could ask to renew my temporary vows again. But this thought does not appeal to me. At the head level, intellectually, I have no doubts. Only self doubts.

Poverty I can handle. I lack none of the basics and have no need of personal possessions, nor can any passing material thing hold a candle to the possession of God. Obedience? I can visualize situations where this could be hard, although up to now my Superiors have always been kind and reasonable in their requests. I do trip over my chin on occasion over such things as being sent for a stint in the ironing room. Or being sent to sort eighty cases of mostly rotten job lot raspberries that had been donated.

However, Sister Immaculate Heart was there to work side by side with us, so what could I say? Perhaps the yuckiest obedience that came my way–for me as well as the other Novitiate Sisters–was the year something went wrong with the twenty-five acres of potatoes we had stored in our root cellar. They were nearly all bad and stank to high heaven. But because they were needed for food, we were sent to sort them out. We were a pretty glum bunch to start with, until Sister Celeste reached into a bin to pull out what she thought was the sprout on a potato and it turned out to be a very agitated mouse. After that we giggled at everything without rhyme or reason.

But what if one day Sister Clare is voted Superior? A competent, classically beautiful woman with a sparkling personality and a great deal of strength; she certainly has leadership qualities. But I have never succeeded in getting behind her armor to where she still nurses the injured nerve that I somehow aggravated. For a year I have been sitting beside her at meals and she has responded to my occasional forays into conversation with apparent deafness. When she is asked to drive me somewhere, the car is taut with tension; holidays when she is present are exhausting affairs. I wish I could let the whole thing slide off my back, simply not care. But I have such wonderful memories from when we were friends. I admired her so much. Now I simply cannot withdraw into a position of not caring. It bothers me in a human sense, and also in a spiritual sense. It violates the love and peace that I truly want to live. Anyway, it is not simply that she is ignoring me. It would be simpler if it was. No, when we are alone together, she averts her eyes, but when we are together in a group she presides as a mocking judge, imitating my laughter, caricaturizing my gestures. I feel wooden and hollow and despised around her. And what if she should be my Superior one day? Am I ready for that? I don't think I could ever be ready. Could I then, endure? Perhaps, with God's help. I have endured so far. Christ was despised and He warned us that we would be despised too. But it hurts. Somehow I must have unwittingly stumbled against something in her past, some point of sensitivity and pain, and it seems she has displaced all the anger of her life on to me. It would be easier if she and I could only talk it out so I could understand. But she refuses to talk. I would happily apologize if she would accept my apology, even if I do not understand what I have done to hurt her. Sister Divine Heart always said: "The supernatural builds on the natural. If we are neurotic, we will love God neurotically."

Christ said that you cannot put new wine in old wineskins. You cannot slap on perfection as you would a coat of paint. The creases in the wall still remain; the unfinished ridges and the holes that held the pictures of our past will disfigure the future until they are dealt with. It seems there are no shortcuts. "The grain of wheat falling down into the ground must die or it remains alone; but if it dies it will bring forth much fruit." But in the end, we can't do it for anyone else; it is hard enough just to do it for ourselves.

And Chastity? How am I going to handle chastity for the rest of my life? Sometimes I ache for a shoulder to lay my head on, for the loving touch of a human hand. This is a sacrifice. And I can only pray that Christ's promise will be fulfilled in me when He said; "I will become in you a fountain, springing up unto life everlasting." Or as St. Augustine said, "If you are hungry, He is food; if you are thirsty, He is drink; if you are naked, He is your cloak of immortality." This much I know and have experienced, again in the words of Augustine: "You have made us for Yourself, O Lord, and our hearts are restless until they rest in You!" My restlessness has become my peace.

But so many people are leaving Religious life right now. These are the sixties and there is tumult and upheaval in the world and in the Church. America has lost faith with what it sees as the exaggerated heroics of the past. We are tasting the dust of our own disillusion. We have capitulated, and canonized the anti-hero, the theatre of the absurd, the meaninglessness of Sartre. It is okay, we are assured, to wallow in our own weaknesses, to indulge our passing passions, to worship our own intellects. The Pill has given us pleasure without price and freedom without responsibility. Science is our cathedral and our egos are our Mecca. If these are houses of straw we build, what matter. Our world seems poised to self destruct anyway. We will go out partying. This is the prevailing wind, the zeitgeist of our times.

Up until two years ago we had a dream. We felt we could work together for a better future. But that dream disappeared in a burst of gunfire on a startling November day.

They said he could never be elected. He was young, and he was Catholic. It was not long ago that Catholics were outcasts in the deep South and had to sit at the back of the buses. He was reviled in the press and was given no chance by TV pundits. Catholic jokes became the order of the day. A Catholic president would change the face of North America one wag promised. Soon every house in the U.S.–and in Canada too–would have three faucets instead of two in their kitchens; one for hot water, one for cold water and one for holy water. I grinned. It was a good joke. But some people probably believed it.

The incredible happened. He was elected. And for those heady days of Camelot he held the hopes of North America in his hands. He faced off against segregation, against the militaristic aspirations of Kruschev, defused the Cuban missile crisis, and brought about the first limited nuclear test ban treaty. He was our hero.

Little clots of icy snow hugged the curb in front of the administration building on the University campus as I stood waiting for the bus that would take me back to the monastery. There were streaks of brightness in the glowering sky, a day undecided upon its fate. I shivered and wrapped my mantle around me, my mind jumbled with statistics, psychometrics and upcoming exams.

A tall student in a plaid jacket was running crazily toward me, ricocheting back and forth across the street.

"He's been shot!" he shouted hoarsely, his eyes wide with horror. "Kennedy's been shot!"

The people on the bus were hushed and crying. What will happen to our fragile peace we all wondered? Our house of cards has collapsed. Our dream is extinguished.

So, is there still a dream worth dreaming? What about my dream? What about the exodus from religious life? What about all the girls that are entering and leaving. It bothers me. Will I alone stay? The problem hits me in a particularly sensitive way because I have been asked to be a confidante and a counselor to the young Sisters. There is no closeness like the closeness of those who hold a common faith, a common love, share the struggles of their spirits, the vulnerability of their hearts. In searching for God we pray and play, bleed and laugh. Still, on some mornings I find a letter left on my pillow:

***

Dear Sister John of the Cross,

Finding myself unable to say all those things I feel so deeply at this moment, I will attempt to write a few of them down for you. I would prefer that no one knew about this note; of course that doesn't include Sr. Divine Heart, who knows what I think of you anyway. First of all, I must apologize for the terrible script (which many a teacher labored in vain to correct) and for the rather nauseating sentimentality contained in these lines. Forgive me, I cannot think of the subject without being a little emotional. You will never be able to grasp the depth of the influence you have had upon me; I can hardly understand it myself. But I will carry away with me a secret glow of admiration for the courage, the faith, the vibrant and living love of God which animates you. Perhaps some of it will stick to me. I hope so, for I am afraid I envied you more than a little at times. But a pebble, no matter how shiny it may try to polish itself, cannot become a diamond. It is my sincere hope that you will not think too badly of me, but will remember me in your prayers, for I will have great need of help. I will never forget you, I know (nor that vicious stroke in badminton).

Goodbye, Sister, and keep laughing. Beware of trees on the toboggan slide and don't forget to beat Sr. Anthony at tennis.

With sincere affection,
Sister Rae Anne

***

And so another one was gone, and I am left with an aching void in the center of my being. They leave for many reasons, reasons as varied as their own personalities and the environments that have nurtured them. Rae Anne had come to do penance for her family who had much need of prayer. But she found it hard to suppress all her own humanity and needs out of a negative motivation, no matter how well meant. Some came searching for answers, for assurance, for sanity and sanctity in a crazy world. Most are starry eyed with ideals but uncertain about what love might demand of them. Always, at a certain point, they become frightened, so frightened, that God might ask from them the sacrifice of that very part of themselves that they are most loathe to give. The difficulty is not so much with the idea of the vows themselves–they are at least crudely understood–but often rather with the trappings of the ego, the petty habits and blind spots that become idols in each of our lives. They are afraid of the future. They do not trust themselves. They are not sure how far they can trust God. Some stay for months, others for years. Always in the search for self knowledge and growth there is struggle.

***

I see a white veil flashing through the crack of the door, and can tell by the light tripping knock that it is Sister Celeste.

"I almost went again last night," she plunges in recklessly, wasting no time in preliminaries. Her freckles and willowy shape fill my doorway like an exclamation point. "I had made all my plans–where to stay–who to phone. Then, when I picked up the phone my hand was paralyzed. The next minute I was telling myself I would never leave here."

But she had a steely nonchalance, a toughness like buffalo hide, a scab hiding the war of the body and the antibody. I know I was in for it again tonight because I had watched her move through the day with a flippant grace, squinting around callously.

"But you're still not at peace," I observe.

"I plotted my whole trip through Europe," she reflects out loud, staring at the ceiling and leaning on my closet door. "I would leave my parents over there and stay on awhile myself. My parents have always been generous. The fountains of Rome will be beautiful at this time of year."

"Are you running away?" I ask. She is like a restless wave, and I am the coastline she has chosen to crash against. "Is Rome real or is it a dream?"

"My whole life is a dream, Sister. You know that," she says sardonically. She seems to give me credit for reading her mind. "When I was growing up it was always more pleasant to live in my dream world, at the movies, staring out the window at school,"

"And when do you begin to wrestle your dreams into reality?"

"Oh, I don't know if I'd want to do that... You'd be shocked at some of the things I think. Do you know why I came here? It was because everybody thought I couldn't live without guys and pleasure. I love pleasure. I love the world. I probably would have backed out if Mother had not jumped in the car first and called me. I can see their faces. My friends–all those who knew me best–said I wouldn't stay."

"That is for you to say, not them. What's past is past. There is no point in looking back at your motives. We've all learned a lot since we came here. What does your heart say now?"

Her chin erects a barrier against me.

"How should I know? Don't you know I can't make a decision? Everyone has always made my decisions for me before."

"No one can do this one for you. Your call is between you and God. Dreams are wonderful. They give us inspiration. But they are seeds that have to be planted in the soil of this world and then nurtured before they can grow into reality."

"What? You suggest I exert myself? You jest!" she laughs raucously at herself. "I wouldn't hurt these dainty soft hands. They're me. They're the only me I know."

I feel her struggle as though her skin and mine are one, but I can not reach her.

"Why all this self hate? God doesn't make junk. I have known you for two years now, and I know you are not as black as you paint yourself. I'm not going to tell you to leave. When you were created in the thought of God He poured so much love in you, so much creativity and vitality, so much strength and potential, and so much joy to share."

"Yeah, well that's what everyone's told me all my life. Potential. "You could do better if you'd only apply yourself". Every teacher I've had has said; "You should be at the head of the class". But I've never made it. I think I'm afraid that if I tried, if I really committed myself, in the end I might fail, and then I wouldn't even have my dreams."

"But you're not doing this by yourself, alone. Or maybe you are, and that's where the problem lies. By ourselves surely, none of us stands a chance. If you are just seeking to prove yourself through self discipline and personal excellence, you would be better off applying to West Point. You are not here to prove how good you are either. You are here to answer an invitation to a relationship with God, an incredible romance beyond any earthly romance you could dream of. Don't be too proud to ask His help."

"Proud? Yes, I'm proud. I'm proud even to admit I'm proud." She begins to make little circles with her shoe on the floor. "But I've decided to stay. I'm not a contemplative. I have trouble keeping my mind on God. I'm lucky if I think of Him twice a day. But I'll stay."

I know here must be something I should say, but my thoughts do not fit neatly into subjects and predicates. I don't want to see her go. On better days she is a lovely person. We are good friends, truly sisters. But I know that her sad resignation is no victory. It is only a pause before the next battle. Her feet are already half way out the door.

But now it is time for my decision. The sanctuary is wild with peonies and clouds of pastel flowers. Their gentle presence wraps the waiting crowd in a heavenly scent. But there is nervous anticipation rippling among all the friends and relatives sitting on the dark pews in the golden light of this spring morning. The Sisters stand facing each other in the Choir stalls lining the back of the chapel, and their singing is glorious, like the sound of angels. I wait in the doorway, remembering my Clothing Day when it all began. It, too, was a day of celebration like today. But that day I had entered dressed as a Bride, and at this same altar I was handed my religious Habit. I had felt gawky and awkward as a bride because I didn't much like the dress I was wearing, and the hairdo I had been given did not suit me despite Sister Magdalene's best intentions. How I cringed later when I saw the pictures! I did not look like myself. But when I re-entered the Chapel, wearing a religious Habit for the first time, flanked by Sister Immaculate Heat and Mother Francis, I felt good, comfortable, and right.

Five years have passed since that day. Now Archbishop Jordan stands in the sanctuary smiling at me, a portly man with electric eyebrows, dressed in his full regalia. I move up the aisle with an assurance I do not feel and prostrate myself on the crimson rug before the altar. I feel the rough carpet against my cheek and I tingle to know the moment is here. The Sisters place a white funeral pall over me and I feel its light warmth cover me, signifying that I have come to give the final gift, my perpetual profession of vows.

The Sisters intone the words of the psalm that my heart sings:

***

One thing I ask of the Lord; this I seek:
To dwell in the house of the Lord
All the days of my life....

***

This is it, I say to myself in wonderment. *I bring myself the best I can. Lord, this is a blank check I am giving You. I don't know what the future holds, but I know You hold the future. Please help me to battle my weakness and to be faithful to You until the day of eternity.*

Music swells and envelopes me:

***

"Thine, my Jesus, thine forever" come the words of the ancient hymn in the pure clear voices of my Sisters;
"Precious chains, thrice holy vows,
From the world my heart ye sever
To bind me to my heavenly Spouse!"

***

Then I am standing, repeating my vows, and a crown of flowers is placed on my head. The Superior drapes the long ceremonial mantle across my shoulders. The choir bursts into the triumphant 'Te Deum', the Church's exclamation of praise and joy. It is all over...and it is just beginning. I am leaving the Chapel, surrounded by celebration, and the crowd spills into the gym across the hall. Uncle Ernest is here, my family and family friends, old school chums and university buddies. The decorations and lunch have been wonderfully done by the dedicated hands of my Sisters and I feel very blessed. One of my honors seminar friends comes over for a shy hug and whispers to me, "You are the best hope of our generation, Sister!"
His words will come back to haunt me.

CHAPTER 13

Memories of graduate school....

***

The mist hung like a curtain, seeming to weigh the hulking branches of the ancient trees down toward the tips of the grass, which was lush and glistening with dew. The mist penetrated everything, leaving the gray, rough hewn stone of the church wall mossy and wet. It penetrated my spirit too like a pernicious fog, and I wondered where I was headed. My eye admired the graceful, dramatic sweep of the steel spires that formed the Ambassador Bridge, as it heaved into the sky and arched down into the twinkling lights of Detroit. Haloed street lights nearby reflected back from the shimmering, shining surface of the Detroit River. Massive dark hulls of ocean going vessels cut smoothly through the night water, shuddering the air with mournful impetuous bursts from their foghorns. Despite the fresh pungent fragrance from the bushes along the shore, the joke was that anyone could walk on water here; the river was that polluted.

The pollution was more than a physical thing. There was an air of uneasiness, of stagnation, at the University which sat in the shadow of the Ambassador Bridge. Its hopes of greatness had lapsed into the orgiastic excesses of the late sixties, and it now pampered its menial existence with the spawn of self indulgent promises. In an effort to improve its image, and to exert some control over its freewheeling graduate students of the hippy era, the administration decreed that all teaching assistants must arrive at their classes clad in pants, shirts and ties. One rebel did them one better by appearing at his teaching post wearing a tuxedo–and bare feet. But at the women's residence where I lived there were streams of verve and fresh air, and I enjoyed sharing the fun and the friendships I found there. I did miss the open, no holds barred, interchanges that I had enjoyed with the faculty at the University of Alberta. Here, many on the faculty seemed defensive, preoccupied with building their own little empires, walling up their egos behind a brittle sophistication. A couple of the priests who taught there seemed to be priests in name only, intent on furthering their own secular agendas, without love, without warmth. Ex-seminarians roamed the campus trying to relocate their ideals in their tottering worlds. More than one young priest battled with problems of his own sexuality in a society where sexuality had become the golden calf. It was a surging, unsettled stew of the human condition that brewed there.

I saw telltale cracks in the veneer of sophistication during a doctoral level group therapy however. It confirmed for me that remarkably similar needs and rudimentary fears flow like common subterranean rivers through all of our lives, no matter how erudite or practiced. During the first half of this course we had to take part in group therapy ourselves so that we might better understand the process, and the feelings of people participating in such a group. The graduate students in the program were joined by practicing psychotherapists from the community who were in the process of upgrading. One thirty-something Greek participant had been a practicing psychologist for ten years already.

We all sat around in a circle self consciously, eyeballing each other and wondering what to do next. Out of the awkward silence, anxieties began to bubble to the surface. I was quiet for the first few sessions, feeling I had little to say, but studied the flow of thoughts and emotions, wondering where I fit in and what meaning this could have for me. My silence was interpreted as a threat, and after initially ignoring me, people began to question me. Their big question seemed to revolve around my sex life, or lack thereof. One fellow told me sharply that there was no way I could be normal, living such a life as I was. Another, a girl, questioned if I could ever be fulfilled as a human being. Another girl tossed out that she had toyed with the idea of becoming a nun but had rejected it, and assured me I was missing the big picture of life. Suddenly, a young, black haired, Italian man, who looked like a former star in a Tarzan movie, became irritated and told everyone to leave me alone and to go bother someone else. He smiled at me reassuringly.

As the sessions wore on, it became more and more apparent that these psychotherapists were just as vulnerable, just as afraid of personal rejection, just as floundering in their personal relationships as anyone who walked the streets of this earth. The Greek began to voice dark fantasies about me, unveiling thoughts of kidnapping and seduction. My knight in shining armor, the Italian, came again passionately to my defense, vehemently warning him to stay away from me or he would break his neck and every bone in his body. The others accused him of hiding his own dark desires in gift wrap. And so it went. It was intriguing and fascinating and made me wonder if the concept of normalcy even existed in the hearts of men.

The pictures of those days flip by quickly, like the faces of a deck of cards: the medical library in Detroit, walking alone there at night without fear, intensive study and sleepless nights, giggling with the girls, special home Masses through the community where we shared the Eucharist in the form of real bread and where we were joined in a happy joy.

I linger a moment now as I come to the picture of Joel. From the background of our history he came into my life, the remnant of a war. In him became real the gutted cities, the dispossessed peoples, the treaties that children could not read:

Intense, moving about with cat-like grace, he made the usual social gestures. As I entered the room he was handing a delicate glass of champagne to a girl leaning provocatively toward him, but he met my eye:

"Come in! Make yourself at home," he demanded almost caustically.

I returned his look readily, and read in his eyes a bitter, mocking, wordless challenge. He was a long, lean, blonde lion with an early receding hairline. He was suave, sophisticated, a man not of our continent, but strangely of my world. Above the moody, exotic and international music, through the passionate statement of a Mozart's Requiem, I was aware of the stunning collision of our two worlds.

I watched him, laughing, casual, reaching out to each guest as they arrived, offering a drink with a flicker of his eye. His speech tumbled out quickly, self conscious in some ill-defined accent. It was his party in a corner of an ancient university residence, covered with posters from all over the world and peopled with a collection of books, offbeat artifacts and one drowsy bird. His dry, cynical, argumentative style dominated the ensuing discussion until most of the guests had drifted off, and he had sunk in a stupor on the floor in front of bookshelves full of political dreams.

Joel and I were in conflict from that first meeting.

Yet I was fascinated by him—drawn—attracted—hypnotized. I heard from friends around campus that he was considered 'different'. His brusque aloofness, his air of superiority, had made him an impressive quota of enemies. His behavior towards girls was reported to be a mixture of continental gallantry and inconceivable boorishness. He fled the very ghost of attachment; and when some current date threatened the sanctuary of his seclusion she found herself stranded at a party, ignored, insulted. Joel rode equally roughshod over the feelings of the small, faithful cortege of friends who sat with him at lunch in the cafeteria, involved in the interminable discussions of assignments and politics.

Yet, for all his boorishness, his harshness, his worldly disillusioned air, he had some sort of power over people. Something came through his callousness; it was akin to passion or pain.

Between us there was some sort of painful affinity and elasticity that pulled us together. He would come and join me in the cafeteria, and suddenly the air was alive with electricity. He spoke to me, taunted me, but he kept coming back. He could not ignore me—nor I him—though two thousand students milled between us.

"So you believe in people," he stated flatly, mockingly, as he sat down. The trees outside the sweeping cafeteria windows were heavy with hoarfrost.

"Well, I don't have the same opinions about them that you have!" I grimaced and then laughed. "I do believe in God, and I believe that in Him there is a treasure house of love that we can plug into if we have a mind to. I believe that God loves His people without reservation with a Father's infinite tenderness—and I guess I'm unpopular because I do believe in 'heroes', in people who have risen up to this love."

"You are very naive."

"Perhaps."

"I once believed in God." And then he launched into a vicious diatribe against churches and the inconceivable probability of a God existing in the midst of our corrupt world. Let alone a caring God.

I stared at him, wondering what fresh disappointment, what new inner war, had brought this on. His tone was sardonic, but was he not trying to cover up some vulnerability?

"Why are you so bitter? Who have you loved that has disappointed you so badly?"

He reared back in his chair and was silent for a long moment.

"Yes," he nodded, "there was somebody."

"A girl?" I asked.

"Yes, there was one of those...but before that...."

"Who was it Joel? Was it one of your family? You never talk about them."

"There is only one other person in this country who knows."

"And you are trying to tell me that you don't know if you can trust me too?" came my quiet question.

"Nobody can be trusted," he pronounced feelingly. "People are treacherous and self seeking. The world you believe in is a fairytale, illusory."

"And so you go on nursing your hurt, taking it out on yourself and everybody else."

"Taking it out on everybody else?"

"Yes you do. You stalk around the campus like a ravenous wolf looking for fresh targets to devour. But then, isn't it just a little contradictory, if you really have no belief or trust, that you are studying so hard to pursue a career in international diplomacy?"

"I have to do something."

"Like that?"

He raised his eyebrow and the unique accent said, "You don't like me then?"

I could hardly believe my ears.

"I think you know better than that. I like you very much—I guess I love you, Joel.... Why don't you love yourself?" And his eyes caught the blaze in my eyes that reached out to him like some aching hand.

His voice softened slightly and he leaned intently across the table. "Alright," he said slowly. "I will tell you—but you must never tell anyone—no one...."

His eyes turned back to a boyhood recorded indelibly somewhere within; and a succession of seasons passed over his face. "I was born near Brussels, where my family lived...."

"Were you a close family?"

"Well, I was the only one, and my father was away a lot because it was war time. But I admired him. I can remember sitting on his knee...and him making little soldiers for me. To me he seemed so good, so...."

"Full of integrity?"

"Yes—upright, honest. In his uniform he impressed me...." He looked up to the ceiling searching for the proper superlative. "I was a boy and my father was a great, noble man. He fought for the Nazis, of course, but he did not have any choice. Belgium was one of the first countries to go down. Then the war ended and our lives became happy. But one day the police came to the door and asked a lot of questions. My father was taken away to prison that day. I screamed and held him but they ripped him away from my arms. There was a trial.... When I was thirteen my father was condemned to death. They said he had been responsible directly for the death of many Jewish people. He had held a very high position...I couldn't believe it...."

"And your world, your credulity was torn apart..."

There was a muffled sound like a deep roar within the earth.

"And you don't like yourself—is it because of your father? What do you feel about your father now?"

He shook his head, unable to speak. He was caught in a terrible conflict of love and hate, regard and recrimination in which his identity and his father's melded into one.

"The father who loved you...who seemed so gentle, good and wise...."

"You asked me why I am bitter about the Church," he continued vengefully. "We tried to get the Church to intercede for my father. They did nothing. We went to the local bishop and the—what do you call it—hierarchy, and they said they could do nothing. The truth was that they could have. They had a lot of power, of influence. The local bishop said he could not stand in the way of civil justice, and, after all, my father had been responsible for the death of many.... God? Churches? We never went again."

I was speechless in response to his bitter grief. What could I say? His face was taut, but in the semidarkness of the cafeteria I felt tears—the tears he could not cry—falling down my face, into my heart, opening such a vast hole there that it seemed that all the pain of the world had fallen on me.

"So you have been betrayed—by your father—by the Church—by everything on which your world depended. By the fear and weakness of people. I guess I can share that feeling with you. I know how it feels to be hurt, I have not lived in a glass cage either. Sometimes I have felt like hiding in my own cocoon. The world can be so hurting.... What happened to you? Have you never trusted anyone since then?"

He stared at me with his barriers beautifully down, some softness, some yearning, standing exposed to the wish to return to earlier happier days. To belief. To the love in my eyes.

"I was sent away to boarding school," he said. "It didn't work out very well. I spent the rest of my school life in boarding schools—in England, France, and finally I was accepted here."

The shadows grew long and black, and the torment of his hushed voice contrasted strangely with the distant indifferent sounds of busily clattering dishes. We left the cafeteria to the supper crowd and made our way under the silent trees to the brilliantly lit library. As we took our separate desks, with a wrenching sorrow I thought I saw the dam gates closing again. The time of magic was over.

I was all too right. In the next few weeks Joel was silent. He avoided me. He lashed out at me. He threw himself deeply, compulsively into his studies.

"How are you, Joel?" I asked.

"Busy," he replied. "I've got four papers to be handed in by the fifteenth."

But he knew that was not what I meant. I was part of his consciousness like an arm or a leg. And I was feverish to walk again within his sanctuary and to bring the heat of my life to his great frozen ocean.

"You came too close," he finally stated tersely. "You know, I have hurt everyone who has ever come into my life. I would hurt you too. I cannot afford other people in my life."

"Do I look afraid? Do I have any choice?"

I stood there understanding that I, with all I stood for, was the embodiment of all his remaining doubt, of his hope, the specter of his disillusion. For a moment he had opened himself to a daring new hope, and suddenly he heard the outside winds and felt the pain of new blood throbbing through the numb limbs of his spirit. It was too much....

He stood in the background of my days like an omnipresent angry shadow, haunting me while I strove to study. One day, in a parting thrust he stalked up behind me in the library and suddenly a magazine was dropped in front of my face.

"Here's what they have done, the people whom you have such confidence in," he challenged bitterly.

The article was entitled 'Napalm'—ten full-page pictures of napalm victims—scenes of such incredible deformity that they nearly froze my blood. There they were, in color, without faces, or what could be recognized as such, without necks, gaping, puss-filled, raw open flesh. I was stunned. "Look what they have done," the sardonic mocking voice had said. It echoed in my head. I took the pictures to my room and spent long hours looking into the night. Who could doubt the incredible evil and ugliness in this world? On every side it conspired to magnify his disillusion. It was reality.

But, Joel, is it the whole of reality? Do we have other choices? And less confidently—how can I answer this latest indictment? How can I explain this choice?

I stared at the pictures and my flesh crawled with the horror of them. What reasoning can justify this manner of warfare? There are people with hopes and dreams like mine buried in these pictures of the living dead. I wondered where I was, what I was doing in my safe sanitized world, the day those injuries were inflicted? I had not heard their cries.... I could see from the captions that many months had elapsed at the time the pictures were taken from the time of the original injury. And still so much suffering! Still so much pain! It unmasked the mystery of evil in our world. It amazed me that these afflicted bodies could still support life.

I wondered who stood in the background, supporting that life? What an odious, thankless, overwhelming burden that must be. But someone—families—medical teams—volunteers—someone was out there, working in seclusion, without fanfare, trying to bring some comfort, some help to these people, keeping them alive. How would I face up to a task like that? It must take incredible courage, incredible perseverance, and incredible love. I stopped. Indeed, what manner of men stretched out their human natures to stem and cure that tide of death? Someone is out there on that alien island trying to counterbalance that evil, giving life, giving help and supplying the necessities of life to those tortured bodies.

Perhaps that was Joel's answer. It didn't explain the evil, but it demonstrated that there is something else too, something better and stronger that exists. But Joel had escaped from answers. In the disfigurement of his family, his skies still screamed with bombers and little could be heard above the chaos. His armored tank continued to fight its way down cluttered, embattled highways. The world would always yield more irrational evils to feed his voracious cynicism. Amidst the quietly lengthening days graduation would come, and our lives would hang like unfinished pictures on the easels of time.

And so they were destined to remain. Youth could not run fast enough to capture the victories of maturity. But because Joel was, and is, he still haunts me like some vexatious spirit. He is somewhere still in your world. Still angry, irritable, and irascible, no doubt. But I see his shoulders hunched at his stereo, clutching to his soul the inspired beauty of Mozart, or the controlled passion of a Gregorian chant. I see a drowsy bird, a room covered with books, ice covered trees. I hear the clang of the gates crashing down upon me and the ache is fresh.

Someday I would tell my daughters wisely that all girlhood dreams of love are not obtainable. I would remind them that pollination can only take place when the bloom is full. In the face of their brave loves I would point to the tangled skeins of wool in my cupboard, forgotten from babyhood days. I would recall napalm scars and closed gates...and many wise things.

But then, as now, there is one certainty. One day in an ecstasy of sun the gates opened. Behind his eyes, slashed by the heavy winds, I have seen one candle in some dark canyon withstanding yet the storm.

Remember that when you meet him. Perhaps you can catch him—the solitary figure, the runner, the embodiment of war.

CHAPTER 14

Choices.

***

"What will you do? Will you leave too?" my Superior asked in a tone of grim resignation as she chronicled the departure of still more of my Sisters. It was as though she expected me to leave. I had returned to the monastery for the summer and found a ship that seemed to be sinking. The government, too, had cut back the number of girls it was sending to us, sending many instead to the new Alberta Institute for girls, a government run institution.

"I don't know," I said awkwardly. Everything looked murky.

"I would like you to stay in a convent for your last year of graduate school," she said. "I have talked to the Ursuline Sisters down there and they have agreed." She handed me a piece of paper with an address on it.

I felt my face grow pale and my stomach felt taut.

"But this is on the far side of the city. It is miles away from campus!" I protested. Suddenly I realized how much I had enjoyed my unfettered freedom of the last year and chafed at the thought of being deprived of it. "Maybe I will take a year of exclaustration to think things out...." I said it without premeditation, in the impulse of the moment.

The words, the halting uncertain words, had been spoken, and I shook, knowing that I had said the words, and that like an arrow that had left the bow I was launched toward an uncertain destination.

I found myself on a jet plane noisily descending through fluffy cumulus clouds down into Pearson Airport. I took the subway, with my empty suitcase, to the University of Toronto.

A rotund woman, with gray streaked hair that had escaped its moorings at the nape of her neck, busily swished her string mop in circles down the long corridor.

Room 342. I checked my slip of paper. It must be near. I looked up at the numbers on the door.

The cleaning woman looked at me with that look that had grown so familiar to me. The long swinging religious Habit tended to cut through conversations and call people to a state of aroused attention, however furtive their glances. She quickly returned to the making of circles, but they were more energetic, more purposeful now.

I nodded to acknowledge her as I passed, but was glad to find her eyes averted. The last thing I wanted to do now was encourage a conversation. So often people seeing the Habit would bond with you instantly and want to reminisce a moment or share a thought.

But the cleaning lady had another priority right now. Stealing a look at her watch, she discovered it was time for the mid morning coffee break. As I knocked, and was admitted to room 342, I saw her lean her mop against the wall and tuck in her errant hair.

Judy was waiting for me anxiously because she had a summer school exam to write shortly. But she greeted me with a hug, concern, and apologies.

"I'm sorry I just have to say hello and run," she said. "But here's my extra key. I will see you back here at five." She hesitated, uncertain how to make the offer: "If you would like to borrow anything, feel free. I don't know what you need. I mean...have you brought anything to wear? I have a pink dress here that I am certain would fit you ...." she added shyly.

"Go! Go!" I urged her. "I'll be alright. Thank you for the use of your dress. I'll be doing some shopping this afternoon."

She looked at me intently and hurried out.

I looked at the sparse furnishings of the student room, and the picture seared itself into my mind with its myriads of details. I slowly removed my black traveling Habit for the last time. *This is not final,* I told myself to ease the burden of the moment. *I still have a year to make up my mind.* But my heart was numb as I opened the empty suitcase, and I placed into it the familiar robes, lingering, caressing the slight roughness of the black fabric, removing the pins that held the veil and the white bandeau and gimp; putting into that suitcase eight years of my life. I had the sense that something vital, like an arm or a leg, had been amputated. But still, like a train rushing through the night, seeing nothing clearly in the darkness, the momentum of my hastily spoken words carried me forward on shiny steel rails into an undefined future.

I studied the pastel pink dress on the bed with fascination. My friend Judy was close to the same size as myself, but taller. The dress was long, but even then, as I put it on, I became aware for the first time in a very, very long time that I had legs. My hair hung long, dark and straight to my waist. Although it had been initially cut when I received the Habit, there was no specific prohibition or ruling on the length of hair so I had simply let it grow. I searched the bathroom counter for something to give some color to my very pale face. Finding a bit of blush, I wiped a trace on my cheeks and lips. In the mirror now I was just any young girl, looking younger than my twenty five years, and anonymous.

My adrenalin had started to pump. Nervously I stepped out of the room, back into the corridor of the student residence, and fumbled as I tried to lock the door. I looked both ways furtively, like a child afraid to cross the street, hoping that the cleaning lady would not be back yet at her post. But there she was. Although I lowered my head as I approached her, I could see her eyes peppering me quizzically, my appearance having obviously set off a startled internal debate. Her mop was making erratic swoops hither and yon, and I could feel her eyes burning holes in my back as I stepped out of the residence into the bright sunshine of the University of Toronto.

I'll always remember that long walk across campus. The slanted rays of late summer splayed light patterns on the deep green grass under the tall gracious trees. Clutches of students stood or sat here and there, idly engaged in endless debates about studies, purposes, beliefs, identities. There was a young man leaning against a tree reading a book. Another lay napping in the welcome shade. A more social group were sitting around playing guitars and singing softly. They looked over at me with casual interest, nodding and smiling as they sang. I was just part of the usual scene. For the first time in eight years I felt the breeze blowing through my hair, and I felt my ears exposed, and my hair tumbling around my shoulders. It was a novel experience and I felt free and exhilarated.

By the time I had mastered the subway and reached the downtown Eaton's I was again more inhibited. Heading down to the bargain basement, I prayed I could avoid the gaze of well meaning salesclerks.

But it was inevitable. "May I help you?"

"I'm just looking," I said uncomfortably.

"What size are you? Perhaps I can direct you to the correct section." The exact question I did not want to hear!

What was I supposed to say? I no longer had any idea what size I was? Like Rip Van Winkle I had returned after a long sleep.

"I don't know... I'll just look around," I said vaguely, feeling foolish. What was I supposed to tell her? That I hadn't worn 'human clothes' since my teen years? I plotted my course to the most deserted corner of the basement.

I didn't need to have done things this way. When Sister Maureen had left, the Sisters had provided her with a beautiful wardrobe, in charity and love, and knowing she was not from a well to do family, they sent her home in style. But for me to have cast off my religious garb in front of the Sisters would have been acutely painful for them, and for me. I had spent nearly a third of my life with them and I had no quibble with religious life. It had been good to me and for me, and in no way would I have wanted to undo the past eight years. My decision at age seventeen to leave home and enter a monastery was still a valid one. I was not repudiating my beliefs or my God. I ached with regret at the pain I must be causing the Sisters and my very kind Superior. I flinched. No, since I would be leaving for another year of graduate school anyway, it would be easier to make the change over quietly and inconspicuously here in Toronto while visiting my girlfriend, Judy.

But why now? I didn't have to leave. There was no real crisis in my life. Life in the monastery had not become unbearable. So why? Fear.... The fear that my monastery would disintegrate in the undertow of history. The renewal of Vatican 11 had brought welcome changes, but also, upheaval. Vocations were decreasing, not increasing. The thought pursued me: what if I waited until I was 35 or 40 and then had to leave? It would be so much harder to find new opportunities for myself then. Now I was in the peak of my womanhood. I had a full scholarship and a teaching assistantship as well, so I could manage on my own. And I had begun to doubt my ability to live honestly and faithfully and fruitfully a life of perpetual chastity. Everyone in the outside world was telling me I was missing something. Was I? Or had the siren call of the sixties, with its ferment and turmoil and fantasies, just warped my soul?

I picked up a green plaid skirt, a matching sweater, a loose crocheted style black top, and headed for a change room. I discovered I was a size seven, so that problem was solved. But when I went to buy stockings and underwear I was lost again. It was a different sizing system. While I had been away, stockings had become pantyhose, and what was polyester? I found the terminology used by the salesclerk confusing, but how could I explain my ignorance without making a spectacle of myself? Crinolines were gone, and what was a 'tank top' anyway?

I muddled through and managed to leave that department with an armload of clothes that fit. But now—what shoe size was I? I had no idea. And I approached the make up counter gingerly. What a selection of colors? Where do I begin? How do I know what will look good on me? I cringed before the pushy probing of the sales girl and exited quickly with a pale pink lipstick which would do double duty as a rouge—which I had discovered was now known as 'blush'.

Judy returned at five and looked me over approvingly.

"Okay," she said, "Now let's go get a bite of supper."

There was a small Greek restaurant just on the periphery of the campus, the only place that was close. It felt so strange to walk in there. Several young Greek men were leaning idly against the counter, waiting, it seemed, for some game to appear. It became rapidly apparent that I had become that game. Was it because I looked vulnerable? For the first few moments I felt flattered and reassured that I still had some feminine appeal. But whistles and winks soon became a brazen broadside. Judy grabbed my arm in alarm:

"Let's get out of here," she said. We did without supper.

For two days we visited Judy's mother at their cottage on the lake, and there my wardrobe blossomed further with some clothes that were too small for Judy.

I still had another hurdle to pass; my first appearance back on my own campus. It was still early September, and the hallway of the science building appeared deserted. I was relieved, but still the click clacking of my shoes on the shiny floor sounded deafening. A white lab coat appeared in the open door of the physiology lab at the end of the hall.

"Hi, Johanna!" Herb grinned. Then he winked, shook his head approvingly and disappeared back in the lab. His dusty blonde European sidekick, Curt, looked from behind his right shoulder and stared.

I was stunned. How had he recognized me immediately in secular clothes? How did he know my civil first name?

But, I was pleased. Herb was a doctoral student with whom I had shared a passing hello over the past year. Although we had never so much as had a conversation, he was one of those people that I felt immediately comfortable with. Short, and laid back, with a resounding mischievous laugh, we seemed intuitively to be on the same wavelength. Curt, wearing his trademark blue Innsbruk Olympic sweater, would always echo his hello each time our paths crossed.

I had made the plunge. The water was fine.

CHAPTER 15

"Are you Canadian citizens?" the customs officer barked, leaning inquisitively into a car packed tight with bodies.

"Yes, yes, yes!" came a chorus of voices.

"Where are you off to?"

"To a retreat in Dearborn."

"Have you birth certificates or other identification?"

"Sure!" and people jostled each other, attempting to get into their pockets for their I.D. Judy elbowed me and grinned as I struggled to get out of the car.

"Excuse me," I said, "this is a bit complicated. May I please use your countertop?"

The young custom's officer looked at me in askance, his eyebrows cocked curiously, but he humored me. He pushed the door open and waved me in to his garishly lit office behind the window.

I leaned over the counter, and from my wallet, in bits and pieces, I extracted a poster sized birth certificate that predated the birth of plastic. In jigsaw fashion I meticulously assembled all sixteen pieces.

The faces of my friends hung expectantly out of the windows of the car, watching the officer's reaction. He knew he was playing to an audience.

"What is this?" he quipped, "the Canadian flag?"

We laughed our way through the tunnel into Detroit.

"Look," someone shouted, as we passed the corner where a towering statue of the Jolly Green Giant heralded canned vegetables in America. "Footprints! Look at the footprints!"

Sure enough; huge fluorescent green footprints were leading away from the statue, down the street and around the corner.

"Let's follow them," we commanded the driver.

The footsteps, reflecting eerily in the streetlights, led us past the stately glass and concrete cathedrals of the business district. They ended abruptly at the feet of a lovely stone statue of Aphrodite, the Greek goddess of love, whose graceful nude shape reached up to Olympian delights.

"The engineers have been busy again," we commented and giggled.

I felt like a yearling, drunk and foolish with youth and possibilities, dancing in the sun. A friend had taken me to Hudson's Department Store, Detroit's consumer Mecca, where she introduced me to a visiting make-up artist from New York, a man who worked on models and movie stars. He did a make-over for me, and taught me how to use make-up to enhance my eyes and pale features. Uncertain of myself, but trusting in his expertise, I soon began to feel good about the way I looked, and I enjoyed experimenting with clothes and hair styles. I felt a part of the big city, of its throbbing heart, of its excitement, of its sophistication, reveling in its theatres, its nightlife, its élan.

This excursion, however, was to be for prayer and sharing. Sensitivity sessions were in vogue, and our retreat, given by a young avant-garde priest, borrowed some of these techniques to foster openness between us. We had an enormous need for closeness with each other, to huddle and to hug. We needed to feel a solidarity with each other in a bright neon world that stood on the edge of nuclear eclipse, a closeness to reassure us who we were. Attracted by what had been a common call, I found myself gravitating to the ex-seminarians, but it was like chasing shadows; every time I came close, the shape of their reality had moved further away and I was left grasping nothing. They, too, were trying to decode who they were in the privacy and confusion of their souls. We hugged, but we could not reach each other.

Simon and Garfunkel were the prophets and seers of our age, voicing our emptiness and anomie. No matter how we chattered, how loudly and feelingly we sang, when we stopped for breath everything that we had created together was swallowed up by the 'Sounds of Silence'. Under the show of warmth and hilarity was an edginess, a defensiveness, a sense of impermanence, as if there were no tomorrow. Or perhaps it was that we had lost the yesterday of our faith and ideals. We were like leaves dancing in the autumn winds, skittering here and there, on no special course, responding to any sudden gust. We reached out to each other like neophyte swimmers, looking to each other for support, then pulling away because we could not hold ourselves in the pitching sea, let alone someone else. I could see a flickering of the Divine Light in those I met, but we were all disconnected, each radically alone. On the surface we melded and shared the same adrenaline rush, but each pursued his and her own agenda of pleasure and gain. I had become a member of the 'me generation'.

The novice who had been Sister Maureen in the monastery now lived in Windsor, not far away from the university. We resumed our friendship and she invited me to her wedding. She told me that she liked me better now the way I was; or rather, she felt that now I simply loved her for who she was rather than for some ideal above her head.

"Before, Johanna," she explained, "I sometimes felt that you were looking through me to the mysterious God within Whom you loved in me, but I wondered if you loved me for myself, just for me."

I mulled over this. Had I learned something I needed to know? Had something really improved in my life? Or is it that our common bungling humanity is the great leveler? Is our fragile human bond to be preferred? Or is this the key to why Christ was born in a stable, one of us, vulnerable, looking up through shivering baby eyes at oxen, asses and humankind? Can it be that our human relationships are the bedrock of something Divine? Are they needed to prepare our hearts for the great call to be in relationship to God? I hear the echo again of my Superior's voice: "The supernatural builds on the natural ...."

So human relationships are invaluable.... Is this what my confreres in my group therapy class were so enthused about: relationships with all their vivid color and Hollywood glitter? I saw that in my growing up days, my extra-family relationships were based simply on fun and good times. They were shallow, and as I look back I realize that we did not really communicate with each other on the level of our hopes and dreams and beliefs. The deeper shared dreams of the monastery were thousands of miles away now in linear miles, and sitting on the rim of another universe in terms of the reality in which I now lived. I hungered for a relationship that would enrich my life and give it solidity. Where would I find it?

"Please," said a deep voice behind my shoulder, "please, may I speak with you? My English is not so good," a handsome, dark, curly haired stranger leaned over my desk at the library, and I noticed with curiosity that the hand he laid on the desk was clad in a black leather glove.

"Sit down," I invited and smiled. It was not difficult to smile at him, because he had wonderful eyes that were dancing like a friendly puppy.

"I am new in Canada. I do not know anyone. There is a faculty party on Friday night. Dr. Smith has suggested to me that I might ask you to accompany me. My name is Jerry."

"Well," I shifted in my chair in surprise, "tell me something about you? Where are you from?"

"I come from Prague. I am a doctoral student. I am allowed to come now, because there is fresh air and hope in my country since Alexander Dubcek is in power." He saw my eyes returning to his black gloves. "Yes, you are asking why I wear these gloves. I had an accident. Every person must serve two years of compulsory military duty in my country. One day, just two months before my tour of duty was completed, I was to throw a hand grenade; it had a defective pin, and my arms, from below the elbow, were blown off."

He absorbed my startled reaction with matter-of-factness, but the lines of his face hinted at his suffering. I was touched by his honest candor and his sad story, but he shook his head and shrugged his shoulders as if to obliterate the memory of that time. He smiled at me. He was intent that I know that there was nothing disabled about his mind and spirit, and that it was his future, not his past, that concerned him now. And right now, he was focused on getting a date for Friday night.

He showed me how he could put his thumb and fore finger together in apposition to allow him to eat or write, and as he did so I heard a faint sighing from the air that powered his artificial limb. I admired his positive attitude, even his pride in the workings of his man made hands that gave him independence.

I began to spend a lot of time with Jerry. It was fun to be with him because he was so excited about even the most trivial details of life in Canada. Toast. He was wild about toast. "Surely," I questioned him, "you must have eaten toast in Czechoslovakia?"

"It is not usual. It is not like you have here."

I bought him a toaster. Cheese whiz. Peanut butter.

He was in awe of stores that were piled high with goods that anyone might buy. He was moved, to tears, to stand in bookstores where he could buy anything he wanted without government interference. He soon collected all the titles that were forbidden to him in Czechoslovakia. The freedom made him dizzy with joy. He studied ravenously.

I found myself, with unaccustomed boldness, arguing with the US Ambassador so that Jerry might be allowed to go across into Detroit with me to do research at the medical libraries I used over there. It seemed strange to me that he didn't have the freedom of movement that I had. But he was from an iron curtain country, and as such was considered an undesirable alien. After several probing interviews, we managed to wangle several day passes for him, and I entered into his excitement as he put his foot for the first time on American soil.

Occasionally Jerry was a bit melancholy, which I attributed to the exhaustion engendered by culture shock. A Czechoslovakian priest was pastor at a parish bordering on the campus, and I brought the two together so Jerry could have someone who would understand him from his perspective, and be able to speak to him in his own language.

We went for long walks along the river in the sunshine, and his loving eyes kept seeking me out and prodding me with their invitation to intimacy. We talked endlessly about our two countries and compared our peoples. In Czechoslovakia, he told me, when young people want to rebel and assert their independence, they would put their lives and futures on the line by attending clandestine Masses held in the woods or in abandoned buildings. How different our lives were! But needs and emotions are a universal language and they bound us in a common bond. One day, by the river, Jerry stopped, and his eyes drew me to him, and he kissed me, and I felt my resistance melting away. I felt giddy and alive.

Then, as the months went on, I noticed a reticence beginning in Jerry, unexplained silences, and I became troubled. "What is it?" I asked.

"I have something to tell you," he said finally, with reluctance, but also with relief to get it out at last: "I am married."

My shock was total. "Who is she?" I asked incredulously.

"I married the doctor who looked after me when I had my accident. But it is okay," he hastened to add, "She knows I am lonely and I must have friends over here. I am sure she is not all alone either. These things are done in Czechoslovakia. It is not like over here. Marriages are not so exclusive."

I turned away. My heedless euphoria was gone. Things could never be the same. Jerry knew that, had struggled with it, and cared enough for my feelings not to let the relationship continue. I saw little of Jerry after that, and soon I saw another girl following him around campus. I felt oddly

detached, flat, and despite some injury to my pride, I was surprised to feel
so little. I dimly understood that this could not have possibly been the
relationship I was looking for. It had no future. Only in my wishes and
hopes had it had any reality. I was grateful, too, that I had not been trapped
in a dead end relationship. Besides, my social life was burgeoning and I felt
no lack of male attention. Still, I look back at this time reluctantly. What
had seemed full of color and excitement at the time, in memory's residues
remains like a choppy sea, dark and unsatisfying. I was thirsty for love and
I chased mirages and found meaninglessness. With thoughts of Religious
life on the back burner, I only succeeded in undermining the life God had
given me and coming up empty.

One night, however, as I sat at my desk struggling to keep my mind
on my studies, a scene from the cafeteria kept popping into my mind with
great persistence. It over rode everything I was concentrating on, and its
clarity surprised me since I am not a very visual person. I kept seeing myself
sitting in the cafeteria, and Herb and Curt would come in, glance around,
then stride purposefully over to my table and ask to join me. This kind
of socializing went on in the cafeteria all the time, of course, but in this
instance I knew that Curt had come especially to see me. I tingled with the
feeling that something new and definitive would begin this evening.

How foolish! I told myself. *This is all just in my own mind!* But I could
not convince myself. Finally, surrendering to the urge, I left my books open,
work incomplete, and wandered into the back section of the cafeteria where
a couple of dozen students were having a late coffee. With fascination, and
a sense of déjà vu, I watched the scene unfold there just as I had seen it in
my room. I was only there a couple of minutes before Herb and Curt had
joined me.

Other people came in, pulled up tables and we got into one of our
hot, but good natured, philosophical debates with lots of haranguing and
friendly digs. Curt sat across from me and watched me intently as Herb tried
to engage me in verbal combat. As Curt turned his head I noticed that his
blonde hair curled at the nape of his neck, and that his features were regular,
even distinguished, marred only by a slight scar over his right eye, and a
tiny mole that sat on his left cheek. His slightly formal English betrayed
his European roots. He was the Student President, a highly motivated and
self directed man of twenty six who joined in enthusiastically with the

traditional engineering antics of his fellow students, but also worked hard in the killing heat of a foundry to pay his own way. Very forthright and outspoken, he voiced a lot of opinions which his alter ego, Herb, enjoyed challenging with a puckish humor. Herb would tackle Curt's point as if it was a football, and head for all he was worth down the field in the opposite direction, finding the intellectual aerobics stimulating, and often satisfyingly outrageous. Curt never failed to rise to the bait, but he tolerated the abuse good naturedly. In a way, Herb was like Curt's reality check in this new culture which he had embraced.

"What a mensch!" Meyer, a Jewish professor who was a friend of ours, thumped the table, bringing the diatribes to an end.

People began to drift off, but Herb and Curt stayed on. I mentioned that a vacancy had come up in the grad residence, a dilapidated building next to the cafeteria, and I was planning to move back on to campus. To my delight, Curt immediately offered to help me move. The logistics of moving without a vehicle had been pushed to the back of my mind pending the end of midterms, and now the problem had solved itself!

This was the beginning. It set me on the road that would end in the nightmare I face today.

"May I join you at Mass?" Curt asked with the cultured politeness of central Europe.

Could I refuse?

"The cafeteria food isn't the best. Will you allow me to take you out to breakfast? ....to dinner? ....for a drive?"

I was telling him about my thesis project. "How will you construct it?" he asked.

"I don't know yet," I furrowed my brow.

"I'll build it for you," he offered. Then, an almost shy request: "I need help typing my thesis. Do you think you could possibly....?"

So I, with my minimal typing skills, reciprocated his generous friendship.

On Valentine's day there was a bouquet of flowers and a box of chocolates. This guy was worming a spot into my life! In Curt I saw strength, solidity, trustworthiness. He had the rare and wonderful ability to give of himself without expecting anything in return. He never pushed me, but was always there for me. Like sunrise and sunset he circumscribed my days, a tall blonde presence leaning over my days. While others had tried to use me to fulfill their own needs and fantasies, Curt was just there as my friend. And he made me laugh! To learn English he had memorized every commercial on TV and could sing the lyrics too!

There was a dark side. Curt bore the scars of a family torn apart, and the marks of violence and deprivation during the war. His earliest memories were of fleeing bombs, of devastation, of seeing Russian soldiers raping women in the street, of hunger, of waiting in interminable food lines. Of becoming deathly ill for months from a hard gotten meal of flounder that had gone bad from lack of refrigeration. His moments of greatest happiness during those years came from listening to the Voice of America, learning rhythmic upbeat songs in words he could not understand. An American soldier gave him the first chocolate bar he would ever taste in his life–it was as vivid as yesterday. A dear woman, Dora Pittman, who lived in New York, whose face he had never seen, sent the care packages that had kept him alive. He described those precious parcels, filled with canned corn, with horsemeat and gravy, biscuits and marvelous Cadbury chocolate. A lifeline had been thrown to him from America. He arrived in America two days after his twenty-first birthday determined to meet and thank the woman who had given him his life back, but found she had died just three short months before. Yet, all that she had stood for was already written in his heart. Although born and raised in Vienna, the city of music, it was the music of Glen Miller and the gravel throated rasp of Louis Armstrong that echoed in his brain. The American dream ran in his veins like a river aflame. All his dreams were of a better life.

I realized that the little boy who had survived the crumbling of his family and his world still had the debris of war littering his soul. He had redirected his powerful survival instinct into becoming the top student in his country. Here, too, he excelled in his studies, by dint of hard work winning the Governor General's Gold Medal. But he had done all this by locking himself in a time warp, impervious to the intrusions of society. Forthright and indomitable, his powerful personality often crackled with anger. I yearned to find something soft in him, something tender. Could I tackle this? Could I deal with this? It consoled me that he had a steely and irrevocable determination not to repeat the mistakes of the past, either those that were made within his family, or those which had nearly destroyed his country. But he lived in a black and white world.

Graduation began pressing in on me, and with it, decisions I did not want to make. I wished I could play a tug of war with time and hold it back. But the days and months only seemed to rush all the more quickly to spite me. I was not ready to return to the monastery. Nor was I in a hurry to make up my mind about Curt. I was comfortable with things the way they were. I felt like someone standing in the hatch of a plane, scared to make their first parachute jump, awed by the immensity of space.

What did I want in a man? I knew that Curt would always remain faithful to me. I knew he loved me with all the love of which he was capable. It also encouraged me that he went to Church with me, even if we were not exactly in the same space spiritually, so that our love would be grounded in something stronger and better than both of us. I believed that love, lived nobly, and even sacrificially, could heal and build and soften and bring joy.

I had received a job offer in Toronto. Curt was looking at a number of offers, but kept being drawn back to an NRC fellowship he had won at McGill.

"Montreal!" he enthused, "is the most cosmopolitan city in North America. It has the richness of the culture of Europe and still the best of North America."

I was not so enthused. My feelings about Montreal had been colored by a bad experience I had there during Expo. I realized I was reacting from an emotional bias that might not even be rational, but I did not speak French, having taken Latin in school, and I did not seem to be on the same wave length as the French culture.

"Are you coming," he asked finally, his blue eyes staring at me calmly.

Beg me, plead with me; don't leave this decision on my shoulders, I cried within myself. But the stakes were too high–he could not take the responsibility for my happiness–my decision could not be forced. It had to come from my heart.

But what did my heart want?

What my heart didn't want was to say good-bye.

The faculty directed me toward a couple of promising job opportunities in Montreal. One was with the Federation of Catholic Charities, the other with the Behavioral Therapy unit at Douglas Hospital. From a career point of view, the offer at the Behavioral Therapy Unit was prestigious and exciting. Behavior Therapy was making a big splash in psychology, and Clark Braddock, one of the protégés of Wolpe and Eyesenck, the trail blazers in this therapy, ran the unit in Montreal. On the other hand, although I had made top marks in Behavior Therapy, and did appreciate its usefulness, my personality shrank from its highly structured methodology, its repetitive, and somewhat mechanical application. The thought of doing behavior therapy full time made me feel slightly claustrophobic. But what a stepping stone to anything else I might choose to do! This was the cutting edge of psychology; I could do worse.

Curt and I packed up our few belongings and pointed the old red and white Oldsmobile toward Montreal. Our buddy, Herb, was already working there, and had invited us to stay with his family until we each located an apartment of our own.

I was fidgety and excited as I prepared for my interview with Dr. Braddock. With great care I selected a light and airy emerald green dress that seemed to express the essence of springtime. I fussed with my hair, trying to achieve a casual sophistication. I looked so much younger than my twenty six years that I was anxious to add an element of maturity to my appearance.

The hospital loomed, a great brick and stone megalith in a sea of green and concrete. I found the street level entrance to the Behavioral Therapy unit, as instructed, and was quickly greeted by a distinguished looking middle aged man in a gray suit. Sleek and urbane, with a touch of gray at his temples, Dr. Braddock reached out to me with a solicitousness and cordiality that surprised me. So this was one of the movers and shakers in the world of psychology! He walked me through the unit, introducing me to all and sundry as the newest addition to the staff. That I was hired seemed to be a foregone conclusion. He explained to me that the pay would not initially be very high, but they would be making new requests when the next budget came up. As a new, experimental discipline they were still carving out their niche.

All this should have made me feel quite happy, but somehow as I walked around the unit I was chilled by the sterility of the place. Long strips of fluorescent light fixtures flooded halls and offices with their harsh artificial light and there seemed to be no substance behind the polite smiles and desultory conversation I encountered. It was not a happy place. The apparent warmth did not feel genuine. I was relieved when Dr. Braddock, with profuse apologies, asked me to come out to his car so that we could sit down and could talk further, explaining that his office was, unfortunately, in the midst of renovations, and there was not, at the moment, a comfortable private place to sit. I was more than happy to go out into the fresh air and sunshine.

Doctor Braddock led me across the parking lot to a long gray sedan. As he reached over to unlock the passenger door he touched my shoulder casually.

"So, are you married?" he asked, sliding into the drivers seat.

"No, engaged," I answered.

"That's alright," he said, smiling a too bright smile.

As he outlined the position I was to fill and the expectations he had of me, alarm bells started to go off in my head. It appeared I was to belong to the hospital, that is, to him, body and soul. The discussion was professional but his gestures were overly friendly. He dropped a proprietary hand on my knee. I froze in horror. In the spirit of free love of the 60's, did he consider me just another blossom free for the picking? Is that what he thinks I am about? Is that the price of a job here? Filled with revulsion, I looked furtively at the door handle, wondering how I could salvage my dignity and exit with some grace.

Sure of himself, as a man who is used to getting what he wants, he appeared totally unaware of my discomfort, but he finished his briefing quickly. I nearly catapulted out of the car. The bright sunlight outside curdled like sour milk on my shoulders.

"You just give my receptionist a call tomorrow morning and she will give you your schedule. And you have my private phone number," he called after me.

"Tomorrow ...." I murmured, feeling breathless as if I had just fought my way out of the tentacles of an octopus.

Three days later I left a curt message with his secretary that I had accepted another position. Had the sexual revolution reduced the female to dead meat, to carrion to be devoured by circling vultures?

I settled in at the Federation of Catholic Charities, in an old building close to the Montreal Forum and the Atwater metro station, on Boulevard de Maissonneuve. My mentor at university, a former seminarian himself, had warned me emphatically not to tell anyone about my 'past'. I did not understand why he would feel so strongly about it, but I decided to take his advice since he seemed to feel it was in my best interests. Still, used to being up front, this made me feel uncomfortable, as if I had a deep, dark, unacceptable secret. It put me on the defensive, because inevitably things would arise in casual conversation of which I was totally unaware– movies, TV personalities or programs, music, nothing important in itself, but it was hard to explain my ignorance short of saying I had come from a different planet. I had missed the entire era of the Beatles, for example, and did not recognize any of their music. Nor did I have any time in my busy schedule to play catch-up. It was a time of great stress. I was adapting to a new city, a new job, a new life, a new culture. I was about to get married, and because I was still, in fact, bound to a Religious Order, I required a dispensation from Rome. My request had just been mailed when a long mail strike ensued. Having decided to subscribe to the theory that two can live as cheaply as one, we had set our wedding date for the end of July. In retrospect, it was a good thing that we did. Just days after we moved into our new apartment on Grande Boulevard, the apartment building where we had maintained our single apartments burned to the ground and two lives were lost.

Curt would have liked to provide a big wedding, but the reality was that we could not afford it, and our relatives and friends were too far away anyway. Herb and Kit offered their home for the reception, and the one thing Curt insisted on was that I have a proper wedding dress even if there would be less than a dozen people in attendance. Doing everything on a shoestring, we rented a dress. Curt had chosen it–it was lovely, and just right for me. Father Joe from St. Monica's would marry us, and would remain a part of our lives for decades. Curt decided he would make a profession of Faith at our wedding, returning to the Church he had been born into, but his family had left. He promised me he would attend Mass faithfully–unless, of course there was a late party the night before. But he cautioned me not to expect any deeper involvement from him. There were still things he had difficulties with that had been inculcated in him from his family. Meanwhile, our plans set, I was getting anxious and edgy waiting for the dispensation to arrive. I had no doubt that it would be granted, but would it arrive before the wedding? The mail strike went on and on, and we prayed and continued to make our wedding plans. The blind faith that it would arrive in time paid off. Just in time. But still I was incredibly nervous. After getting my hair done the morning of the wedding I ran off to St. Joseph's Oratory, Montreal's glorious shrine, to talk and pray, still trying to make peace with my decision. The wedding party: Herb, the best man, and Eva, Curt's sister, who was my maid of honor, did not know where I had gone. Eva, a sensitive and mercuric strawberry blonde, was always poised for disaster, so I found myself abandoning my own nervousness in the end to calm her down. Eva had left Europe at seventeen to escape her bitter family situation. Unlike Curt, who had left later, and who was esteemed by his mother because he was male, and intelligent, Eva was denigrated and abused. When the family broke up Eva fell apart emotionally, failing in school and putting on a lot of weight, becoming a social outcast. But with the encouragement of her father, who cared for her, she found the strength to leave her home and her country to make a new life for herself in Canada. Still, with every letter her mother wrote, she continued to drip vinegar into Eva's still festering wounds, and those letters left Eva in emotional upheaval. But despite being tormented by feelings of inadequacy Eva worked hard, and she had achieved far more than she would give herself credit for. She had found Dan, a fellow who loved baseball and who idolized her, a laid back and easy going man who could accept her as she was, and someone who would become for Curt the brother he never had. Eva and Dan were the only family who were able to be with us for our wedding.

The wedding itself passed like a blur. Father Joe said a wonderful prayer in which he prayed that our home would be blessed with the gift of hospitality—the words were beautiful and I wish I could recall them. They could have also been prophetic.

Unfortunately, Drake, a friend who offered to be our photographer, got so drunk at the stag the night before that he only arrived at the Church in time to catch us exiting the Church. Then Herb's son, Mark, an exuberant five year old, wanted to carry the long train on the back of my dress, so he became part of the wedding party. Entranced with his role, he looked from side to side excitedly, tripped on the top step and ripped the train off the back of my dress! It made for a memorable finale.

Lest we forget our paltry four day honeymoon camping by Lake Champlain, hurricane force winds swept over the lake in the wee hours to create another memorable experience. Sleepless and terrified, we spent the night holding on for dear life to our borrowed tent, and worrying about our own air worthiness. But by dawn the only remnants of the fury of the storm were fallen trees and battered boats. In fact, the morning mellowed into a sparkling clear hot day. The lake was glassy and inviting and like two tired but exhilarated kids we tumbled in. Splashing around, we caught the attention of two huge Chesapeake Bay Retrievers from the adjoining farm. If I had ever wondered why they were called Chesapeake Bay Retrievers, I was soon to find out. Once discovered, every time we made a foray out into the lake they would come and retrieve us! There was no arguing with the big mastiffs, who were duty bound, it seemed, to grab us by whatever arm, leg or other appendage that they could reach with their powerful jaws and they would pull us back to shore, wagging their tails all the time with great satisfaction. After spending a couple of hours trying to dodge, outwit and reason with these honor bound hounds, eventually we had to concede defeat, and instead set out by car to explore the other faces of Vermont.

Thus began the next chapter of my life, a life that was overshadowed by dreams of the monastery I had left in the hours I slept, and crowded during the day with the demands of my work with the poor and the desperate of Montreal. Every form of social and psychological distress paraded through my days, all the sorrows and malformations of humankind. There seemed so little I could do; I was only one drop in a vast ocean. I felt emotionally drained. I could not go home and rest in front of the TV to clear my head; TV was no longer entertaining. After the real life dramas I witnessed in my work, I was satiated with the miseries of the world, and could take no more. Besides, next to reality, the TV was insipid and superficial.

In trying to be a good psychologist, I listened and applied the best of what I had been taught, but I often felt my efforts fell short. The crux of the matter is best illustrated by a story from a radio program, 'The Hour of St Francis', that played on Sundays when I was a child. One episode remained burned in my mind and it spoke to my professional quandary: in my head I can still hear the echo of his footsteps along the wooden wharf.

A middle aged man is bewildered, distraught, contemplating suicide. His mind travels back, as mine is traveling now, to twenty-five years before. He was kneeling in a confessional. The priest was curt, abrupt. He tells him he must return the stolen goods to receive absolution. Disappointed, and offended because of the priest's manner, he flees the Church, never to return. Despite his spiritual void, he goes on to become fabulously wealthy and successful. His life revolves around the one person who means everything to him in the world; his only daughter. Through the years he has doted on her, showering her with every extravagance money could buy. The girl buys into the good life, moving from excitement to excitement, becoming a jetsetter, a connoisseur of relationships, and of drugs. Now he has just come from the hospital where she lies dying of an over dose.

Mystified, and wracked with grief, he implores his dying daughter, "Why have you done this? What else could I have done for you that I have not done? What else could I have given you that I have not given?"

And his daughter, her eyes deep pools of anguish, answered, with the voice of one who has already died inside:

"Daddy, can you forgive sin?"

For so many of those hurting people I saw, I was not the final answer. They needed more than human compassion and human wisdom. They needed the caress of the Divine Healer, the assurance of Divine forgiveness.

The growth of the spirit of French nationalism in Quebec, as embodied by the FLQ, began to make us uneasy. The first time I phoned the University of Montreal to ask the location of a meeting on campus I was surprised that no one would speak to me in English. A type of virtual reality was beginning to suck Curt and me into its circuitry. It started with the bombing of the computer center at Sir George William's University. This was followed by the kidnapping of the British Trade Commissioner, James Cross. Later the body of the Quebec cabinet minister Pierre Laporte was discovered in the trunk of a car. To this point these were still just things we read about in the paper or saw on TV. Then it began to come closer to home. Word was broadcast on the street that 15,000 of the separatists were marching from Montreal East. Destination? The English bastion of McGill. The QPP, the RCMP and the Montreal police all declined their services, saying that the university was out of their jurisdiction. It had, after all, its own campus police. But what were they against 15,000? Now Curt became involved. Faculty and students armed themselves and positioned themselves on the rooftops to defend the campus, and in particular, the computer center, the nerve hub of the campus where their research lay vulnerable. Fortunately, once word filtered back to the marching hordes that their intentions had been discovered, and unprepared for a bloody conflict, the marchers dispersed before they reached Sherbrooke. But they did not forget. In the summer of '70 in a more surreptitious manner, they did manage to plant a bomb in the computer center.

The terrorism grew. One night Curt fell asleep in front of the T.V., waking up alarmed and annoyed because he had slept through an engagement he had at Loyola College, where he also maintained an office and did some work. In a foul mood, he stumbled out the door, only to return, ashen faced, forty-five minutes later. The building where his office was situated had been blown up as he slept.

Riots were breaking out with increasing regularity. One evening every window along St. Catherine's was broken, and looters frolicked with impunity. Drunk with the excitement, some families brought their children with them in their cars to watch the mayhem! Things were growing out of control. Every day now we saw armed tanks going down the streets, not only in the core of the city, but out in the suburbs where we lived. The army was everywhere. It all culminated with Black Tuesday, when it became apparent that the force of law had broken down. In the years that have elapsed since that October Crisis, some people have criticized the then Prime Minister, Pierre Trudeau, for invoking the War Measures Act. Checking over the dusty chronicles of history, they have concluded that he over reacted. Not so to those of us who were there.

All this only served to unlock all the memories, all the terrible recollections of a little boy caught in the crucible of war. Suddenly all the intervening years were smudged and erased, and the little boy, now a man, found himself again threatened on all sides by the same dangers, the same horrors that he had known so long ago, and he seethed in anger and disillusionment. It was time to begin thinking about leaving Montreal.

Our solace during our three years there was an incredible and wonderful group of friends, whose homes and lives we shared. They joyfully helped us welcome our first son into the world, and were there to buoy me up in my fatigue as I struggled to work and care for a child who was convinced that four thirty A.M. was happy hour. It was at a party at one of their homes that something peculiar happened that has stuck like a thorn in my heart. It was a rousing get together with an English pub theme. I had played my first game of darts, and with unabashed glee I had beaten my husband, who otherwise excels at everything. Everyone was in high spirits, so it was with shocked amazement and a chilling sense of prophecy, that I heard Sheila, our hostess, turn to Curt with a sudden intense look, as if she was responding to some inner voice, and say: "You will have a lot to suffer."

The remark was so out of context and so startling. It just suddenly came out of the blue. Later when I gained the courage to ask Sheila why she had said it, she had no memory of making the remark.

CHAPTER 16

The manner of our leaving Montreal came suddenly and unexpectedly. My father phoned one night. Mom and Dad had now semi-retired to Kelowna in the Okanagan Valley, but tonight Dad was bubbling with the news of a lucrative contract he had landed.

It is amazing how the power of a few casual and inadvertent words can influence the course of our lives.

"Do you think your Dad would like to go into business again?"

"I don't know," I looked at my husband searchingly. "He sold his business and moved with the idea of slowing down and doing some of the boating and fishing he has always dreamed about."

"Well," my husband was beginning to look excited, "it wouldn't hurt to ask him. I know that one of the disappointments of his life has been not to have a son to carry on the family business."

"That's true," I said dubiously. "But he is in a different line of work than you are...."

"That doesn't matter. The future is not looking that bright here–and it sounds like things are happening out West. Do you think I should I call him back?"

"If you want to...." I said hesitantly.

Dad, as it turned out, had bought his boat, a sleek and jaunty cabin cruiser, had taken it out on the lake twice, backed it through the garage door, and sold it the next week! That was the end of his fishing. Work remained his creative outlet, and the orchard was not enough to keep him busy year round. It seems that a man's life is shaped more by his habits than by his dreams.

My mind was going into overdrive. Should I blurt out my misgivings or just support my husband? I kept seeing flashes of my Dad through the years; hurried, harried, always in a dither. I wondered if this was a future I wanted for our family. Perhaps it was just because Dad was such a perfectionist, and took everything so seriously, that he paid such a high emotional price to succeed in business. But Curt was cut from the same cloth. True, he could relax. I had been delighted to find out that he had what we call his "silly inner life". He was earthy, and did funny impressions, and communicated in his own 'grunt language' when we would lie in bed vegetating on a Saturday morning. But nevertheless, his expectations were high and he could be hard hitting, intolerant and irascible. He was a fiercely loyal person and would not understand the fickleness that is part of the business world. His past had left him with a hefty dose of negativity too, and I wondered if he had the tact for business. A lot of his growing years had been spent in emotional isolation and this gave him an appearance of aloofness or arrogance.

On the other hand, I would be glad to leave Montreal. The agency in which I now worked catered to the English speaking populous of N.D.G. But day by day the government was closing in, and we were advised that whether we needed it or not in our job situation, that we would not be allowed to hold a job in Quebec unless we spoke fluent French. One day three ingratiating, and then surly, members of Curt's professional organization visited him and ended by telling him categorically that there was no place for him in Quebec unless he would speak French. This was just enough to complete the demise of any vestige of positive feeling Curt had toward Quebec. With enthusiasm and good faith Curt had enrolled in a French course as soon as we had arrived in Montreal. He had enrolled me too, but the course was too advanced and I lacked Curt's affinity for languages, so I did not last. By now Curt could speak French passably well, but refused to do it under duress. He noted that while the rest of Canada was putting up bilingual signs in recognition of the French fact in Canada, all the bilingual signs in Quebec had been replaced by French only. It began to irk him more and more.

If we were to move, I wondered how we could get out of the renewal of our lease that we had just signed for our duplex. I phoned to ask. Somewhat grudgingly the manager of the properties agreed to let us sublet–provided that I was very careful who I sublet to. We placed an ad, and out of six applicants chose a fine looking gentleman who was most anxious to move in. However, when he went to the general office to sign the lease, it was only in French and no English translation was available. The man felt squeamish about signing something he did not understand. But not to worry, they would have an English lease for him in ten days. The man waited, growing increasingly impatient, but we implored him to hold on. At the end of ten days they told him coldly that the owner was out of the country and it would be a few more days. By the time our moving day had arrived, our renter had disappeared to find greener pastures. There was nothing we could do at that point but proceed with our plans. As we stood out on the street, coming to grips with the sad realization that there was no way our straining Olds could pull the loaded U-Haul across Canada, a police cruiser screamed up the street, lights flashing. Someone had reported us for skipping out on our lease. All my fears had crystallized into reality. The situation was so unpleasant that I began to feel physically ill. I ran to the bathroom in alarm, and to complete our misery, found that I was having a miscarriage. No one seemed concerned. I huddled in the bathroom and cried with our little son, and let Curt deal with the police and the strident manager.

Finally we were allowed to leave, after giving the manager a forwarding address and promising to pay out the rest of our lease. Now our alienation was complete. We watched our bank account dwindling as we hired United Van Lines to transport our goods, and we said goodbye without regrets to the duplex, with the snow of that bitter winter still up to the balcony of what had been our home. It was April 1, 1971.

With the sound of crunching snow beneath our tires, we sighed in relief knowing we were on our way. I put Justin down in his car bed for a nap and put our kitten, Bunky, down between the luggage hoping he would find the litter box. Bunky was an anonymous donation who had appeared on our doorstep on the coldest day of winter. Having heard him cry, I brought him in, warmed him and fed him, recalling at the same time the many pleading negotiations I had gone through with my mother growing up. I had passionately wanted a cat. My mother passionately didn't. Helpful neighbors often sent me home with a new kitten "just in case...." and my mother sent me back with it just as fast. It was like living in a revolving door. This donor obviously knew his people: my son had to have a pet.

But Curt was firm. He hated cats. A cat had jumped down on him from a stone wall in Europe one time and had scratched him badly. He grabbed the kitten and canvassed every house within three blocks. No one admitted to knowing anything about the little tortoise shell kitten. By this time, the kitten had figured things out. When Curt, tired from his excursion, fell asleep on the couch, the kitten crawled up on his chest and fell asleep too. Sofia Loren could not have been more seductive. When he woke up and found the peaceful little animal curled up on his chest he was forced to concede: "He is kind of cute."

"So....?" I prompted him.

"Well, we can keep him—but only if he is a male." He inverted the cat and did an inspection.

"Well?" I held Justin back from pouncing on the cat.

Curt smiled a defeated smile.

So Bunky became a fellow traveler, and as we set out I wondered how Curt and I, and two acrobatic, squirming beings, full of the exuberance of life, would manage to survive together for six long days on the road.

"Do you know what the agency bought me for a going away gift?" I asked Curt.

"No, you didn't tell me. What?"

"A crystal cigarette lighter."

"But you've never smoked."

"Exactly," I said ruefully.

"Never mind," he said, "Take out the map and check it over. I've decided to take the northern route through Ontario. It will be quicker and less traffic."

"Are you sure?" I said doubtfully, studying the map. "There are just miles and miles here without a town or any human habitation. What if we should get car trouble and get stranded?"

"Don't worry. This car is in A-1 shape. I had it checked out by the best mechanic available—you know, that French fellow up the street. I explained about our trip and told him to go over everything with a fine tooth comb."

He turned out to be the mechanic from hell.

The car stalled, not to be restarted, on the outskirts of a little hamlet in northern Ontario. Fortunately for us it did not happen somewhere in the empty wilderness. Unfortunately for us, parts to fix the car were unavailable and would take five days to bring in. In the meantime the last of our money was being eaten up by food and the motel. We spent the days watching Bunky chase rabbits. And fidgeting with frustration. But finally it was fixed.

Happily for us our trip across the desolate prairies was broken up by visits to relatives. Finally on April 10, with the sun high in the sky, we turned the corner into the Okanagan Valley of British Columbia and discovered a different world. Fluffy cumulus clouds lazed across a sky of infinite blue. Clouds of blossoms crowned the fruit trees covering the slopes, and the sun was warm on the luminous fresh green leaves. Miles of lake twinkled and shimmered under the spring sky. To our road and winter weary eyes, it was the Garden of Eden. Kelowna called us home.

We settled in with Mom and Dad, and they were content and happy to have us. I, for my part, was happy to have the freedom now to use my training and talents in ways for which funding was unavailable, and soon assembled a youth group that met weekly in my parents' large basement. Before long I also began teaching at the college. Dad's large contract, however, proved to be a flash in the pan, and the business did not take off. Dad was unknown in the Valley, and we found the community very ingrown. From the time of the first settlers until, finally, a long floating bridge was built across Lake Okanagan a decade earlier, the people of the Valley had lived in isolation. A few tourists would brave the challenging mountain roads, but for the most part the valley people were a kingdom unto themselves, intermarried and tied to each other by several generations of bonds. New business was either ignored or made to feel unwelcome. Mom recalled her visit from the Welcome Wagon. After what seemed a most amiable visit, and being loaded down with coupons from local businesses, the matronly lady with the bright smile turned to leave. As she bent down to fasten her shoes she murmured, "Yes, the Okanagan was such a nice place before all these people started to move here."

Mom couldn't believe her ears.

"Don't be impatient," my father counseled us. "Statistics show it takes three years to get a new business on its feet, that is, before you can make a living out of it."

"Great!" I thought, "Three more years of being penniless." True, we were comfortable with Mom and Dad. My teenage sister and brother were still home, but there was plenty of room for us. And Mom, through her understanding of our position and her compassion, tried to keep everything going smoothly. The fly in the ointment was their dog. Timmy was a small golden Pomeranian with a yipe that was non-stop. From his spot in the front window, across from a school, he felt it was his calling in life to greet every passing vehicle with a high pitched crescendo of excitement.

Unfortunately, our little son Justin, who had problems sleeping at the best of times, could never nap or enjoy a night's sleep without being jarred awake. He became more and more irritable and his frequent crying got on my Dad's nerves, putting us all on edge. He began to hate his crib, and once he learned how to climb out of it we would find him in the morning sleeping under our dresser, in a closet; every morning somewhere new. One morning I found him standing in a free standing sink getting into the medicine cabinet.

"I am not asking for something outrageous," I pleaded with God on a rainy day as I rode the bus downtown. "We need a home of our own—just an average house—nothing special. Like that charcoal gray bungalow over there with the For Sale sign in front," I said, jumping up and craning my neck to get a better look.

What I was asking really was quite outrageous. We didn't even have enough money coming in to pay rent, let alone a down payment on a house. But that didn't stop me from asking. Nor from falling in love with that little charcoal house. I watched it with a proprietary air each time I rode the bus. It did not sell quickly; it seemed to be waiting for us. But one day the For Sale sign did come down, and it seemed my praying had been in vain.

But now I was in the eighth month of my next pregnancy. I could no longer work and we urgently needed a place of our own. The prospect of two babies crying each time that dog barked was more than I could deal with. We had a family council and while Dad was quite taken aback, and could not understand why we would even think of moving out, Mom understood. We found an old house, a former butcher shop, near a creek downtown, and Mom and Dad agreed we could take just enough out of the business to pay the modest rent. Poor as it was, it had an apricot tree, a little garden space and an abundance of glowing red tulips. A walnut tree swept over the fence and luxuriant flowering shrubs made it beautiful to me. The sound of the rushing water was enervating, yet peaceful. That is, until I discovered that Justin and his new found friends had invented a new game; throwing his toys and sundry household articles over the fence, for the joy of seeing whether they would sink or float down to the lake.

So it was to this little house that I brought Angel, our new daughter, home from the hospital. I looked ruefully at my still ample tummy, and noted that Bunky, no doubt in some deeply symbiotic way had also grown a rather ample tummy. Or, was it the ampleness of his diet. Or... could it be...that I would have to call into question the credentials of our resident kitten-sexer?

"I think he's pregnant," I said, smirking at Curt.

Curt didn't like to be caught short in anything. "Who?" he asked, a little aggravated.

"Bunky, our male cat," I rubbed it in.

Curt rolled his eyes to heaven and sputtered, "Well, make HER a bed somewhere!"

Using a moving box, and my creativity, I managed to design her a box that was the cat equivalent of the Waldorf Astoria, soft and plush, lined with an old kimono. Apparently she wasn't much of a Waldorf Astoria cat. As a matter of fact she wasn't even a good old Holiday Inn cat. She wanted our bed. I put her in her box. She jumped out. I put her in. She jumped out. It became a relay race. All it proved was that she was in considerably better physical shape than I was. And she continued to circle our bed like an ancient Druid performing a ritual dance. Our bed was covered by a lovely native crafted bedspread that had the interesting peculiarity that every time we washed it, it grew larger. By now there was quite a sizeable overhang on the floor. Bunky loved it. I wondered if it had been spun with catnip. I rolled it up; Bunky went under the bed. I suggested, it being springtime, that we could put her outside. My husband said it would be inhumane. By now, when Bunky laid on her side it looked like a game of ping pong was going on inside of her. My encyclopedia suggested that the birthing box have an overhang to keep it dark. I was certain I now had the answer. Which proves you can be certain about nothing.

It was four A.M. when the yowling started. I checked under the bed. Nothing! Luck! A surge of triumph swelled up inside me. My husband slept on peacefully at my side. A second yowl. Suddenly a dark, dark thought, a black, black conviction began to take shape in my head.

"What is it?" my husband muttered semi-comatose as he did automatically whenever a baby cried.

"Bunky is giving birth," I said.

"Is she under the bed?" he asked, half sitting.

"No," I answered.

He rolled over to rejoin his dream.

"She's in the closet, I think." I had, in fact, peeked, but was feeling particularly vindictive since it was, after all, his idea that the cat remain inside...

Another unearthly yowl. "Number three," I counted. I nudged my husband. "Did you ever unpack that box of ties in the closet that I've been nagging you about?"

"Oh, shit!" My husband ejected from the bed like a rocket. I heard his retreating steps and the plaintive mewing of new born kittens as he headed for the laundry room. The washing machine went till dawn. The ties, of course, were ruined.

So did I enter into the next chapter of domestic bliss. Finally I had the chance to be a homemaker, to cook and plant and smell the earth again. But I was a mother, a wife with a difference. For at night, in my dreams, I wore a Religious Habit and continued my life in the monastery. The bells rang and I did my work and prayed with my Sisters in the golden light of the chapel. By day my life proceeded under a cloud, in a state of spiritual numbness. I felt I had backed away from my pledge, reclaimed my gift, abandoned the high road I had chosen. In the end selfishness had won out. For five years I had had no comfort in prayer, and the sky of my spirit was bathed in a wan and dying light. There was no one I could talk to, and I hungered for deeper communication, for an existence based on more than shallow material things. Even the Church here seemed to be stagnant and uninspired. And what about the people I had disappointed? So many had counted on me and I had let them down. I ached for them. Was I a source of scandal to them now?

My mind went back to a meeting of the Canadian Psychological Association I had attended in Winnipeg. Curt and baby Justin had accompanied me. As I stood in the elevator, holding Justin, I realized with a start that I was eyeball to eyeball with Dr. Willy Runquist from the University of Alberta. I froze. But surely he would not recognize me anyway....

"Babe!" he shouted exuberantly.

His greeting was jovial. But what was he thinking? What would he go back and tell the rest of the faculty? Had this chance meeting undone all the good I felt I had accomplished during my years at U of A. Had my leaving left a wake of injured souls?

How can I heal them? How can I put my hands on the hearts of those I was given to care for? How can I let them know that nothing has changed but surface appearances?

I am not abandoning my cause, my friends. I am not leaving the ship I have sailed so long. I am not carrying a different standard. I am not boasting of a better way. I am not repudiating the way I have traveled. Many others will walk this way of light to their graves, and I will envy them and wonder why for me it has been different. I have taken a different path and I cannot explain it right now, but it is the same faith. Somehow I am still an expression of the Church of the twentieth century, and my life must still articulate the Word of God for our times.

But I think I will drag my feet in this new place until I know that you are alright. In some way I must know that my new path has not destroyed the hope within you–that you are not bewildered or discouraged or sunk in cynicism. For everything has changed, and nothing has changed. All the things we have discussed remain the same. What is Perfect cannot be destroyed by what is imperfect.

I remind myself of one of the axioms of our Religious Order: 'One soul is of more value than a world'. Now I am entrusted with more than one soul. I think of my husband whose support I am, to help him resurrect from the deaths of the past and build his future. He has still so much negative debris from the past. I would like to boast I have been a channel of light to him. So many discussions—arguments, actually–we have had…I try…. Sometimes I think, after an exhaustive session, that we are making progress. We have unveiled prejudices, and made steps toward understanding. Then two weeks later the same argument rears up its ugly head and we are back again at step one. I would like to say I handle this heroically, I keep my cool and respond with a loving calm, but I do not.

These things form the burden of my days. Curt goes to Church with me, as he promised, but our spiritual lives are as different as our backgrounds. It can't be helped. Right now he is engrossed in his work and making a living and there is little else left to give.

Then, suddenly, unexpectedly, a watershed experience occurred that formed the Great Divide in my life; my spiritual travail came to an end and I was able to embrace my present and my future.

One early spring day when I awoke I became aware of an incredible luminosity filling the whole house, penetrating the barriers of my skin and lighting a wonderful light within me. It seemed as if light was coming from the floor, the walls, the ceiling, everywhere! All day I walked about, as if on tip toe, as if I walked on holy ground. There was a hush, the noise of children notwithstanding, and a sense of vibrant and complete Life embraced me. It was as if the barriers had been erased between heaven and earth, time and eternity. Best of all, an irrefutable, unmistakable message was somehow clearly transmitted to my understanding that said: "My Daughter, you are where I want you to be."

Everything was okay. It was alright. Truly.

From that day on, although I still dreamed at night of the monastery, I regained the interior peace that had been lost to me. And the most amazing, exciting, ratification of that special day came when Curt returned from work that night:

"I've had the most extraordinary experience today," he said in awe and fascination. "The only way I can describe it is to say that it has been as if a telephone receiver has been off the hook between earth and heaven."

In a happening that bore the stamp of the same Spirit, the dead leaves of winter began to be stirred up that spring through the light cast by the humble father of the L'Arche communities for the mentally handicapped, Jean Vanier. In a series of retreats through the Valley, Jean Vanier's simple but extraordinary love reached out to help us embrace our own woundedness and the woundedness of others—for we are all in some manner wounded—and it resuscitated spirits numbed by routine and mechanical observance. Although I had not attended the retreats, the waves of love unleashed there spilled over to me from the lives of others.

It had been a year now that we had lived in our little house by the creek. As we had been spiritually enriched, we had also been warmed by our friendship with Peter and Eve. I had met Eve the year earlier as she was strolling by my parent's home, heavily pregnant as I was, with her little girl dancing around her. Tall, blonde, with an endearing English accent and a lilting laugh, we shared together the conundrums and joys of motherhood.

Her husband, Peter, entered our lives in a more spectacular fashion after he nearly sent my canine nemesis, Timmy, to the happy hunting grounds. As Peter headed down the street in his Volkswagon van one day I saw Timmy run out and heard the van screech wildly to a halt.

Dad descended on the van like a bolt of lightning.

"Some sort of a bearded-idiot-delinquent nearly killed our dog!" Dad spluttered irately as he tromped into the house, "Who is that imbecile?"

I cleared my throat and my heart fluttered between apprehension and laughter, "Ah...well, that delinquent is our local dentist.... As a matter of fact, he's the new friend I've been talking about."

We often giggle about the beginning of our friendship. We talked endlessly, sharing fun, feelings and foibles, and though not at one with our beliefs, I sensed that the warmth I felt all came from the same Creative Love, Who was bigger than both of us, and Who gave each of us life.

We were still depressed financially, unable to save, living from day to day but we coped. Peter and Eve were our human angels and passed on their children's clothes to us, since, although their children were the same age as ours, they were taller. At the end of that year it was a big relief when our landlord agreed to let us stay on in the little house for another year.

A week later, on a Sunday morning after Curt had left for Church (we went in separate shifts so that each of us could have an uninterrupted hour without the disruptions of our two active children), the phone rang. I grabbed the children from the bath tub and ran for the phone. With a hurried apology our landlord informed me he was bringing over a buyer for the house later that day! I was thunderstruck, struck dumb. We did not have a written lease, but only the week before he had agreed to another year!

What will become of us? I cried in panic. *If only we had a down payment maybe WE could have been able to buy this house.*

I grabbed the newspaper and raced through the classified ads. I had to find some answer for us before Curt came home. If I was upset, he would be more so. To be homeless would be especially hard for him as, in the aftermath of the war, he had grown up in a magnificent house, jointly built by his father, who was president of one of Vienna's foremost banks, and his maternal grandfather, who was the chief electrical engineer of the city of Linz. Curt had been bred for success. His expectations were high.

Someday, of course, he would inherit that house—it had been willed to him, his sister and his mother equally after his grandfather died, but his mother, who lived in it now, was not inclined to sell it, and Curt had too much manly pride to ask her to move. He felt sure he could make it on his own—after all, was he not the top student in Austria and the recipient of a Governor General's medal in Canada? The inheritance would come some day. But, for today, he needed a house to house his family.

"Emergency sale," the ad read, "Private sale by owner, three bedroom house, fireplace, basement, one year old, assumable mortgage, $22,500."

A crazy hope began to stir within me. Still, we had no down payment, and could we even afford the monthly payments?

Curt went pale when I told him the news.

"But look," I said to him, shoving the paper under his face, "Look what I found?"

"Forget it!" Curt said roughly. "We have no down payment, and there's got to be something wrong with the house at that price."

"Well, we could at least drive by and look at it, couldn't we?"

"No!" Curt said emphatically. Then seeing my hurt look, he softened and said, "Look, this is foolishness. It is impossible. We cannot afford to buy a house and you know it. There's no point in going to see a place that is probably a dump anyway, and you'll just be disappointed."

"Well," I said, trying to smile as if nothing was wrong, "we are going for a Sunday drive. I want to go for a drive."

By now Curt knew I would leave him no peace. He shook his head and reached for his jacket.

I held my breath as we drove down Clairmont Drive, a new subdivision in an area that had once been orchards. To my astonishment the For Sale sign was standing in front of a charcoal gray bungalow, not unlike the one I had prayed about a year and more ago! And it looked so good that even my finicky husband was impressed.

Rushing home, we phoned the owner, asked questions, and made arrangements to meet back at the house. The owner had built a second house which had gone way over budget, and now was about to be foreclosed on if he did not get rid of one of the houses immediately. We explained that we had no down payment, but that did not seem to faze him. If we wanted the house he suggested that we could make the down payment later on. We knew our income was not high enough to qualify us for a regular mortgage, but since we would be signing a sub-agreement for sale and assuming his mortgage this would not prove to be a difficulty.

In the time it took to fill a baby bottle with milk, we were back in the car heading back to the house. We parked out in front, waiting anxiously, scarcely daring to hope, until a beige pick up truck pulled into the driveway. As I stepped out of the car to meet our destiny, with Angel in my arms, eight ounces of lukewarm milk poured down the front of my red wool dress. Angel had gnawed her way through her rubber nipple! Perhaps my nervousness had transmitted to her. No matter. The disaster of the morning was blossoming into a most special answer to an almost forgotten prayer. God was giving me my charcoal house.

Chapter 17

"I have some bubble gum, but I can't bubble," my three year old son declared tragically.

I didn't know what I should do about that. Fortunately, since I frequently don't know what to do, my son did not wait for a reply before bounding out of the door.

"Let's play dump trucks," I heard him shout to his friends.

"No, let's not," came the rejoinder.

"Yes!"

"No!"

"Yes!"

"No!"

"Yes!"

"Noooooo!"

"Hey, guys," I stuck my head outside the door, "cut the noise!"

"They won't play dump trucks," my son said, aggrieved. He spun around at them again: "You play dump trucks!" he shouted at his friends. "I'm boss!"

Since he was born our son has had the unshakeable conviction that he is boss.

"I'M BOSS!" he shouted again before his beleaguered pals could rally their resources.

The miniature human beings glared at each other in a stubborn stand off until Preston, a serious four year old, offered: "No, Justin," he said, "You're not boss. The government is boss."

So far has socialism pursued us!

I was finding motherhood to be an interesting challenge. I thought it was only right that I should have some advantages with my background in psychology. For instance, it is known that one of the chief ways a child learns is by association. Common sense really, because whenever two things happen together they become linked in the child's mind. If a stimulus behavior is linked to a negative reinforcement, that is, a punishment, the child, to avoid the punishment, will avoid the stimulus behavior. At least, that's what the theory holds. One of my first forays into practicing a psychologically enlightened parenthood involved teaching my son, Justin, then a toddler, to stop pushing over a six foot rubber plant, known affectionately by its German name, Goomybaum. Every time Justin touched that plant I tapped his fingers and scowled at him. After some time, I felt I had got the point across, so the next time he trundled into the room I sat back and watched. He stopped. He looked around at me sitting on the couch and looked at the poor fractured Goomybaum. It was like a light went on in his head. He toddled over to me, slapped me sharply on the fingers, headed over to the rubber tree and bounced it joyfully onto the floor.

All in all, parenthood is a humbling experience.

It is also very educational.

Take yesterday.

"Does God make cookies?" my son enquired. It could be that he has become theologically minded from eating the religious medals my old Superior had sent him.

"I don't know if He makes cookies, but He isn't around making any cookies today," I growled. "What's the matter with the angel cake I just baked anyway?" I expected him to overlook the fact that it had only risen two inches.

"No, no, no!" my son interrupted me impatiently. "Not he. She! God is a girl."

"Oh," I gulped, "Why do you say that?"

With a beatific expression in his blue eyes he gazed up at the picture on the wall of his most generous benefactor. "See," he said serenely, "GodMOTHER."

Justin's godmother, my old religious Superior, always managed to remember him in special ways.

Meanwhile something disinterred itself from the fireplace, looking like an ambulatory bag of peat. It appeared that Angel was doing a little vocational training as a chimney sweep. But it wasn't like ashes she smelled—and it wasn't like Evening in Paris either. It was more like Night in the Sewer. Toilet training was my nemesis. It was only after I had changed many hundreds of diapers that it occurred to me that maybe there was a plan in all this. Diapers, and all the other demands of motherhood, I realized, were stretching me as a person, and I began to understand that the heavy investment of time was essential for a profound bonding with my children. Left to my own devices, I knew, I'd be apt to cut corners, be around for the fun times, and end up being a 'fair weather friend' to my children.

Nothing has really changed, I think to myself. *It never really ended. It continues even now.*

I am still called in obedience to the needs of my children and the service of my husband. I am still learning to surrender to the demands of circumstance, to the austerity of the necessary. In days gone by I could trust in the reasoned requests of a Superior. Now my nights and days are ruled by the sometimes capricious demands of a growing family. Crying babies tear me from my dreams, and their necessity is my necessity. Although I am aching with sleeplessness, there is no negotiating with a sick child, or one in terror of a nightmare. I can see now, with an acid clarity that I needed this family of mine to rip me from the core of my self centeredness and set me free. There is nothing like a baby's unrelenting cry, or the petulance of a child, to stretch one's patience, and to call forth new awareness and fresh giving. It is like God's Tough Love program for me. It has forced me to do things I would not otherwise have done, and grow in directions I would not otherwise have grown.

And poverty. Tell me about it! My vow continues unabated. Poverty may have more to do with inner detachment and the setting of ultimate priorities in our lives, but I have also found it to be a rigorous test of my trust in God; a test which has become a wrestling match for me. When I married the accomplished and educated man that I did, I had no illusions that the rose would be without thorns, but I did not anticipate stresses over money. Or the lack of money. In fact, our business has taken us on a wild roller coaster ride of uncertain highs and scary lows. Although there is fresh air here now, with many newcomers arriving in the valley, there is no regulation in the refrigeration and air conditioning industry and many unqualified people are price cutting and botching up jobs, creating suspicion and a negative ambience in the whole business community. Aside from this, there is the basic problem of establishing a large enough clientele to support a family in an economy that flip flops like an unsteady penny. But the hardest blow to bear has been people defaulting on payment. When a person robs a service station of fifty dollars it is recognized as theft and it becomes front page news. Yet when a customer leaves you holding the bag for thousands of dollars of goods and services rendered, it becomes a hidden crime which has only a long and expensive recourse in law. There is an imbalance here, a lack of appreciation for elemental principles of justice. "Blessed are those who hunger and thirst for justice, for they shall be satisfied," Christ said. *When, Lord?* I feel the lack of security keenly. One of the hardest prayers I have ever had to pray is "give us this day our daily bread". Am I lacking faith? *Please, Lord, take care of our needs! You have said, 'The laborer is worthy of his wages'. Curt is a creative and dedicated worker and deserves to get paid. Touch the hearts of those who trample on justice and truth, and those who say with patronizing arrogance, "I tell you what. I'll pay you half...."*

Hurtfully, sometimes it has been people who wear the label of Christian that refuse to pay. Claude Benoit was such a man. Not only did he proclaim himself Christian, but he helped lead a weekly prayer group. Unfortunately his financial adviser was one of the most unsavory characters in the business community. I was beside myself how to reach through to Claude's conscience. His large debt was driving us into bankruptcy. Finally I took to going to his weekly prayer group and simply stared at him the whole time.

"Why aren't you paying us? You are causing so much suffering to our family." I said to him, trying to unmask his soul with the frankness of my gaze as he sat at the hospitality desk.

The smooth veneer of his cordiality cracked for a moment as he struggled with his speech, succeeding only in sounding like he had a speech impediment. "Why are you here?" he rasped hoarsely, and then looked away with feigned nonchalance, his brown hair disheveled by a careless hand.

Claude eventually paid us, but the price for him of playing on the dark side was his mental health. It strikes me that our psyches are so finely orchestrated and honed to truth that even when instructed to tell a deliberate lie on a lie detector test our bodies involuntarily perspire, sending the polygraph needle soaring. What is not truth causes a stress in the body, a state of dis-ease, which is a step toward the breakdown of what we are and what we were created to be. When we do violence to truth and justice, we not only violate society, we violate ourselves, planting the seeds of death in our own bodies. In the end, the hypocrite is his own executioner.

I see that in the throes of every circumstance, and beyond every effort of my own, my life remains in God's hands. His hands have crafted my being, designed my parameters. His life has infused my soul. Everything I am or have is gift. This is the great truth. This is my poverty and ultimately my limitless wealth. As the Father of the prodigal son said to his eldest son, "Everything I have is yours...."

But what of chastity? I am a married woman now.... Yet even here my vow continues, for in all of our flawed loving there is incompleteness. In the second of our creation we must have caught some vestigial glimpse of God, because we yearn for this ultimate Love ever after. Human love is like a workout at the gym; it takes effort and sweat, discipline and perseverance, to build up the muscles of our spirit. All our loving, our tangential unions, are preparation for a great invitation that has been etched into our spirits. In faithfulness, forgiveness, commitment, there is a celibacy that prepares us for the greatest Love of all.

The harsh ring of the telephone interrupts my reverie. The children's tousled heads are bent over their morning breakfast cereal, and the sun streams through the windows framing the flowers on the wallpaper with glory.

"Hi, good morning, Johanna," It was my Mom. "I thought I'd better let you know that I've just had a call from Saskatchewan. Uncle Mike died last night."

"Ohhh...When, how? Did he come out of his coma before he died?"

Mike, Dad's oldest brother, had been found on the couch in a semi-comatose state three months earlier. It was discovered, that, along with cirrhosis of the liver he was severely diabetic. Mike never went to doctors. I suppose, to him his symptoms were indistinguishable in his drunken haze from all the other ills of alcoholism. Or he had just given up. I was always frightened and repelled by him.

"Yes, as a matter of fact, he did! It was quite remarkable. The doctor had no explanation. For all those weeks he couldn't talk; he was like a prisoner in his own body. But they could see in his eyes that he understood, and he tried to follow people with his eyes." Mom was excited.

"Who was there with him?"

"Everyone. The boys had come in from Winnipeg, and Eileen, and of course Aunt Tillie."

Aunt Tillie was a saintly woman who had remained calm and dignified through a life of abuse, empowered by a higher Love. Her children adored her, but none of them had had the courage to get married themselves. I think marriage frightened them. Eileen, her daughter, a brilliant, competent young woman, crackled with hostility toward men. She nearly decimated Curt the first time she met him. They tangled like a couple of mountain lions. Mind you, Curt also proudly lays claim to a Viking warrior ancestry and is no slouch when it comes to battle. Still, Eileen took the side of her mother when it came to high principles and ideals. As a nurse she had donated years of her life to nursing the poor refugees of Cambodia. She told me, with dread flashing in her dark pained eyes, that she expected she would have to nurse her father too when he died of cirrhosis of the liver. Graphically, from her nursing experience, she described what a death from cirrhosis would be like. She spoke of the horrid smell that emanates from the bodies of cirrhosis sufferers and the utter misery of their last days.

"They all held his hands," Mom was saying, "and they told him they forgave him. Though he couldn't talk, they saw two big tears roll down his face into his moustache. And then, the next day, against all expectations, he was able to talk again briefly, and he asked to see a priest. I believe that through the gift of her faithfulness and forgiveness Tillie has reclaimed her husband's soul."

I felt two tears edging down my face. "I know that some people will say that he was such a beast he didn't deserve to be saved. But it is so wonderful that they were able to forgive him. And, obviously, their forgiveness transformed him. If his suffering of the last months does not satisfy the demands of justice, then maybe he will spend some time in purgatory, but in the end his cruelty and brokenness has finally been replaced by an answering love! And that is wonderful!"

If Uncle Mike found healing on his death bed, it turned out that the forgiveness of his children also healed and freed them. The sweltering coil of animosity within Eileen seemed to have been washed away in her father's tears.

Justin cocked his head as I put down the phone, "What is purgatory?" he asked with little boy curiosity.

"Hmmm," I pondered. "What if I was to send you to Peggy's birthday party next week with motor grease on your hair and face and dirty tattered old clothes?"

"I'd hide!" he said solemnly.

"That's sort of what people do when God calls them and they are not quite ready. It's a place where they can clean up and get ready for heaven."

That was the first of two deaths that would occur that spring.

We were on our way to Victoria for a family outing when the police tracked us down with an urgent message. We were to fly immediately to Winnipeg where Curt's sister lay dying in the Heath Science Center.

Eva had had a mole removed the summer before because it was being irritated by the elastic on her bikini. It was a total shock when the doctor phoned the next week to say they had found cancer. But she had surgery, had it removed and life went on. After all, she was only twenty nine. She joked that now, with a sizeable portion of her buttock extirpated, that she was "half-assed Eva". Life was just beginning to come together for her. After postponing having their first child for years: until Eva's insecurities were assuaged, their freezer filled, they had a home of their own, everything prepared, Dan and Eva had a baby boy whom they named Colin. Her dreams were coming true. The doctor gave the baby a clean bill of health, and Dan was thrilled with his new son.

One morning as Eva and Dan awoke they were surprised to see the sun already high in the sky. Colin had not woken them up for his morning feeding. Dan stumbled sleepily to the nursery. The next moment Eva was electrified to hear Dan screaming hysterically, lying down on the hall floor. At thirty nine days Colin had succumbed to sudden infant death syndrome. It was a dreadful blow. It took time for their life to mend, but eventually it did, and later two healthy baby girls arrived to delight their hearts. And now?

"Everyone is here," Eva said in surprise as she opened her eyes from a fitful sleep. "I must be dying."

She looked wan, weak. "Where are you staying?" she turned toward me.

"At the house," I said softly, thinking to myself; *The house you waited for so long which you will never see again.*

But ever the consummate mother and housekeeper, Eva tried unsuccessfully to hoist herself up in bed, "Is it clean? Do you have everything you need?" She looked questioningly at Dan. He nodded and smiled reassuringly.

"It's fine, it's perfect," I murmured and caressed her head.

"Papa!" she said, and her eyes widened in wonder as she saw the tall white haired man who had flown from Europe to be at her bedside.

The hours passed and Eva's life passed on to another dimension of being. But Eva was not the kind of person to abandon her family before she had made provisions for them. Dan, of course, scrambled to find a housekeeper who could cook, clean, and care lovingly for his children while he worked. The first two tries were not very successful. But, answering his third ad was a lovely young woman named Bonnie who was everything he was looking for—and more. They fell in love. By the strangest of coincidences she happened to have a son the exact same age as the son Dan had lost. The little boy's name was Colin.

The only person who had not come to be with Eva before her death was her mother. Mutti said she had a phobia about being around illness, and, furthermore, she did not want to be around her estranged husband who she knew would be there.

Several years before, I had had a chance to meet this mother who had been such a thorn in Eva's heart. Presumably she was not overly enthused about our marriage because when informed by Curt of our impending marriage her sole comment was, "Do you have to?" There was no other acknowledgement of our wedding. A year later she sent Curt an airplane ticket to return to Vienna for a visit, no mention of me. We assumed she could only afford one ticket and we managed to scrape together enough for a second ticket for me.

I was excited about meeting Curt's parents, and I was curious to see Vienna and the splendid house I had heard so much about. As the DC 8 circled above the airport, Curt pointed out the Danube River, a silver blue necklace passing through the center of the city. Faster than my eyes could follow, his finger went from the Prater, with its huge ferris wheel and the adjoining soccer stadium, to St. Stephen's cathedral, the domed roof of the Opera, Belvedere Castle and the Parliament whose buildings looked like a Greek temple.

Curt found himself surprisingly awkward using the language of his birth after so many years of speaking English. His parents, who had each arrived at the airport from their separate directions, joshed him about his grammar. On the way back to the family home, Franz, Curt's Dad, followed us in his vehicle. As our car whipped wildly around corners and dodged around other cars, vibrating madly all the while on the cobblestone streets, I felt like I was riding in a blender. I began to understand why European doctors cautioned pregnant women about riding in cars. Beads of sweat were scattered across my face by the time we pulled up in front of an ornate wrought iron gate, which provided the only access to a square three storey house sequestered behind seven foot white stone walls. Inside the gate a profusion of roses of every hue led around to the back garden. A plethora of trees, some heavy with golden orange apricots, filled the back yard, along with a giant birdhouse which looked like an African hut, and a tiled swimming pool attended by a life size stone mermaid. Inside, a stunning eight foot high mirror stood in its gold baroque frame by the stairwell. The house was decorated lavishly with antiques from Marie Antoinette, the hunting castle of Crown Prince Rudolf and the Palais Auersperg.

What puzzled me was the miniscule kitchen in all of this. Was this where the famous Austrian strudels and tortes were conceived? It turned out that Mutti (Trudy) abhorred cooking. After a sumptuous meal the first night, we woke to find the refrigerator empty. It became apparent that we were expected to supply the groceries and to cook for the three of us. I felt awkward and ill at ease in the unfamiliar surroundings, and was particularly intrigued by the fact that each kitchen cupboard had its own individual lock. What mysterious spices and ingredients lay hidden behind these cupboard doors such that they must be protected from thieves?

Blonde, blue eyed and vivacious, like a cat ready to spring, Mutti could not wait to show us all her jewelry and furs. She showed us closet after closet crammed with beautiful clothes. I was particularly interested in the array of embroidered dirndls that were the Austrian national dress. It was obvious that her house and her possessions were her greatest passion. But I found her likeable and charming despite my own discomfiture. She had a way of getting excited and speaking quickly in a high pitched voice that was both child-like and enervating. When our friends, Herb, Kit and family, who had been touring Europe, arrived for a visit, her excitement reached a fever pitch. She gave the children each a gold coin, but the much larger one went to the boy, explaining that she liked little boys but she found little girls shrill and silly.

Between jet lag, being four months pregnant, and experiencing culture shock, I felt interminably tired. But Mutti would not have us sleeping in because she wanted to be out and about town to sight see and visit her favorite cafes. So I propped open my eyelids and dragged myself along, telling myself I would be sorry later if I missed anything. I found the July heat sweltering, but I preferred that to shivering indoors. The house had unbelievably thick stone walls, built to withstand another war, and the air inside the house always felt cold and clammy. No wonder some of the houses in Vienna have stood a thousand years!

We visited Curt's old haunts, his school, his friends, his relatives, drank black espresso with whipped cream at sidewalk cafes, and saw an incredible number of castles, palaces and fountains. One afternoon we were invited over to the neighbors' house, where a man, who looked like a bearded elf, and a buxom, ruddy faced woman, had just returned from mushroom picking in the Vienna Woods. Their entire table was covered and piled high with orange, ecru, strange shaped and textured mushrooms, the like of which I had never imagined. During their long conversation in German, I gazed at those mushrooms and developed one of those powerful pregnancy cravings. I loved mushrooms and prayed they would give us a sample. But the old couple were not so inclined, and I left disappointed.

"Someday you'll have to find me some mushrooms like that," I scolded Curt.

He laughed and told me how good they tasted.

We visited Salzburg and saw the fountain featured in The Sound of Music, and did a car tour of Austria. Near the end of our visit we spent several days with Curt's father in his downtown apartment, decorated with his wonderful paintings and wood work, and from there were taken out to his mountain cabin. There our presence was a huge annoyance to his pet cat who marched stiffly out of camp at our arrival, only to reappear three days later with as much lofty disdain as a cat could muster.

With our return to the family home, Trudy's mood had turned morose. She obviously resented the time we had spent with Curt's father, taking it as a personal insult to her. I was rather glad I did not speak German so that I could not follow the recriminations that fell upon Curt's head. I was aware that our trip here had provided Trudy the opportunity to get Curt's father back into the family home for the first time since he had left fifteen years before. I had sensed some chemistry operating between them that first day, and Trudy had been blushing and flirting like a schoolgirl. But that visit had been followed by a phone call which left her in a rage. The way I figured it out was that Franz, Curt's Dad, had experienced a flickering of his original attraction to Trudy, then, in alarm, calling himself short, he reminded himself of the reasons he had left. Simply put, she was a bitch. To prove his point to himself, he phoned her, pressed old familiar buttons, got the response he had grown to expect, and ratified his original decision to leave. He had made a new life for himself with his secretary, and he was not about to give it up.

Trudy retaliated by dragging out every bit of dirt she could about Curt's father, and told us how she was going to get him back in court to get more money out of him. I listened to her and saw a woman who had been rejected at birth by a mother who wanted a son, who was thwarted in her attempts to gain the support of her father whom she loved, and abandoned by her husband. She told us, further, how her first great love had been a Czechoslovakian boy, but her father had put a halt to that relationship because he was still seething with anger over the seizing of his family estate by the Czechoslovakian government. Trudy had demurred to his wishes, and eventually met the young promising student who was Curt's father. I felt sorry for her, and wondered how I would have fared under similar circumstances.

That trip to Vienna was destined to be only the first of many trips abroad. As our business slowly began to grow, I discovered that one of the perks in this business was the opportunity to win all expense paid trips to exotic and far away places. Suddenly I found myself able to travel as many people can only dream of traveling. We were able to experience the excitement of Rio de Janiero and the haunting nasal cry of the muezzin in Tangier. We saw the red light districts of Amsterdam and the alpine meadows of Switzerland. We traveled from Brussels to the Alhambra of Spain, from Picadilly Square and the Tower of London to the ruins of Chichen Itza. Between the mundane tasks of motherhood, we danced in the world's most celebrated nightclubs. I had the chance to wear glamorous gowns, cruise in the Caribbean and snorkel in the Mediterranean. In the midst of this, I came to be aware of the incredible sameness of humanity in all its manifestations. One city became like another city, each country another habitat where men struggled with the same problems of living and dying, pain and pleasure, searching, always searching, for some sort of glue to hold it all together, some meaning through which it would all make sense.

For our marriage, however, one of the best journeys we took, was a spiritual journey. Something called the Cursillo movement had swept into the valley in the mid-seventies. My father was the first to go—unwillingly—tricked into it by Mom. He had promised to give her anything she wanted for their anniversary. He was thinking in terms of jewelry or furs. But there was something Mom wanted more. With his life always roaring at fever pitch, his nerves shot, she wanted my Dad to find some peace and serenity within himself for the sake of them both. She asked him to make a Cursillo.

"I'm here under protest!" Dad complained that first night, glowering at Father Bernie, his chin set stubbornly, ripe to find fault with everything.

Cursillo was started in Spain, and it means 'a little course in Christianity'. It is a weekend spent living Christianity as it ideally should be lived: full of love, music, prayer, humor, fellowship and sharing.

By the end of the weekend my father had been mellowed, humbled, and chastened by the touch of Christ and his fellow men. When he, and the other men, came out to rejoin their families their faces looked strangely scrubbed, clean and shining, like choir boys. We were frankly awestruck by the change in them. One of the priests, Father Charlie, in his inimitable Irish brogue, gave this testimony: "As a priest," he said, "I've often been lonely. After this weekend I will never be lonely again."

With results like that, it did not take much to convince Curt to make a Cursillo. So, one frozen morning, Curt set out with some buddies for the town of Trail where the next Cursillo was being held. Upon his return, Curt was as radiant as Dad had been, and full of talk. Excitedly he told me of an unusual happening that served to ratify his experience. At one point in the weekend, each of the men had received a carnation. After packing his suitcase in the trunk to return home he inadvertently laid the carnation on top of the outside of the trunk. Many hours later, after a rugged drive through the mountains in a blinding, blowing snowstorm, he arrived at our doorstep and found the carnation still sitting securely on the back of the car.

Several weeks later Curt was sitting in his favorite chair, and in a rare introspective mood he said, "You know, those men at Cursillo told me all the things that you have been trying to tell me for all these years, but I couldn't take them when I heard them from you."

From this point on, Curt and I grew closer in our faith, and were able to do things together, sharing our reading, giving marriage preparation courses and participating in things that would have been unthinkable before.

From somewhere in my head the words tumble out: "I will heal the broken hearted... The crooked ways will be made straight and the rough ways smooth." How can I deny my own experience? How can I deny that He has done this for me, untangling the tangled skeins of wool in my life, listening to the voiceless whispers of my heart? My faith should be like granite.

And yet it is so dark tonight.

CHAPTER 18

I thought I was taking driving lessons, but perhaps I was living out a parable.

"Where are the dual controls?" I asked anxiously. I was thirty-three years old and my mother had finally browbeaten me into learning to drive.

"Relax!" he said, but the driving instructor did not look relaxed. "I'm sitting right beside you. Just take it slow. Check the rear view mirror, turn on the ignition, and step on the gas pedal...."

"But," I said fearfully, looking at the quiet residential neighborhood I was about to devastate, "human beings live here...children...." I was seven and a half months pregnant and very conscious of children. Why hadn't he taken me on a country road somewhere?

I touched the gas and the car jumped forward. My heart lurched. I leaned into the steering wheel and glued my eyes on a spot on the road just in front of the hood of the car.

My driving instructor was becoming unglued.

"Look ahead! Look ahead! Down the road!"

"I am looking ahead!" I said, weaving crazily from one side of the road to the other. What did he think? I was looking backwards? I was so pregnant that I couldn't turn to look backwards to save my life!

He probably equates me with the local woman who put twenty-two pints of water down the oil pipe when her car overheated!

"Look ahead down the street—to the end of the block," he insisted.

"But," I protested, "if I look that far ahead, how will I know where I am?"

"Trust me!" he said, sweating profusely.

With great misgivings I did what he said, and miraculously the car straightened out. And though he told me I was the most over-cautious driver he had ever run into, I was, in fact, now a driver.

Later, when I thought about it, I realized I had learned one of the great truths of life. And it wasn't about driving a car. While I have my eyes glued firmly on myself and my immediate surroundings, I have no point of reference outside of myself to guide me. Unless I keep my eyes focused on the horizons of life, on the bigger picture, goals and destinations, I will never find my way and never know ultimately who I am. Unless I look ahead and accept the Eternal Creative Plan, I will never be a whole person.

I find it easy to get lost in the every days of life, the immediacy of my feelings and occupations, to be lulled by chores and tedium, to be swept up and mesmerized by the reach of my shallow intellect. And now I realize that who I am is becoming lost in the present terror. I am losing my identity, my perspective. I feel I have no resources left to face tomorrow. Or is it that I am just fixated at that spot beyond my hood? Yet to look further fills me with dread and pain—such pain. I am sinking into a great dark abyss. Are today's and tomorrow's events the sum total of who I am? Have I no future that is not darkness? I yearn for the taste of normalcy, of peace. Where can I find a drop of comfort for my spirit? Through my rear view mirror I see the footprints of God. I must try to retain faith in the reality of the past, and color my darkness with its hope.

Color: the years on Clairmont Drive, in the charcoal house, in the shelter of a pine covered hill, are a kaleidoscope of color. Like the cars of a swiftly moving train those days streak by hypnotically, carrying the cotton candy of headier days.

Normal days: Curt wangling ten loads of topsoil to cover our boulder strewn backyard so that a garden, flower bed and grass might emerge. City boy that he is, not realizing that the topsoil he chose is riddled with couch grass... After months of eradicating it, bit by bit, the ground eventually is ready for planting. What an exhilarating day! In anticipation and excitement I look out the back window...and see the rich black loam of my garden covered with hundreds of gaudy red and yellow plastic flowers.

"Nice garden you got there," grinned George, our neighbor.

George, a balding fellow with mischievous eyes, was home with a disabled back, and we were his entertainment.

For some days he kept tabs on Curt through the day as Curt wrestled with a boulder the size of a small armchair. Between heckling him and offering unhelpful suggestions, George kept himself well amused. He had gone in for supper by the time Curt had finally managed to get the big rock out to the curb where it could be taken away by truck. Exhausted, Curt fell into bed that night, content at least that the worst was over. In the morning he happened to glance out the window and saw the rock back in the same place it had always been, surrounded by several smaller boulders.

"Fertile valley," stated George, grinning over the fence.

Curt was speechless. And confused—until he heard George's brawny sons laughing around the corner of the house. The boys obligingly moved all the rocks back out to the curb.

But the coup occurred on Curt's birthday. I was waving him off to work in the morning as usual when his white van stopped as abruptly as if he had hit a brick wall. Curt was gesticulating wildly and waving, but I couldn't figure out what he was trying to say until he stepped out of the van and pointed up to the roof. While we slept, our mischievous neighbors had put a twelve foot diameter weather balloon on our roof.

I managed to win my own place in the spotlight the day I asked George for some advice as to why my strawberry plants were not producing. The plants were green, healthy, well weeded, but nary a blossom had set. My neighbor managed not to snort or to make any other rude noise, but his face was twitching as he informed me that I had weeded out the strawberry plants and had been cultivating the weeds all season. In my own defense I've got to say that they looked a lot alike!

Still after the elusive mushroom, I finally decided that now I would become a mushroom farmer. I appropriated an old sandbox and ordered some spawn from the Dominion Seed House catalogue. The list of instructions that came with it made me gag. Growing mushrooms, I found out, is not the same as growing lettuce and carrots. Mushrooms will only grow under very precise conditions; specific light, temperatures, humidity, soil mixtures. I did my best, but not a single mushroom ever grew.

At growing a family, however, I was substantially more successful. We now had two more children, Christian and Kelli. And kittens. Non stop kittens. Bunky was obviously a very promiscuous cat, to the boundless delight of all the neighborhood children and numerous nieces and nephews. When it came time for the birth of the kittens the children would flock over, and I had my own virtual neighborhood sex ed clinic. One niece, Danielle, who never managed to make it over at the right time, finally got a ring side seat as Bunky assembled all of us around her. Bunky had decided she was a show cat, and if any of we labor coaches left the room while she was giving birth she would follow us and bring us back, dragging afterbirth, and whatever else was coming, with her. Finally, after a textbook display of prenatal breathing, a tiny kitten emerged, still enclosed in its amniotic sac.

"Oh, look!" squealed the enchanted niece, "It came in a plastic bag!"

But even then the steel edge of another reality intruded into our lives.

One night, as I scolded the children, trying to hurry them up for bed, we heard a series of popping noises. As I headed toward the living room to check it out, Curt brushed by me at great speed and grabbed the telephone:

"Hello? Police? I am phoning from 800 Clairmont Drive. I have just witnessed a murder!"

"Oh, come on," I grabbed my husband's arm, "You are over reacting!" I was embarrassed. People didn't go around murdering other people on our street! "What do you think you saw?"

"I heard a sound. Like the crack of a gun. I ran out the front door. I saw a man lift a gun. It fired. I saw the burst of fire. Someone fell. The body is lying on the driveway up the street!"

I was standing in front of the living room window. My husband yanked me roughly. "Get down! There he is!"

I hit the floor. But I had to know what was going on. I peeked cautiously over the edge of the windowsill. A man was walking by the front of our house. He was walking casually as if he was just going for a stroll. In one hand he clutched several letters. He dropped one in front of our house and bent down to retrieve it. In the other hand he held a revolver.

"That's Mr. White!" I said in shock. He had been at our house for a New Year's Eve party. I thought for sure it would have been someone like Craig Langdon. Langdon was a drunk who also lived up the street and had broken his wife's neck the year before. Ernie White was a quiet, seemingly inoffensive man who lived common-law with a nice social worker up the street. Her two kids, a nineteen year old boy and a thirteen year old girl, lived with them. What, I wondered, had gone on behind their silent doors that had led up to this? What stresses and pressures had exploded this ordinary day into a bloodbath?

We stayed there, sitting on the floor, bathed in a sense of stunned unreality, as we watched the police arriving on our street, marching by grimly, two by two, guns cocked. On the radio we heard that our whole area had been cordoned off. Within an hour they had picked up Mr. White, whose only comment was: "I did what had to be done."

White, it turned out, had killed his common-law wife in front of the garage doors, and then chased the son around the car. It was the son's murder Curt had witnessed.

Now what? Curt would surely be called to be a witness. Mr. White's darkness would intrude into our own lives. I was very afraid for us. And the next day I was in total shock to hear that White had been let out on bail! The condition of his bail was that he stay in Calgary where he had another family. My stomach churned as I watched three slick Calgary lawyers in their expensive three piece suits pace off the distance between our house and the White's. I had such a bad feeling about all of this. I knew that they would make this a terrible ordeal for Curt. I prayed something would happen so Curt would not have to testify.

Something did happen. First, White tried, unsuccessfully, to have himself killed by walking in front of a bus. After his injuries healed, and another court date had been set, he failed to show up for his hearing. When police went to his apartment to apprehend him, they found he had blown his own head off. My first reaction was one of enormous relief.

The house of the Whites' remained abandoned for a year, like something unholy and untouchable. The grass remained uncut and turned brown. Flower beds became overgrown with thistles and tall ragged weeds. People passed by the house with hushed voices, and called back their dogs if they strayed in that direction, lest they be contaminated by something that passed understanding. How long would the sense of oppressive darkness surround that house?

One day a government agent came to our door. With great courtesy he enquired whether we had a young son, and if this young man would be interested in a job. The real estate, he explained, were going to try to sell the White's house, but they couldn't do anything with it while the yard remained in its present rundown condition. Other neighbors, whose grass Justin had cut, had recommended Justin as an enterprising and responsible fellow.

I choked. Justin? Four foot eight Justin?

"Well, please speak to him—I suppose he's at school right now—and let me know. I imagine it would be a blessing to the whole neighborhood if we could rejuvenate that property." He handed me his card. "Tell him that if he can water, weed and get that grass in shape, he can earn some money. When he is finished he can write out his bill and bring it to me at the Justice Building."

I couldn't wait 'till Justin came home for lunch that day. He was quite taken with the idea.

After school his friend Preston came by. I thought he had come because he had smelled the cookies, but Preston had other things on his mind. He was a little embarrassed:

"Mrs. Meuller," he said, "Justin is going around telling everyone he has a job with the government." He lowered his eyes.

I rolled the thought around in my mind like a wad of gum, and I felt laughter bubbling up. "Yes," I said, with as serious a voice as I could muster. "Yes, Preston, he is working for the government."

Justin and I walked over later to assess the job that had to be done. It was a big one. It would be a test for my young son. We made the sobering discovery that there was still blood congealed on the driveway, and even more gruesome, I found splotches of whitish sinewy looking matter adhering to the dark brown garage door. It looked like dura mater from the dead woman's brain.

It took weeks before the grass started to revive, and I had to prod Justin to weed the flower gardens, but at last the yard looked presentable. Curt printed up a special billing form for his son and they sat and figured out the hours spent, and discussed what Justin should charge an hour. With the bill completed, I took Justin down to the Justice Building. I stood back as Justin, whose eyes barely cleared the high counter, told the girls behind the counter that he wished to see Mr. Manson, the Government Agent.

"May I enquire the nature of your business with him?" the pretty blonde girl asked, trying hard to keep a straight face.

"I've been working for him, and now I've brought him my bill." my son said seriously.

"Um hm," she said, looking at the other girls whose eyes were twinkling merrily, "I'll just check if he will see you." She returned momentarily with an expression of mild surprise: "Go right in," she invited.

It was a big official looking office, and Mark was almost lost in the huge leather chair. He introduced himself and slid his bill across the desk.

Mr. Manson checked it over in a cursory manner and quickly wrote out a check, which he presented along with his thanks and a hand shake. Justin walked out of the office and passed the tall counter with a new dignity, immune to the curious gaze of the giggling girls.

I was proud of my son—I was proud of all my children. I enjoyed their individual personalities, the innocence of their love for us and their love for each other. The two boys shared a room and I heard them talking to each other before bed, addressing each other by the nicknames that were a trademark of our household:

"Do you love me, Oog?"

"Yes, Woog, I love you. Do you love me too?"

I thought of all the loving and happiness that Curt's Mom was missing. She had never seen her grandchildren, although we had often begged her to come. I could not help but feel that her life would be so enriched by their youthful joy. Her letters always sounded so glum, to the point that I asked Curt if she was suicidal. He shook his head. "I don't know," he said, bewildered as he always was, with her letters. The roof in the big home in Vienna had begun to leak, and she had written to ask for money. We sent her some money, all we could manage, but not enough, I knew, to replace the whole roof. Curt phoned her and begged her to sell the big house.

"But I have worked so hard to save it for you," she said defensively. "Your grandfather wanted you to have it."

"Mutti," Curt said as kindly as he could, "That big house has not succeeded in making you happy, and I don't think it would make us happy. We have another life over here. Now you say it needs so many repairs. Why don't you sell it and build a smaller house, one that you can care for more easily?"

Trudy hemmed and hawed and continued to complain. But the idea took root. Before the year was out she had found a buyer for the house. In 1975 the house was sold for over $400,000. She moved to another area of Austria and built a new house, only marginally smaller than the one she had sold. We wondered why she had built another big house, but her mood was upbeat when she wrote to us. I waited and scanned Curt's face as he read her letter.

"Translate, translate," I begged him.

And he began: "Dear Curt,

First of all many greetings from my heart for your very long letter, which has given me buoyancy and which has given me courage again. That I received my Christmas gifts on time and in good condition also created a lot of joy which I appreciate and am happy about."

I sighed with relief. "Maybe things are truly changing for her. I was so nervous that she'd react like she did over last year's gifts. I did not know what to buy her! I could not believe that anyone could be so angry after getting a gift. I really thought that the red velvet towels, carved bath soaps and perfume I had bought her were beautiful. But she said it was the kind of gift she would give to her maid. Anyway–go on!"

"Well, I guess things are looked at differently in Europe," Curt said ruefully. "So she goes on to say:"

"I have informed Herr Doctor (Curt's Dad) that I will fight until the very last despite my rather second rate state of health, even if it has to be in front of a court. I also wrote him that under all circumstances I will maintain the inheritance for you. I am not such a bad father as he is, who would rather deny you your inheritance in order that he could put it down the throat of the whore and her son. The last portion of this I have, of course, not written to him, but I only write it to you. That I will now put this whole thing in a new court case he is now informed. I would really like to know how he is reacting to this letter. You must know that I could not get a divorce done from him because the statutes of the Central Bank say that at the point of your father's death, she only who is presently his wife will get his pension. In the present court case, which looks very positive, I hope to get my legal right which is an alimony of 33% of his income, not just the 25% that I have been getting.

In regard to the next point in your letter, about the sale of the house and building the new house. Your opinion is that I have built the new house so big only in order to fulfill my pride. No, my dear boy. There is another reason. I have promised your Opa on his deathbed that I will keep the inheritance for you, not to reduce it, but will keep it under all circumstances. We Muellers do have character, and therefore there is no question that I will stick to this promise. I have done therefore what I have done. The house and inventory is worth over 3,000,000 Austrian Schillings and is your inheritance maintained for you as was Opa's wish. I have, in order to keep the Vienna house, denied myself food, but it was not worth it. With the new one I will not have repairs and I have a low estate tax. I have, of course, a reserve saving for emergency which I will not use up.

Regarding the work in the new house, I can put your anxiety to rest. It is much easier than in Vienna. I have the flat to go in from the ground floor and no stairs, and the upper floor I need dust but once a month. Although we had the most snow in ten years, the overhang did not let snow by the entrance.

Now to a very critical chapter regarding belief. Dear Curt, I do not often talk about my inner thoughts, but your assumption that I do not believe in God brings me out of my reserve. It is very good for me to know that you and Johanna include me in your prayers. I do believe in God, but on my terms and in my own way. I do pray each night before I sleep, but I deny the Church with all its glitter and pomp, and I do deny that categorically. I have seen my own mother behaving like a hypocrite, going there only to be seen. I must say I am sorry, too, I grew up without the love of parents. My mother pushed me away from herself in the first moments after birth because her wish was denied and no boy was born. When I was three years old I was sick with diptheria and the doctor had given me up, and I was told my dear mother was already talking about having a boy. That Opa, my father, has saved me with eight lemons was her bad luck. But motherly love I never knew. My mother's secret hate went so far that she also knew to bring Opa so that he was denied ever showing me his love. Once it came to a big fight between my mother and me, and then Opa said to me, word for word, "I know, of course, that you are innocent, but your mother is my wife and I must stand by her side." Then I knew what the situation was. When I finally believed that I had found someone to love, Herr Doctor's mother threw in my face that her son had only married me for the house."

"Excuse me," I interrupted, "That doesn't make sense. Weren't you about twelve when the big house was built? And wasn't it 'Herr Doctor', your father, who carried the mortgage on it? So how could your Oma have possibly said that to her? And wasn't Oma dead by that time?"

Curt threw up his hands. "That is so, on all counts. But you asked me to translate what she has written, and that's what I'm doing," He shrugged and shook his head. "Anyway, she carries on:"

"Then I have helped Herr Doctor obtain his doctorate. Even his mother said the title should actually be mine. He would never have been able to obtain the doctorate himself. Then came the separation. I have seen it as my responsibility in life to educate you children into good people. Now, I want to tell you the following secret. I have dearly loved Uncle Bob from Canada and we wanted to marry, and for that reason he also returned the second time to Austria. He wanted to convince me. I only wanted to say yes so badly. He held me in his arms, and told me I would inherit his businesses and I would never have any worries. But with heavy heart I said no, and only to save you the lot of children of divorcees, and from playing both of you into the hands of Herr Doctor, which I would not have been happy about. So I denied this happiness for myself to save you from an unhappy lot."

"Or to deny your father the satisfaction and let him off the hook! For all practical purposes as far as you and Eva were concerned they already were divorced, it seems to me, and Eva told me she loved her Dad and would have preferred living with him because her relationship with her mother was so difficult. It seems to me to be a classic case of Mutti being rejected by her mother and passing that rejection down to her own daughter whom she also resented because she was not male. And did you not petition the court at the time of your parents' separation, to make your grandfather your guardian because your own relationship with your mother was so rocky?"

"That also is true. My father did have a special feeling for Eva because he understood the problems she was having. And she was very close to him. Which didn't make her any more popular with Mutti. I tried to remain neutral and stay out of the whole mess. But there were times she drove me crazy. Once after I had spent three months rebuilding and refinishing my first motorcycle she got angry at me and threw a bucket of paint at it."

"I guess you weren't too pleased. Did she ruin it?"

"Pretty well. I didn't talk to her for months. I just ignored her." Curt's face tensed at the unpleasant remembrance. "But that was a long time ago. Shall I go on?"

"Please do."

"Well," she continues: "After my mother's death I spent the most beautiful three years of my life with Opa until he died. I have spoiled Opa

201

and have really blossomed in my care of him, and in thankfulness he did say to Ralph, my boyfriend: "I have never known what a good and worthy daughter I had". This was for me the best acquittal. When Opa went from me I thought my world would collapse. Then Eva, at that point, provided me some joy. Every week arrived a letter from her, on every occasion a little present, photos, always encouraging words. You are right when you say that she has died because of the break up of our family. But I could not have prevented that from happening even if I had wanted to. Eva hated her father very much and her shame about his doings and his deeds she went to Canada about. Therefore also has he become the murderer of his own child. The saying that it takes two to make a quarrel does not apply here as Herr Doctor behaved himself like a pig and was not bearable to me any more. His miserable character brought my own lawyer to a boiling point as your father wanted to bribe him to let the court proceedings go to his side. Also General Pickler, who was able to get him back to his homeland when he had wounded himself, said to Opa that for this swine the first bullet would have just been good enough. You have asked: "How can two people hate each other so much?" I have not hated. I have written to Herr Doctor entitled "Dear Franz", and have ended with "Loving greetings", and he has answered by typewriter and signed "Franz". After this, I answer in kind.

In regard to the loss of inheritance from Herr Doctor, Eva had been very sad, but I had assured her that I would provide myself. It is too bad he has put his house in Miss Schindler's name. I have told Herr Doctor that I have received a letter from you that has given me great moral buoyancy and courage, so that he does not believe that I stand here alone and without any help. Perhaps it would not be so bad if you would provide a shot in front of the bow of Miss Schindler's ship as Herr doctor is a willing tool in her hands. Miss Schindler and her son are the reason for this whole tragedy.

Now, dear Curt, I have opened up my innermost, and I leave it to you to write Herr Doctor. I thank you from my heart for the birthday wishes, and I have spent today's day in all quiet.

Hugs and kisses, also to Johanna and the little ones,
Your Mutti".

"Wow! This is the first time she has ever acknowledged the children and me in a letter! Things definitely are looking up! A welcome surprise! Sometimes I've wondered if in her mind's eye she still thinks you are a bachelor?"

But Curt wasn't listening. His brow was furrowed and he was staring intently at the floor.

"I'm going to phone my Dad".

"Just a minute," I suddenly realized what Curt was contemplating. "Do you think it's wise to become her hatchet man? You've always maintained that it was best to keep a position of neutrality and stay out of their scraps."

But Curt was already on the phone.

The conversation was short, clipped and angry.

"You told him off?"

"Yes."

"How did he respond?"

"He just said, "Some day you will understand."

That was the beginning of an estrangement from his Dad that would last almost ten years.

Mutti's letters would continue to be sprinkled with the news of their court battles, and also, inexplicably with the sale of the new house she had built:

***

"Dear Curt,

Today it is especially difficult to write to you. But first, many thanks to you and Johanna for your loving letter.

I have sold the house. Fourteen days I have cried about that. I am over it now. I have bought myself a penthouse in Saltzburg and I will now try and better my health if this is possible. Because of the latest exciting, in a negative sense, happenings, I am totally at an end with my nerves and the doctor says it is about five minutes to twelve. Now you may ask what these negative excitements are. Well, it is the court case which I must fight against Mr. Meuller, your father. He refuses to increase my portion of his pension, and I don't have any other income. As he does not see his way clear to follow the law, he has thought of a meniality. He accuses me that I have sold the house in Vienna for double the price and did not report the proper sales amount to the tax department. He says I could now live on the interest income from that investment. I have to start a defamation of character suit against him now, and the high cost of this court proceeding will melt to a minimum your part of the inheritance. Then, of course, Miss Schindler has reached her aim. First, she has got Mr. Meuller to a point where you will lose your inheritance from him, and now you shall also lose your inheritance from me, that is, from your grandfather. I am very sorry I have saved and hungered for the last 20 years to keep your inheritance intact. Now I have to muster all my left over forces as I will be again alone for the move to Saltzburg. Please, Mr. Meuller does not need to know where I am. You see, I am fully exposed to his bad attitude and the meniality of this couple of gangsters. Pray for me that the good Lord give me the strength to see all of this through. I wish you and your family all best greetings from your sad Mutti."

"What do you make of that?" I asked Curt. "Why did she sell the house?"

"I'm not sure, but I did get a letter from Uncle Rolf saying that she had been really taken by the builders, and he has been worried about her because of the state of depression she has been in."

"What do you mean 'taken'?"

"Well, according to Rolf, the builders charged her about a third more than they should have for the house. But he didn't go into any detail about it."

"What about your Father's charge against her regarding tax evasion? I do remember you telling me what she got for the house in Vienna, and it does jibe with what your Father is saying."

"Yes, well it is a very common ruse used by people in Vienna to avoid taxes. I would say that most people underestimate the sale price of their homes. A lot of business is done under the table in Vienna. It is a fact of life."

"So your father is right in his accusation."

Curt's eyes twinkled, "Well, how do you think she was able to build a $300,000 house if she only got $200,000 for the house in Vienna?"

"And is she as poor as she says?"

"I don't think so. She has at least $100,000 left over from the house in Vienna that I know of, not to mention the money she said she "put aside", as well as many priceless possessions. The mirror you saw in Vienna may be worth more than the house. It is a masterpiece and its twin hangs in the Louvre in France. The point is, she does not want to be made to appear in a poor light in public, especially by my Father. And, still less, does she want to lose this court case she has brought against him."

***

Saltzburg, May 1979

Dear Curt,

For your lovely letter of the 3rd of May many, many thanks. It is now the 99th letter I got from you from the far distance. In this letter you have spoken in terms of human feelings for your old mother. It was not just the businessman speaking. A thousand thanks for your heartfelt greetings for Mother's Day. Your flowers arrived punctually on the 13th. Your letter arrived, I am sorry to say, two days late, and I could have been spared many tears.

Slowly things are looking up again, especially since people here welcomed me in such a wonderful way. I feel they like me and I couldn't be such a bad person after all.

Now regarding a visit to Canada. Yes, dear Curt, I would very much enjoy finally to see my grandchildren. But if it is not possible for you financially, that is, a flight ticket, then we will have to postpone it once again. I cannot afford it with the present court case still carrying on. Mr. Meuller is behaving like a pig and I ask myself how it was possible for Miss Schindler to change him so much. In two months they will marry and she already accompanies him and plays herself up as Frau Doctor. She is trying to kill me with her looks from up there. My lawyer has requested only my legal rights, but Mr. Meuller says he is not a welfare organization. My lawyer has said in front of the courts, "When you marry this other woman you will have with her 42,000 schillings per month." Mr. Meuller has screamed: "This woman here has worked for her own money for thirty-five years and she has well earned it." I have not worked, so I must be happy with what is given to me! Up to now I have not hated, but now I do. I will curse him with my dying breath. You can write to him, but do it deeply and through his heart. I will now have to start court proceedings against him that he has swindled the war veteran's pension. I have witnesses about this and perhaps I can even get him in jail. It would be very satisfying for me because he has never paid me a penny from it. Please write him about this; perhaps he will get a bit scared and is then willing to give me more money. It will take a long time before I can put a closing line under this black chapter in my life. With what did I earn this? General Pickler has rightly said that he has saved a swine from the battlefield. It would not have been bad to lose him out there. No, on the contrary. But enough of this. Please do not wait so long to write. Greetings and kisses for you and your loved ones from all my heart.

Mutti

***

Curt was growing increasingly concerned about her. We decided that it was time she had a change of scene and something else beside court cases to think about. We sent the plane tickets and met her at the airport on a steamy July day. I had been looking forward for such a long time to sharing her grandchildren with her, and I felt they would bring her some happiness. The children, on their part, were fairly bubbling with excitement. Our house shone, and our roses were in bloom. Even my strawberries in the garden were now strawberries!

As Mutti walked in the front door, she paused, looked around disdainfully, and sniffed:

"Oh," she said, "I would never live in a house like this!"

There was a shocked silence. I couldn't believe my ears. We did not have a grand house, true, but it was a pretty average North American bungalow. Then she began to unlatch her suitcases and the ambience changed as she began to bring out gifts for the children.

I realized where Mutti was coming from and I psyched myself up not to take personal offense to anything she might say. I remembered ruefully how she had come to meet us on a trip we had taken to Switzerland. She had embraced her son effusively, then turned to me and looked me up and down: "You have gotten fat," she said to me by way of greeting. Although amazed at her rudeness, I felt secure enough in myself and in my relationship with my husband, to let her behavior roll off my back. Besides, apart from her idiosyncrasies, she could be fun loving and charming. For many years we had dreamed of this visit and I was determined that it would be a loving holiday for us all. We did all the tourist things with her. At the game farm a saucy giraffe with an incredibly long tongue reached his head over the top of the fence and stole an apple Mutti was about to bite. After our initial surprise everyone convulsed in laughter. Mutti enjoyed the outings and the attention that was lavished on her. Still, these were weeks of emotional aerobics for her. Frequently in the evenings she would hold teary vigils on our balcony as she chain smoked and complained that her son did not have enough time for her, or did not understand her, or had said something she didn't like. I, then, assumed the role of comforter and intermediary. When we asked her if she would ever consider moving to Canada, her answer was always an emphatic "no!" After two months the visit was over, and she returned to her world of intrigues and court battles, leaving us to our more peaceful pursuits. We began, in the following months, to tackle the question of a house that had become too small for our burgeoning family.

I looked with appreciation at the surrounding hills that had seemed so hostile in the beginning, and realized with a full feeling in my heart, that they were now home. It had taken me years, but I had finally put my roots down here in the pebbly soil whose richness yielded magnificent orchards and sweeping vineyards, and our lives, while caught up in the whirlwind of our children's throbbing energy, were comfortable lives.

I was hanging fresh fluffy curtains at my kitchen windows, when Curt returned from a job up the valley. "How was your day?" I called out to him happily.

He looked at me with eyes that were disconcerting, and spoke in a voice quavering with uneasiness, "I don't know what is wrong. As I drove today, the sun was sparkling off the lake, not a cloud in the sky, the orchards looked lush and green. And yet it all seemed false, like a facade. I had the strangest, most eerie foreboding of a supernatural evil hovering over the valley, overshadowing everything." He shuddered.

An icy wind blew through my soul, and its remembrance chills me still.

CHAPTER 19

"Well, what do you think?" my husband asked sagely, sliding the design across the table toward Louis and me.

Curt had been fussing over a design for a new house for the past two weeks, but would not let me see it until it was all finished. We had tossed around the idea of an addition to our present house, but an offer had come up to buy a one-acre lot, covered by cherry trees and backed by a lovely wilderness harboring a tiny whispering creek. It was an offer we couldn't refuse. Although large for us, we saw that we could subdivide the acre and come out with a very inexpensive building lot for ourselves. So we stuck our necks out, were almost decapitated when interest rates exploded up to 20 per cent, fought city hall, and eventually found ourselves with a spot of earth on which we could create our ultimate home. At this point we had already perused all the designs Curt had in his office, as well as a mountain of books and magazines, but finally we agreed—no small feat for us—that we both liked the look of a house we had seen just a few blocks away. The only hitch was that it was a three bedroom house, and we needed five bedrooms.

"No problem" Curt assured me, grinning wickedly. "Don't you realize you have married a genius?"

"Uh huh," I replied laconically.

He darted into his office, like a gopher into its hole, and I heard humming and whistling coming from behind the closed door.

In honor of this moment of the unveiling of the ultimate house design, he had invited over his friend Louis, godfather to our daughter Angel, who fancied himself to be both Curt's surrogate father and design critic extraordinaire.

I looked at the design and began to fidget. Louis' mostly bald head was bent over the drafting table, and he was tugging thoughtfully on his bottom lip.

"Well?" Curt repeated, inviting our reactions.

"Well, actually," I said, looking furtively to Louis for support, "you have expanded the bedroom wing so much that now the living room looks like a semi-detached outhouse."

The silence was stifling.

Louis coughed into his sleeve. "Curt, you know I have always been like a father to you and I admire your work greatly, but on this occasion I have to agree with your wife. I am sorry, but it is so."

Curt kept his cool but I had the distinct impression I could see heat waves undulating from the top of his skull. Despite his politeness to Louis, I knew he was furious. Coward that I am, I pleaded exhaustion, a really rough day with the kids, and headed up to bed.

At 4 A.M. I felt my shoulder being shaken roughly, and the bedside lamp was flicked on.

"Here, look at this," Curt said tersely, thrusting a piece of drafting paper beneath my groggy, sleep filled eyes. "And you'd better like it!"

What my eyes saw, as they found their focus, was the most gorgeous house I had ever seen.

"It's magnificent!" I said, startled. "I love it! You've been working on it all night," I added repentantly.

"I presume this doesn't look like an outhouse," he complained indignantly.

"No, no! It's incredible. It's a mansion. But can we afford a house like this?"

"I don't know. We'll have the money from this house, and now that I am back working in my own profession, I am thinking of selling our contracting business. It is getting too much for me, running two businesses. Sam Crockbit dropped by the office a couple of days ago asking if I was interested in selling. I told him I'd think about it."

"He has the money to buy a business like this?" I asked in surprise.

"He was the one that approached me."

I settled back in the pillows, planning, "We could do a lot ourselves, and with you doing the contracting and designing, that alone will bring the cost down significantly."

"We may not get everything done with it initially the way we would want, but I think we can do it. There is only one stipulation I want to make."

"Which is?"

"All this area here, above the garage, is going to be for my model trains. I know we won't be able to get that area finished in the beginning, but it is reserved for me."

"You got it!"

Then the planning began in earnest, haunting plumbing shops, checking out electrical supplies, stone masons, cabinet makers, researching wallpaper designs, tile, and floor coverings. It was a creative extravaganza.

"I think I'll send Mutti a copy of our house plans," Curt said with pride.

I was particularly happy with the indoor tropical atrium that Curt had designed especially for me, where I could grow orange trees and figs and dates under huge skylights.

"But what will we do for a light fixture there?" I asked, 'there' being the two storey entrance.

"I know exactly what it needs. Look!" Curt said, reaching for a pad of paper. "This will be all crystal," he sketched out a long cylindrical pillar, "and around this in a helix rotating left to right are small crystal spheres. How does it look?"

"Like an outhouse?" I laughed, and ducked. "No, really, it looks lovely. But where are we going to get a fixture like that? Are you communicating telepathically with Bavarian lighting manufacturers?"

"No, Silly, I'll make it."

"You'll make it," I repeated, stupefied. "In what year will you make it? In my lifetime? Where would you get the time and the components to make a chandelier like that? I know your intentions are good, but do you walk on water too?"

Curt was unfazed. I redoubled my efforts to locate a large enough, long enough, cheap enough fixture to hang from the two storey ceiling. After three months I was on the point of giving up as I closed the last available lighting catalogue in town, and suddenly, incredibly, there it was on the back cover. It was absolutely the same light fixture that Curt had drawn out for me, only the helix rotated in the opposite direction! I couldn't believe my eyes. "This is uncanny!" I murmured to myself. "Surely, this was meant to be!"

But by the next day it all began to look just like some odd disconnected coincidence. "$13,000," the salesman said firmly. This was definitely out of our league. Too bad.

The following week the salesman called again, "Say, you know that light fixture you were interested in? I am prepared to make you a special offer on it..."

"How special?" I asked in a polite but desultory voice. I knew it was hopeless.

"$7,000!" the salesman could hardly contain himself with excitement.

"I'm sorry," I said resolutely, "it's still beyond our means."

The light went out of the salesman's voice.

"So that is the end of that," I said to myself sadly. "When I found that picture, I really thought it was meant to be, but it was too good to be true."

Two weeks later a vaguely familiar voice identified himself on the end of the line: "Look," he said, "I hope I'm not bothering you, but a supplier down East has gone bankrupt, and I could get you that chandelier for $3,600. I wouldn't be making any money on it, but I want the dealership from that light company, and I need to prove to them that I can move their product out West."

My voice was hushed with awe as I explained the situation to Curt, "Somehow, for some reason, it was meant that we have that light fixture."

But the surprises were just beginning. After we sent the house plans to Curt's mother we received an unusually swift reply. I had a strange, prickly feeling about that letter, and I couldn't wait for Curt to get back home to translate it. I had a feeling that its contents could change our lives.

"She wants to come here to live," Curt said, looking up from the letter.

"But she said just a year ago that she would never move to Canada!" I was incredulous.

"Well, she wants to come now. On condition that we provide a self contained suite for her in our new house."

"How can we do that? You would have to redesign it again," I said, with disappointment in my voice.

"The area above the garage could be made into an apartment...." Curt offered, after a slight hesitation.

"But that is the area you had designated for a train room."

"I know. But she is my mother. She's basically alone now in Europe. How could I refuse her? You know how depressed she's been, even talking suicide. Maybe she just needs to get away from that European mess and make a fresh start like I did. But it depends on you. I will not even consider it unless you are happy about the idea."

"She certainly must have been impressed with your house plans!" I laughed. "Well I know she can be difficult, but she will have her own quarters. I think I could handle it. My training must be good for something. She has always felt the lack of love, and I think we have enough love around here to share. Of course, the culture shock, and a new language to cope with at her age, won't be easy, but it's still a healthier situation than she's been living with in Europe."

"She goes on in her letter to say, "I will make it possible so that you will never have a mortgage. I have given my father a promise to keep the inheritance for you and this I have done. It has been my life's work. Only, if I die in Austria, you will get very little: firstly, you as a foreigner would have to pay four times the inheritance tax; secondly, you would never be allowed to export the antiques; thirdly, possibly a lot of these would disappear before your arrival. So it is perhaps the right time to come so that your grandfather's dying wish may be fulfilled. Please think on these things and, if you agree, you must come to Europe to help me to settle my affairs."

"So what do you think?"

"Wow, I can't believe this is happening! I feel like Cinderella," I danced around the room. "I think it can work, because we will each have our privacy, yet we will be together. You will no longer have to be lonesome, as you are on occasion, for Europe. And we will have no financial worries."

Curt smiled. "It's the right thing to do, and somehow God seems to be blessing our new home already in a special way. With the extra money from the inheritance I can specify triple windows instead of double, and we can use the bulk of it to prepare her new apartment."

"And will she bring all the antiques?"

"It sounds like it. I don't think she could part with them. But she may have trouble getting them out of the country as they are national heritage objects."

"Our house will look like a museum," I protested faintly. I had never been interested in antiques and particularly disliked anything pretentious, glitzy, or ornate. But I did like the dining suite from the hunting castle at Mayerling with its rustic heavily carved wood. "You'd better heighten the ceiling in the dining room," I reminded him.

"I already have, because I knew that someday we would get the dining room suite. But I will have to reinforce the wall for the heavy mirror."

Within weeks we were airborne on our way to Salzburg. Young Justin sat beside us, soaking up the experience of his first flight with every pore in his body. He was now old enough, we felt, to profit by some exposure to his father's past, and to learn first hand something about life beyond our Valley. I knew Mutti would be pleased because Justin seemed to have won a special place in his Oma's heart.

She was pleased. He was a willing captive audience for all her stories, and with great glee she showed him all her possessions. He was amazed, along with us, at the fountain she had in the middle of her living room, and listened attentively to the history behind the various artifacts.

"And look at this desk," she enthused to Justin. "I have bought it for your father. See all these worm holes? It is a true antique and very valuable. It belonged to Prince Eugene of Savoy. It is a special gift for your father. Also this grandfather clock, inlaid with mother of pearl, is for him. I have also two other ones of my own."

The visit was very upbeat. Curt measured all her furniture to make sure it would fit in her new apartment, and they made many plans. She entrusted us with her collection of old Austrian and gold coins to take back with us since she felt it would be easier for us to bring it out of the country.

"How will you be able to get the antiques out of the country then," I asked.

She smiled meaningfully, "A little money under the table. I have friends...."

One thing left me with a bad feeling. When we mentioned we would like to visit Curt's father, she became very upset and threw a tirade that was almost frightening. I am ashamed to say we capitulated to her wishes.

Back at home the basement of our house was dug, and we watched in excitement as the frame rose to the second storey.

Then disaster struck. Water started to pour into the basement, almost with the force of an artesian well. Both floors were in and no access to the basement was possible to do anything by machine. The whole basement would have to be excavated by hand and drainage tile laid its entire length. Fortunately, both for us, and for them, our parish had just sponsored two families of boat people who had been plucked from the Southeast Asian sea. They needed jobs, and we needed their diligence and patience. They were excited and bubbly when they saw the situation:

"Velly lucky!" they exclaimed. "Water...in our country this is sign of much good luck!"

"Good luck?" I whimpered, watching the cost of the house soar by an additional $8,000.

Every night before sunset, we took one last walk to the house, marveling each time anew at the beauty of its lines. We saw cars detouring down our quiet street just to take a look, and sometimes people would stop to talk, ask questions, or attempt to make us an offer.

By the time Mutti arrived it was almost finished. She had only to pick out her kitchen cabinets, tile, and floor coverings. In September she beat the rest of us at moving in.

The great chandelier hung in welcome to all, sparkling, shimmering, with all the colors of the rainbow; and, when it was lit at night, it became, in my mind, the mystical pillar of fire that had led the Israelites through the desert to the Promised Land.

But how could I, who had lived by a vow of poverty, find myself living now in such a magnificent dwelling? I felt uneasy, guilty. But, guilty of what? Would I become too attached to all these things? I did not trust myself. Had we squandered too much money on earthly grandeur? Were we forgetting that 'we have not here a lasting city'? Yet, as a family of seven now, we needed room to live and grow, and to appreciate the beauty of God's creation.

I prayed; *do not let us get lost in our comfort zone. Do not let us succumb to the temptation of Eden, that with knowledge and our own deeds we can go it alone. With Christ in the desert, help us to resist the temptations of power and arrogance, of materialism and independence from You. In eating an apple, Father, let us taste Your love. In the sweet, shrill voices of our children let us hear You calling. In the songs of earth, the extravagances of its beauty, let us see clearly Your signature upon our hearts.*

The words of psalm 103 again coursed through my veins, as a reminder to me to keep all things in perspective: *Man's days are as grass; like the flower of grass he blooms; and the wind sweeps over him and he is gone and his place knows him no more....*

It seemed, however, that God had led us toward this house, had even inspired and procured our chandelier. Is He truly the Lover, concerned and interested in all our tiniest, most mundane desires? Building had been a stressful time, with clashing ideas, battles with city hall, tradesmen who were not on cue, and late deliveries; but in the end He had ensured that everything had come together for us, and that everything was functional as well as aesthetically pleasing. After two near misses at selling the business, sales that fell apart at the eleventh hour, we finally managed to sell the contracting business and totally paid off the house.

But we needn't have worried that the unaccustomed affluence would turn our heads. Two years after moving in to our fine house, the bottom fell out of the economy, and ninety per cent of those working in the building trades in British Columbia found themselves unemployed.

"We'll be alright," Curt assured me. "I have contracts signed for three high rises in Vancouver, so that should keep us going for at least a year."

How mistaken he was! Within three dark days at the end of July, 1982, the recession had claimed our three contracts as well. No one was willing to risk building in those uncertain years. We sat in shock that Saturday morning as the realization of our dilemma sank into our troubled hearts. Self employed as we were, we had no money coming in, no work, and no unemployment insurance to fall back on. Our neighbors, as well, were at the point of losing their home, and many other families were in jeopardy. We were glad the children were still sleeping so they could not see us so distraught as we mulled over our sad fate. True, we owned our home, but how were we to eat? What would become of us?

Suddenly a loud noise jolted us to attention. The whole house shook.

"I think one of the boys has fallen out of the bunk bed," Curt said, furrowing his brow. Even though they had their own rooms, they would sometimes like to sleep together on a weekend on Justin's bunk bed.

Curt ran up to check. "No, they are both sleeping soundly," he said with puzzlement in his face.

"Someone must have vandalized the house," I said with apprehension, heading for the front entrance. Hesitantly, nervously, I opened the door. There on the front doorstep lay three quail, two dead and one still dying. "Look," I said in disbelief to Curt, "they must have flown against the house!"

"But quail don't fly—at least not much—they are like chickens in that way," Curt protested.

"Well, these flew—*and* with enough force that they killed themselves."

What does this mean? I wondered. Somehow, there must be a meaning in this. Even as I asked the question, there flashed into my mind the story of the Israelites, who had been freed from the slavery of Egypt, and whom God led through the desert feeding them manna from heaven. I remembered how the trip had become tedious for them, and they became weary of the hardships of the journey, complaining to God that they had no meat, and pining for the fleshpots of Egypt. That night at sundown, as on many days thereafter, God sent quail into the camp and fed His people. *So, today,* I said to myself, *it has been done for us. We, who felt abandoned in our hardships, wondering what we would eat; for us God has sent quail as an assurance of His continuing care.*

For the next weeks, quail continued to be a living sign for us. Because a high fence was mandatory if one had a swimming pool, we had never seen quail in our yard before. Now when I walked in the front yard I would find a hundred and fifty quail among the roses. I walked in the back yard and I would find several hundred more wandering about under the fruit trees. These meek, mild, little birds, with headdresses that looked like little question marks bobbing above their heads, would be ambling along without fear, despite the presence of our two cats, and unperturbed that I was only an arms reach away. By the time the birds disappeared, as completely and inexplicably as they had come, it was mid September, and another phenomenon had taken their place.

One of the concerns I had raised about the presence of our indoor planting area was bugs. As the planting area was made up of virgin soil that reached down through to our basement, I quizzed the people at Greenworld about what I could do to prevent a house infestation of the same bugs I constantly fought in my garden. They provided a simple–and expensive–solution. They excavated the top four feet of soil, put down a layer of drainage rock, and then filled the top two and a half feet with sterilized soil.

"How do you sterilize soil?" I asked, intrigued.

"It is baked at extremely high temperatures, high enough to kill bugs, weed seeds, everything," they explained as they gently set palm trees and assorted greenery in their designated spots.

Much to my satisfaction their words proved to be true. For two years I had not seen a bug, nor had a single errant seed sprouted uninvited. Then, in mid September, mushrooms appeared from nowhere, unplanted and unbidden, filling the atrium with their huge ridged heads. They looked almost unreal, like something from out of a Walt Disney movie. Many of the heads, when open, were ten inches across. Curt recognized them immediately as a type of parasol mushroom he had picked in the Vienna woods, but had never seen since, and he assured me that they were not only edible, but incredibly delicious. This proved to be true. For the first time in my life I truly had my fill of mushrooms–as did all our relatives, and some of our friends. The mysterious mushrooms continued to grow for more than five years, eventually thinning out and appearing only, uncannily, on special days like Christmas, my birthday, or days when we faced a special trial that needed the kind caress of a hidden but caring God.

"God has updated," I joked. "He gave the Israelites manna, but He knows I've always been partial to mushrooms."

And it was true. Like the gift of the calendar so many years ago, like the charcoal house, like the quail; in so many delicate expressions of a Father's love He has cared for us. He has provided for our needs and tailored His compassion to our weakness. How can I deny the evidence of my own senses–my own experiences?

How can I doubt, in this cataclysm, that Your presence will sustain us and carry us through this night of pain? But I am dizzy and sick with fear.

CHAPTER 20

"Do you really think it is a good idea to have your mother-in-law living with you?" one of my friends asked, balancing a cup of coffee on her knee.

"I admire your courage, but I wouldn't do it."

I wasn't getting much support from my friends.

"I don't think we really had much choice," I defended our decision. "How could we have lived with ourselves if we had refused her request? What if something had happened to her? In her letters she would say things like: "It is the end for me now. I am alone. There is nothing to live for." Where would that leave us if she decided to take her own life? Curt could not live with that. Anyway, you have met her. I find her likeable. She can be really charming. She's sociable and is good company. And it is not like she spends every minute with us. She does have her own self enclosed suite."

In fact, she was with us a great deal. I cooked for her, washed her clothes, took her shopping and she watched TV with us in the evenings. She and I shared a common love of flowers and we spent hours at local greenhouses planning the landscaping. I saw it was best that she have an area to plant that was hers alone and this inviolate area became Mutti's rose bed, a duplication of what she had loved in Europe. To my consternation she immediately put up another fence. I did not like to feel I was living in a fortress, but it was what she was accustomed to, so I decided not to make a big deal of it. She was bound and determined to get everything finished in the yard as quickly as possible, and I was secretly pleased about that. She insisted she needed a pool for her health, and told Curt that she would pay half of it. She had ways of nagging Curt, and lighting a fire under him, that I would not have chanced. When Curt dragged his feet with the plans for the front yard, she waited until he went in the hospital to have a hernia operation, and then organized everything behind his back so it would be done by the time he returned home. Curt was not pleased, because some errors had been made with regard to the sprinkler system, which meant that part of it had to be dug up and redone. He was less than enchanted to find all this work charged to his account. But it was done, and in the end I was glad. Once the house was livable Curt really had little time or creativity to devote to its surroundings. His answer to landscaping was a bag of grass seed. With Mutti's collusion I planted hundreds of multi-hued tulips, swaying daffodils and scented hyacinth. For summer there were flowering bushes, peonies with heads like giant pompoms, scarlet geraniums, salmon colored poppies with hearts of deep black velvet, lofty delphiniums, and sky blue hydrangeas. Apple, plum, apricot, peach and cherry trees dotted the yard, and a large vegetable garden yielded strawberries and peas, carrots, corn, and the vegetable whose name is no longer allowed to be spoken in our household.

I have always tried to put a great deal of creativity in my gardening and cooking, so the year that I ran into a colorful seed package labeled 'Squash Blossoms', my brain went into overdrive. I could see the gleaming dinner plate in my mind, with a lovely summer salad tumbling out of a giant golden trumpet shaped flower. Or for breakfast, blossoms dipped in batter and deep fried, perhaps dusted with icing sugar. Energized by the thought, and cognizant of the many mouths I had to feed, I headed out with my pitchfork and planted a dozen hills.

The blossoms were as beautiful and copious as the package had promised, and it was only when I failed to keep up with the onslaught, and some blossoms wilted and began to form long green fingers, that I realized I was in hand to hand combat with an army of zucchini. Nowhere on that package had it said anything about zucchini.

In morbid fascination I watched as our rambunctious zucchini plants galloped across the beans, over the corn, buried the carrots and tomatoes, and headed over the fence. The next thing I knew, they had found a slit in the neighbor's shed and were hanging from his rafters. Seeking sunshine, however, they exited the other side and picked up momentum to their son's sand box. The last time I had the courage to look, they were headed up the street.

I am absolutely incapable, as it happens, of letting good food go to waste (although my husband has some quibble about any possible link between the words 'good' and 'zucchini'). And I do not easily cave in to pressure. We had zucchini raw, baked, fried, souffled, broiled, stuffed, pickled, barbecued, and mixed with other vegetables. I also found zucchini makes great cake, bread and muffins. But the coup de grace as far as I was concerned was when a friend suggested grating it up finely and hiding it in spaghetti sauce. That friend is no longer allowed in our house.

Everyone who comes to our door gets a hello and a zucchini. Our visitors have tapered off. Curt suggested sending a thank you note to everyone who had accepted one, hoping, I presume, for repeat business. He has taken to leaving zucchinis on parked cars, and has threatened to design a zucchini canon to shoot tailgaters.

My popularity has continued to plummet. My kids are in rebellion and my husband is talking about padlocking the kitchen. I suggested we should maybe shellac some of them and use them for fence posts. We are praying for an early winter.

Mutti wisely stayed out of the zucchini controversy, only harrumphing from time to time about the evils of waste. She was far too busy doing her own creative thing, installing a little waterfall under the cedar trees in the corner, and building a wooden deck there for her lawn furniture. She had a vision of water lilies growing in a tiny pond, and felt that they, too, must be protected by another fence. Once it was all completed it would become a social center for the symphony crowd, where she presided as high priestess. I was pleased to see her enjoyment, and encouraged my friends to take her under their wing as well. Most of them were from Church, and I knew they would be good to her. Initially, of course, she resisted going to Church with us, claiming she would miss her favorite TV sports programs, but Curt begged her to come so as not to set a poor example for the children. Besides, there she could be part of the community. She dearly loved to be in the center of everything, in first place, the focus of attention. Heaven help us if she imagined we left her out of anything.

This latter trait soon gave rise to some ticklish situations. When she had first visited, out of deference to her, and respecting her wish to visit with her son, I had given up my seat to her at table and in our van. Now she insisted that she must continue to keep my seat because otherwise she would get car sick. Incredibly, she also expected to sit with my husband if we went out for dinner or to a movie. Because the children could be annoying to her, she expected me to sit elsewhere with them! Further, there was nowhere that we went that she did not expect to be included. If it was our wedding anniversary, she tagged along. When we were invited to the wedding of business associates, strangers to her, she expected to be included.

Even our bedroom was not sacrosanct. Curt's forbearance wore thin the day she burst into our bedroom while he was changing his underwear. His bellow could have been heard in Buffalo! She was affronted. She seemed to be trying to recapture the lost years. She wanted Curt to be twelve years old again, dependent on her for all his needs, symbiotically entwined. Curt would have none of it, and she would pout and go up to her room and brood.

One day she bounced into the family room wearing her best hostess gown, glittering with its metallic accents, clutching her gold cigarette case. She was clearly in high spirits.

"I have something to tell you," she chirped with great satisfaction, but," she put down her cigarette case with exaggerated precision, relishing her secret, "I will not tell you until after this program. It is a surprise especially for your father." She chided the children as they mobbed her in excitement.

We watched Love Boat, Mutti's favorite evening TV program, with her, and she could be seen smiling as she watched.

"Now," she said significantly, instantly garnering everyone's attention, "I will tell you... I will take your father on a Love Boat cruise." She waited for the expected accolades.

Curt was silent, uncertain how to react. "You mean you want to just take me on a love boat cruise?"

"Yes, just you," she said, pursing her lips in a pleased smile.

"Mutti," Curt said after staring at the floor awhile, "I would not go on a Love Boat cruise unless my wife was along. Why not include her?"

"Never!" she snapped.

"Then I cannot accept your kind gift under those conditions," Curt replied as evenly as he could.

Trudy swept her long skirts about her angrily and stomped out of the room, muttering bitterly. She hid up in her apartment sulking for two months. Every night faithfully we would go up and invite her down for supper. She would refuse. We would bring her supper up to her. The next meal the same thing would happen. She would sit and brood, chain smoking, and nursing her anger like a child picking a scab until it bleeds. Eventually, she sent a note down to Curt that she wanted to talk. She did not mention the Love Boat, but she told him that I was deliberately making supper late to annoy her. If he would allow her to supervise the children's rooms they would be tidier. The children did not greet her properly in the morning, and their friends were not polite. He sympathized. He agreed that she could help the children with their rooms. Having won this concession, she reappeared, all smiles. But the fruit of her seclusion seemed to be that I was the interloper who was the cause of all the dissatisfaction in her life. If I was not on the scene she would have Curt to herself and get whatever she wanted. So the attacks began. Every night, five days out of seven, she hovered by the front door at supper time, pacing back and forth smoking, waiting for Curt to come home so she could unload. A barrage of German would assail his ears the moment he came in the door. He would take her arm gently and lead her to the supper table and promise to talk to her after supper. For a man whose strong point was not diplomacy, he was amazingly patient and soft spoken with her. As I cleaned up after supper they would sit there and talk—in German—for one, two, three hours. I would hear her spit out my name in fits of indignation and Curt would strive to soothe and placate her.

Was this the price I had to pay to allow her time to adjust and heal? If so, I would pay it. But I would not allow her personal problems to destroy my serenity. I knew enough not to take her attacks personally, and that was my saving grace. I felt no compulsion to conform myself to her standards of excellence because I realized I would be no further ahead. My basic sin was that I had married her son. I only hoped by letting it all slide off my back that eventually my love and warmth would outlast her negativity. I counted on it. Even a drop of water can dissolve a rock given enough time. It didn't matter who Curt would have married, she would have suffered the same fate.

Later, when Curt would translate the discussion for me, I would just shake my head in wonder. I was not a good housekeeper, she complained. I was too soft on the children. She did not like my hairstyle. I was not well dressed. I spent too much time talking to my mother on the phone. My bi-weekly phone call with my mother seemed to irritate her particularly. Despite her apparent abhorrence of me, she did like to sit and talk with me by the hour. She felt that any attention I paid to my own mother was taken away from her. And so it went on.

After this carried on for a couple of years, Curt laid down some ground rules. He would listen to no more criticisms of his wife; he had heard his fill. And in future if she wanted to talk with him in front of me she would have to speak English. Grudgingly, she acceded. But she complained he did not pay enough attention to her and did not spend enough time with her.

"Mutti!" I exclaimed, "look how hard he is working! Look how little time he spends with us as well. He is not slighting you if sometimes he is in a hurry."

Whenever she was mad at Curt she suddenly became my best buddy, and I found myself having to apologize for and defend her son. Sometimes she listened.

"He works too hard. He is at the right age to get a heart attack," she began to worry about him.

Two days later she came down into the kitchen in a solemn mood. "Do you have a life insurance policy?"

"Yes, of course," Curt replied.

"It is in my name?"

Curt was taken aback. "No, it is in my wife's name."

Mutti's face turned livid. I couldn't believe my ears. Why would the father of four young children name his mother as beneficiary of his life insurance? But Mutti didn't see it that way. She behaved like someone who had had her human rights violated. "If something happens to you, what will become of me?"

"I will look after you just as I do now."

"What if we are not getting along?"

"Mutti," I explained patiently, "when your son welcomed you to this family, it meant for always. Have I ever been unkind to you, or said a cross word to you? Do you think I would ever do anything to hurt you? If I did, I would have to answer to God." I put my arms around her and tried to calm her down. "Perhaps you could get some insurance yourself, or Curt could get you some, if that would make you feel better."

"No, never!"

"Why not?" we asked in surprise.

"I have nothing to say to you!" she marched off haughtily and sequestered herself in her room.

Curt made several attempts over the next few weeks to see his mother, and renewed his offer of insurance for her. The answer was always an unequivocal "no!" Finally she met him gaily at the door one day with a smile on her face, acting for all the world as if there wasn't a cloud in her sky, and as if nothing had ever happened between them. Trudy was like a chameleon. She had the most remarkable ability to change her mood in a split second. It was back to charm once more.

"Come upstairs," she said, leading him by his sleeve.

I wondered what this latest change signified. Life was certainly not dull since Trudy came to live with us. I waited for Curt to come back downstairs.

"What did she want?" I quizzed him.

He rolled his eyes. "Now she has the idea that if something happened to me that your mother would get her hands on the antiques."

I giggled. "Now, that is really funny. I may not be that enamored with antiques, but my Mom has positively no use for them at all. I think Mutti thinks everyone's mind works like hers does. Or else she is spending too much time watching the soaps, and life has become one big intrigue for her."

"That's what I told her, but you know her: 'convince me but don't confuse me with facts'. Anyway, she had this paper ready for me to sign which basically says that the antiques in this house belong to her."

"But the ones in our part of the house she GAVE to us—those that weren't already willed to us by your grandfather. Even the ones she gave you for your birthday? Did you sign it?"

He shrugged.

"Yes, why not? It's not a legal paper anyway because it was not witnessed, and if that's what it takes to settle her down, so be it. She's here now, and so are the antiques, and we've got to make it work somehow."

"It's your call," I made a face.

You could count on something happening at every family get together or religious holiday. On each occasion we ended up walking on eggshells. The following Christmas there was another incident. The entire extended family were over to celebrate Christmas at our house, as was the custom, when my nephew, a rough and tumble one year old, toddled up to Trudy's knee. Whether his hands were dirty, or what the problem was, I do not

224

know. Perhaps it was just her dislike of children. We saw her push him away so violently that he took a bad fall.

"Mother!" Curt exclaimed in utter shock.

Without a word, Trudy got up, gathered up everyone's Christmas gifts, including those for her astonished grandchildren, headed upstairs, and stayed there until February. At the end of that time she called Curt up to her apartment. They talked for a long time, and eventually she appeared ready to smooth things out. But again she pleaded insecurity, and asked Curt to sign another paper she had prepared. What if something happened to him and she was left on the street? It would never happen, Curt assured her.

"Please," she begged him, "sign this for your poor mother for peace in her heart. I am your mother and I promise you I will never show it to anyone—it is only my insurance that if you die that I will not be ill treated. Your grandfather willed you that money—I have the will right here in my hand—and I will show you where I keep it; in this drawer at the bottom of the grandfather clock. So you need not worry. But your grandfather gave you that money with the condition that you take good care of me. If you sign this paper acknowledging that I have loaned you $100,000 then no one can take advantage of me and put me out on the street."

"That's loony," I said, exasperated. "That money was an inheritance, not a loan. Just like when she gives the children gifts and she uses the gifts to control them—well now she's doing the same with the inheritance money! You didn't sign it did you?"

Curt looked sheepish. "Yes, I did. To keep the peace. The German word used, by the way, only roughly translates as "loan". In German the context is "money advanced for a purpose", and yes, she did advance us the inheritance money for the purpose of finishing this house. Anyway I know she wouldn't break her promise. And I did see the will, in my grandfather's own handwriting, and I know where it is kept, and that is the important document. This other is not witnessed and has no legal weight. I did write on the bottom though: 'The above can be accepted as factual and true until further notice has been given', which gives me the right to rescind it at any time I wish. So you have nothing to worry about!" and Curt leaned over to give me a comforting hug.

But I didn't feel comforted. I was conscious of a feeling of uneasiness deep in the pit of my stomach. I wished Curt had not complied–but if he hadn't, it surely would have meant more trouble. I tried to banish my misgivings but they only rolled like dust bunnies to an unseen corner of my mind where they tainted the house of my soul.

When summer came, Trudy flitted back to Europe for a visit, bringing back gifts for all, including a gold watch for me. She seemed to be trying hard to put to rest Curt's feelings about the way she treated me.

"We will go shopping today? I have something which I will do," she said mysteriously, some time after her return.

Once uptown she directed me to a ladies wear shop, and casually began to point out various coats to me, and asked me to try them on. Finally, I tried on one she liked.

"This one I will buy for you," she said.

"The coat is lovely, but Curt just bought me a new coat last year. You shouldn't spend your money."

"Pshaw! That is no coat. What does he know about fashion? I know about fashion. It is my training. This coat is right for you, and now he may never say I do not like you."

So that was it. I thanked her profusely as we rode home in the car. I tried to speak of things that would make her happy.

"The women told me how much they enjoyed having tea with you in your apartment," I complimented her.

"Yes," she sniffed appreciatively. "Your friends like me more than they like you."

"Oh," I raised my eyebrows and sighed to myself, "I didn't know we were having a competition."

"By the way," I had just remembered: "your friend Marg bumped into me at Church the other day and was very concerned to know how your arm was. She said you were groaning with pain through the entire flight from London."

"Oh, that," Trudy's coiffed gray head bobbed toward me with a conspiratorial air, "You have seen the sling and bandage I have kept from when I have broken my arm three years ago, but I have worn it so the customs men will not bother a poor old woman to see what I am bringing back in my bags." She smiled jubilantly about her charming deceit.

"You are certainly a marvelous actress to have even fooled one of your best friends," I said dubiously, but she did not take offence. When I left her to go in to prepare supper she was still smiling with satisfaction over her exploit.

Justin and Angel came in out of the hot sun just as Curt got home and the supper was ready to be put on the table. They were standing together at the table glancing at each other, obviously embarrassed:

"You tell her."

"No, YOU tell!"

An awkward pause....

I waited. "Well, somebody tell me before I die here of old age," I kidded them.

"Look!" Angel grabbed my arm and pointed.

There, through the window, we saw their Oma strolling around outside casually, smoking, and wearing only a bra and panties.

"My goodness!" I gasped.

"Is she getting...you know....?" Justin looked at me. His eyes were pools of concern.

"What? Senile?"

"Well...yes...."

"No, I don't think so.... Maybe she's just so used to living alone that she isn't aware of how things affect other people." Now, did that sound convincing? But somehow I wanted to allay their fears.

"There's something else...." Angel said in a wee little voice. "Tell her Justin."

Justin blushed. "Well, I wish Dad would say something to her, because it's very embarrassing when my friends come over to swim and she changes right in front of them. Everyone thinks my Oma is mean, and now everyone at school thinks she's a crackpot too."

"Whaaat?"

"Well, she drapes her housecoat over her shoulders, but it's the same thing."

I was floored. She was only a few steps from the door. Why would she go upstairs to get her bathing suit and then come outside to change?

I looked at Curt, who for once was speechless: "I think you'd better have a little talk with your mother."

My biggest concerns about my mother-in-law from the beginning had centered around her behavior with the children. I realized that while we might take her mercuric temperament and peculiarities in stride, the children were far more vulnerable to her influence. For one thing, her treatment of them was very unequal. Justin she had adored from the first day, and she lavished gifts and favors on him to the detriment of the others. Angel, she openly disliked, and she visited on her the same treatment she had given her daughter, Eva. Her excuse was that when she had arrived that first day, Àngel's room was untidy. At that point, of course, we were still in the charcoal house, and Angel, who was eight years old then, was sharing a tiny room with Kelli, who was an exuberant and messy four year old. Ironically, Angel was, and is, the only neat freak among our children. And many a time after that day Trudy has spotted a mess in Christian and Justin's rooms with nary a comment.

Uncomprehending, but with the resilience of children, Angel has forgiven her Oma's rebuffs time and time again. But I have worried about the damage it could do to her in the long term. My mother noticed, with emotion one day, that when Trudy was sitting dejected about something, it was Angel who went to her and put her arms around her to comfort her. But Trudy has never returned the gesture. On Sunday evenings she would often bring down money and treats for the children and hand them out with great largesse, pointedly ignoring Angel. On Christmas and her birthday, Angel is lucky if she gets a card. Curt has taken Oma aside on a number of occasions to try to implore her to be kinder to Angel. Trudy responds with hurt feelings and incomprehension. In the end, Curt forbade her to give the other children any gifts unless she also gave one to Angel. She got around this handily enough though. That year she brought brand new bicycles for the other children. For Angel she picked up an ugly worn brown sun dress at the thrift shop.

When buying the children gifts she always retained careful control of them. The children were not allowed to ride their new bikes to school, and they had to ask her permission whenever they wanted to use them. When she bought them new clothes she kept them in her own closet, and the children were obliged to come to her when they wanted to wear them. In retrospect, I should have seen the seeds of trouble in this pattern of behavior. But if I had seen it, what could I have done about it? No one could have reasonably predicted behavior that did not arise from reason, but rose, rather, from the inchoate murk of some disordered darkness. Besides, as tensions rose, she, smiling, would seek to disarm us, bestowing on us the sunshine of her favors.

As Justin got older, he began to resent the trade offs between gifts and control. He was a teenager now, and outside interests and activities took him away from home more and more. The antiques in her apartment that she had promised him became less and less of an attraction. Trudy missed the attention she was accustomed to getting from him, and her carrot no longer seemed to be effective at drawing him to her. She lashed out in anger now at him, and he became almost as much of an outsider to her affections as Angel. In her irritation, Trudy would complain far and wide about anything and anyone she was currently displeased with. She delighted to talk to any workmen who might be around the yard, and the day the mattress in our waterbed was replaced she spent the entire morning in our bedroom regaling the repairman there with all the faults of her son.

The repairman grew more and more uncomfortable and confused, and I have never seen anyone so anxious to finish a job. As each new disclosure was made he would look at me helplessly, and his eyes and body language communicated to me that he thought he was in the presence of a madwoman. The newest breaking news, according to Trudy, was that her son had torn up her Mother's day card. He had indeed torn up her Mother's Day card. What she conveniently omitted mentioning was the reason. It began when a neighbor had brought us Bunky's body. Our poor old pet must have been slowing down in her old age, and was hit by a car. Trudy hated our cat and made no secret about it. She would hiss at her, and even kick her when the poor animal, attempting to make friends, would come too close. The children were hysterical when they found out what had happened. They had been weeping for about three hours when the word got up to Trudy that Bunky had been killed. Exultant and euphoric she sailed down the stairs proclaiming to one and all: "My prayers have been answered. I've prayed and prayed that that cat would be killed!"

The children were horrified. They could not believe their ears. Nor could Curt, who had heard the whole thing.

"What do you mean by that?" Curt lashed out at her. "We have just lost a member of our family whom we loved. For someone who always claims sensitivity for herself, you have just behaved in a gross and unbelievably insensitive way toward these children!"

Kelli pulled me over and whispered to me, "Mom, if Oma prayed and prayed that our cat would die, she must have been praying to the devil, because I don't think God would answer a prayer like that."

Trudy went wild. She could not see that she had been at fault in anything–she never could–so the fault must be her son's for yelling at her. She flounced out, incensed, and we heard the door to the apartment slam so hard that we wondered if the door frame was broken.

This time, Curt was reluctant to go up to her and be the peacemaker, but as Mother's Day approached I went out and bought a beautiful card, and I urged him to rise above the situation and offer her the card. She answered the door, screamed abuse at him, threw the card at him, and slammed the door in his face. He stood in the hallway, stunned at her vitriolic outburst, and slowly, deliberately tore up the card and left the pieces by her door.

Trudy really got good mileage out of that story. She retold it over and over to everyone that she met, and it got more pathetic with each retelling. Half the town must be convinced that Curt is a real beast without any love or regard for his sainted mother. As she finished this last triumphant story for the waterbed repairman I stood by, humiliated, wondering what I could do to shut her up.

But the waterbed repairman had heard and seen enough. As he brushed by me hastily, with his plastic tool box banging at his side, he hissed in a stage whisper, "Do you have to live with this all the time? I feel sorry for you!"

It was a relief to know that at least he considered ME normal. When you live with a situation at close range for long enough you begin to lose perspective, and the lines between normal and abnormal begin to blur. Besides, I had been so sick with hepatitis for the past six weeks that my coping mechanisms were compromised, my head was fuzzy, and I began to question my ability to see anything clearly.

In retrospect, I think I caught the hepatitis when I went in to get some cervical polyps removed which had hemorrhaged. The young woman waiting ahead of me at the gynecologist's office was a street person who was obviously ill and also dirty. Sometime in the days following I became ill.

Curt whooped at me in surprise one morning, "Look at yourself! Look in the mirror! Your eyes are yellow!"

I looked in startled affirmation. They *were* yellow; the deep color of mustard. And I was as sick as I had ever been in my life. As I lay helplessly in bed day after day, vomiting at the very smell of food, my only distraction was the odd sensation that I could hear a baby crying. Was this sickness affecting my mind? There were no babies in the house any longer. Kelli was already in grade three, and I was almost emancipated. For the first time in many years diapers were a thing of the past. And it was a good thing too, because the recession was dealing us a killing blow. Despite the mushrooms that continued to grow in our atrium, our RRSPS were virtually gone and Curt had precious little work. But, even as I got better, I kept hearing the crying. It was not in the same room—it seemed to come from far off. It was faint, but it seemed so real that against my common sense I even walked down the hall to see if I could find the source of the noise. Of course, no source for the crying was found, and in time it stopped. But, it made me think of babies again, and I wondered. It occurred to me that it was a shame that none of our children had been born in this house. It was a perfect house for a young child to be born into. At the same time, I was grateful it had not happened. Besides being broke, I was forty two now, already slowing down, and enjoying a schedule that was less hectic than the days when all the children were tiny. And now, I had to get well again.

The doctor kept close tabs on me, and even after I felt I was sufficiently recovered, he persisted in having me come in for blood tests. But I began to feel tired again, and wondered whether I was having a relapse. I anxiously checked the color of my eyes. They looked normal. The doctor asked me to come into his office and closed the door.

"Did you know you are pregnant?" he asked.

I choked up with fear. "No," I breathed.

He kept asking me questions. Aware of our circumstances, I could see he was trying to offer me an abortion. I began to cry. It was too much. But I knew an abortion was out of the question. I—we—would survive, if only because in the mystery that was God there was some reason for all of this.

I was working away at the kitchen sink thinking about this new life growing within me when the phone rang.

"Guess what?" my sister sang out merrily. "I'm pregnant!"

I started to laugh. "You'll never guess what... I'm pregnant too!" Then we cried together.

Not an hour later a light knock sounded at the front door and my sister-in-law bounced into the kitchen.

"I've got news," she said cheerily. "We are expecting!"

Is this God's idea of a joke? I asked myself.

"Well, dear Pam," I said clearly and distinctly, "*if* we work this right, and all give birth at the same time, we might make it into the Guinness Book of World Records."

"You too?" she shrieked in amazement.

It turned out we *were* all expecting about the same time. To commemorate this occasion, the humorous types in our family took a side profile photo of the three of us—my sister looked pregnant, but I look like I had swallowed a weather balloon. Pam, on the other hand, looked like she was giving birth to a family of mice. As the grand old lady of the family I came in for a lot of ribbing. My mother recalled that she had had June when she was forty-one, and great Aunt Barbara had had her last daughter in her forties....

"Why didn't you warn me this was a family tradition?" I grumped to her.

Soon after, the doorbell started ringing. The grapevine had been busy, and people I hardly knew began bringing gifts of clothes and necessities for the new baby. Obviously the word had gotten round that I had given away all my baby things and that things were tough for us right now. The result was an outpouring of compassion and emotional support that was like a heavenly hug. Although Curt had been aghast when I first told him, at this stage of married life he was used to rolling with the punches, and he rallied quickly. Not so with Mutti. The night she heard the news she went berserk. She stormed down the stairs yelling at the top of her lungs:

"You got pregnant to ruin my life! You did it on purpose! I hate babies! I hate babies! I hate babies!"

She took my pregnancy as a personal affront and demanded that I have an abortion. I assured her that it was as much of a surprise to me as it was to her, and I asked our mutual friends to talk to her to see if they could calm her down. It took a couple of months before she grudgingly began to accept the inevitable—but only if it was a boy, she stipulated. And I was never to expect her to baby sit, nor even to touch the baby. But when the baby was born, she was happy enough to get her picture taken with her.

Baby Erica arrived a month before her due date by caesarian section. At five pounds she was not the smallest of my babies, but she had the most health problems. She had hyaline membrane disease, a usually fatal lung condition, which meant that she had great trouble breathing. In addition, she became jaundiced as my other children had been, and was unable to suck. She spent ten days in intensive care, hooked up to a gamut of tubes and equipment, from oxygen to heart monitors. She was constantly poked and tested, woken from sleep for yet another blood test or a change of diaper. As I sat beside her incubator I watched her become progressively more and more irritated with all the discomfort, and with the interruptions to her natural biological rhythm. Finally, one day as I sat beside her, I watched as her little body tensed and she went into cardiac arrest. The heart monitor went crazy and her tiny body began to turn blue. In a panic, my heart pounding for the both of us, I called for help. *This is like a TV program*, I thought. A nurse grabbed her, and my day faded into a blur. But Erica was not ready to depart this life yet. My instinct told me that she was just registering her protest at this madcap, frustrating world she had been born into. Further examinations seemed to bear this out, as she had no heart damage or congenital problems.

With all the worry and fuss surrounding Erica, I was hoping that Mutti's heart might be touched, and that she would soften her attitude toward her new grandchild. We tried to make her feel right in the center of all the attention. Everyone emphasized how Erica looked like her, had the same blood type, the same tiny feet. In order to encourage some bonding between them, I sought special permission from the doctor for her to visit Erica in the intensive care nursery, and she was flattered to get this privileged treatment. It seemed to work. Although Mutti showed no more physical affection for Erica than she did for the other children, she did finally resign herself to her existence, and even bought her a highchair. Still, I overheard her telling her friends how much she disliked little girls and wished Erica was a boy.

Life stepped up to a quicker pace, but always we rode the roller coaster of Mutti's highs and lows. I never knew what would set her off next. One day, having fallen asleep in a chair, and not realizing she had gone out for the evening, I turned off the outside lights before I went up to bed. I woke up to a horrible ruckus. Trudy, in tears and fury, had awoken the whole household, yelling at Curt that I had deliberately turned off the lights so that she would break her leg. For weeks she could talk of little else. Finally, one night she, herself, inadvertently turned out the light while Curt was still out. When faced with this evidence of a shortcoming of her own, she treated the whole affair as a huge joke.

The immediate precursor of all the trouble that was to come, came in the innocuous form of an invitation addressed to Curt and me to attend the 25th wedding anniversary of the Johnsons. Trudy knew these friends slightly, but had never met their young daughter who lived out of town and who was the one organizing and paying for this celebration. I knew from experience that Trudy would be terribly upset that she was left out, despite the fact that the daughter's finances precluded inviting everyone, even if she had known of Trudy's existence. Nor did I feel I could ask this extra indulgence of her, even for the sake of family peace. So I kept the invitation secret, worrying all the while how we could escape from the house that evening without Trudy noticing. Unfortunately, a mutual friend innocently mentioned the celebration without realizing she was releasing a malevolent genie from a bottle. Trudy was beside herself with wrath. Her recriminations flowed like a river in spate. She blamed me personally for excluding her, for bearing her ill will, for causing, it seemed, all the sufferings of the world. The day of the party she prevailed on the blundering friend to somehow wangle her an invitation too.

"Good," I thought, "at least she will be there. She will be chilly for awhile, but this too will blow over."

But I was wrong. Six months later she accosted Curt as he was doing some repair work in the basement. I heard her loud and angry voice rise in successive waves of fury.

"*What can she possibly be mad about now?*" I wondered. I was unaware of having done anything to offend her.

Curt was grim when he came back up to the kitchen, and I was astounded to hear that the source of her current anger was still the matter of the anniversary party. For six months, perhaps lacking any other oil for her fire, she had been brooding and seething over this one matter, and it was as fresh in her mind as if it had happened yesterday.

"Well, I can't let this matter go any further. This is ridiculous. I'm going right up to talk to her."

"Be careful," Curt said, laying his hand on my arm in a cautionary gesture. I could see by the flat look on his face that he thought it was hopeless.

"Look," I said earnestly, "there's got to be some way to reach her. One night a couple of years ago, when I was heavily pregnant with Erica, something happened that has become a sign of hope for me. It was an awful night in November, dark and with an icy wind and slashing rain. The kids were with me, and so was Mutti, and I did what I had always dreaded doing: I locked the keys in the car. I was really upset, not feeling well, and the kids were shivering—you were out of town—and I was wondering what I could do. I checked all the doors, even the back door of the station wagon, just in case, but I could see clearly that all the buttons were down as far as they could go. Then, for lack of anything better to do, I walked aimlessly around to the back of the car and tried to open it. It opened without the slightest hesitation.

It occurs to me that this was a parable meant for today; that when all the doors of life close upon us, God still has the key to open them. And I think this applies to Mutti's heart as well. I think God sent this little miracle for Mutti, to tell her that He is still in control of all that is, and that He can open the locked doors of her life too and let in the fresh air. All these things she is always obsessing about—He can free her from them if she so wishes.

I must admit that on the way home that day I wondered if the whole thing was a fluke, and maybe the lock at the back of the station wagon was simply dysfunctional. But when, like a doubting Thomas, I surreptitiously tried the door again after we pulled into our driveway, it was locked solidly and could not be opened."

"Go, do your thing then. Maybe you know something that I don't," Curt said wearily, sinking into his chair and closing his eyes.

CHAPTER 21

I paused apprehensively and knocked lightly on the door.

Feet shuffled across the floor and the door opened to reveal Mutti's raised eyebrows and her lips pursed in a disdainful look. The air was gray with cigarette smoke.

"I would like to talk to you.... ?"

"About what?" she snapped hoarsely.

"Mutti, Curt tells me you are still angry about the Johnson's anniversary party. Please believe me, I have not done anything to hurt you, and I did not deliberately exclude you from the invitation."

Trudy's back was retreating into her dining room. I followed her. "You would have left me out of the party, but I have friends too," she sat down and faced me severely. "When I was a young woman I have gone to a fortune teller, and she has told me many things she could not have known. As she was finishing she turned over the last card and I have seen her face change. "What is it?" I have asked her because I could see it was something that was not good, and she would not tell me. She has told me then: "Everyone in your life will betray you." And it is so. First it was my mother who has said, "Take her away" when I was born. And then my father, whose love I could not get while my mother was alive. Then that swine who was my husband. He has wanted–you know–but I have told him "No way, not until you behave". Then he has gone with the whore and in a single day my hair has turned white with the shock. But I have fixed him. I have gone to the people who have given him his job at the bank, to the highest authority, and they have listened to me, and Herr Doctor was no more the second from the top in the most famous bank in Vienna. They have put him in a branch bank in a not so important district. For twenty-two years I have fought him in the courts. Now he has taught me to hate with his evil deeds, and with my dying breath I will curse him. And now you...."

"But, Muttti, I have not betrayed you! And you must be careful in taking the word of fortune tellers. They have many tricks. If and when they do have knowledge that is supernatural, you can be sure it does not come from God. So you must be careful about listening to them. You are allowing this woman's words to become a self-fulfilling prophesy, to turn your whole life black. Remember also the joys of your life, and I would like to think that the love we have given you these six years is one of them. Many years ago I heard a short poem which has stuck in my mind, and I think it has a great truth. It goes:

"Two men looked out of prison bars:
The one saw mud, the other, stars."

Do not always look for mud, Mutti! The stars shine also for you! Look at our friend, Priscilla. She has had a life as bad as yours–marrying a homosexual man who later tried to murder her. But today she is a happy and cheerful person, unchained by her past. It is possible to be so. But you must look sometimes at the positive and not sit here brooding all the time about things that are past, and about other things that are not important. Real life is not like the soap operas you are always watching."

She butted out her cigarette sourly and reached for another. "You think you know so much, Doctor Psychologist. But I know the invitation was sent to Curt, Johanna and family."

"That is not so, Mutti. For one thing, have you ever met their daughter?"

"No."

"So, if she never knew you, how could she invite you? This anniversary party was to be a surprise for her parents."

"But the invitation was to Curt, Johanna and family," she persisted obstinately.

"How do you know? Did you see the envelope?"

"No. But I know."

"Well, if it was also for the family, why did I not take the children?"

"You were too busy,"

"Well, if I was too busy, all the more reason why I would have taken them. Then I would not have had to cook a full meal for them before we left. I could have saved a few dollars on food too, which would have meant something in these very difficult times. And, did I take my own father and mother? They have been friends of the Johnsons for years as well, but neither were they invited. Sarah, the Johnson's daughter is only working her first job, so she could not afford to invite everyone."

Trudy stuck out her bottom lip. She was not willing to be convinced.

"Okay," I said wearily, picking up the phone. "How about if I phone Sarah and ask her if you were included on her guest list?"

"No," Trudy grabbed the phone out of my hand angrily, "I will not talk to her. She will not remember."

"Alright then, the Johnsons just live two blocks away. Let's go talk to them."

"No, they won't remember either."

I was incredulous. "Let me get this straight," I said, not believing the information that was reaching my ears. "Do you mean to tell me that the person who threw the party would not remember if she invited you, and the persons for whom the party was thrown wouldn't know? You have never seen the invitation, but you alone know?"

"That is correct!" she stated categorically.

I felt a crushing sense of frustration. How do I deal with this? There is no reasoning with her. My head pounding, I went down and joined Curt on the couch.

Within days Trudy had a new demand. She wanted her name on the title of our house. Curt demurred as gracefully as he could. But she would not be put off. She called Curt into her apartment, and with ice dripping from her voice she told him that if he did not concur with her request he would have to get body bags for Angel and myself.

"You've got to be kidding! She threatened to kill us?" I asked Curt. I found it hard to take this seriously. But a thought occurred to me: "Does she still have her gun?" I asked with rising anxiety. In Europe she had always kept a loaded pistol on her night table, but I had asked Curt before she came to Canada to tell her it would not be allowed here. It was not necessary, and it would be dangerous with a house full of small children. We had also put a steel door at the entrance to her apartment, at her request, which she always kept locked, and we assured her she need not fear for her safety, surrounded as she was by a big family.

"I think she disposed of it when I told her about it, because I was very strong on the point. But now she is talking in terms of knives.... She also said that she has stockpiled enough sleeping pills to take her own life."

"I think she is just trying to frighten us into giving her what she wants," I said. I felt certain this was so, and refused to be intimidated by her latest hysterics.

But Angel was not so easily dissuaded. We had not, of course, told her about the threat, but the following day she ran to me, white and shaking.

"Oma says she is going to burn the house down," she cried.

"Wherever did you get such an idea?" I asked her.

"It's true. I just heard her. She is in her apartment and I heard her when I went to put my dirty clothes down the laundry chute. She was saying, "Fire! Fire! I will burn it down...the house...everything." She grabbed my arm, "Come listen! Listen yourself!" I followed her down the hall.

As Oma often did, she was talking out loud–very loud–to herself in the apartment. Though she was talking in English I could not make out exactly what she was saying as she now seemed to have moved and was facing away from the door. I could only distinguish clearly the word "Fire!"

"Don't worry," I put my arm around Angel and comforted her. "She doesn't really mean that. She is just saying that to scare us, so we will do what she wants. This is just a ruse to control us. She would never burn down the house–if not because of us, then at least because of all her antiques that are more precious to her than anything else. So, please don't be afraid. She's just mad, and talking crazy and saying things she really doesn't mean, like people sometimes do when they are angry."

But I phoned Curt at the office anyway and he wrote the incident down in his daybook.

But, having already experienced her Oma's vengeance, Angel was haunted by her fears, and I could not put her mind at rest no matter what I said to her. Bedtime became nightmare alley. She told the others, and as I had done when the children were babies, I found myself running to crying children during the nights. After several months in which nothing happened, their fears began to mitigate a little and I was able, finally, to get some unbroken sleep.

But not for long.

One day in July a letter came from a lawyer's office saying that Curt was to go to his office at 10 A.M. Thursday on matters pertaining to his mother's will. Curt asked her about it, and she was coy and cagey. He soon concluded it was to do with the title to the house again. Both because he had a business meeting that morning, and because he did not want to be railroaded into anything, he did not show up at the appointment that had been made for him.

"You will not do as I ask? You will see what I will do to you! Your grandfather has given you that money only if you are good to me," she sputtered spitefully.

Then Trudy tried a different tactic. As I was driving her up town one day she put on a conciliatory tone and a show of great concern. I was weary with stress and begged her in tears to back down from all her threats and implied actions. I assured her of our continued love and asked her what was wanting in our devotion to her. She promised me that if I did everything in my power to change Curt's mind, and got him to sign the papers that she had her lawyer prepare, that she would make sure that I and the children were never put out on the street.

"*Sure,*" I thought cynically, "*you really have my best interests at heart!*"

"Tell him I have never waited for anything in my life, and I will not wait longer for this. If he does not do this," she added theatrically, "I have saved up my sleeping pills in my safe."

The sleeping pills, however, were only the back up plan—or threat.

In early August we received a registered letter from her lawyer. It sat hot in my hand like some evil thing. I took my muddy feet from the garden and sat down nervously on a lawn chair to open it. Trudy was swimming her daily thirty five rounds of the pool in her usual butterfly stroke. She avoided any eye contact and her expression was smug. I tore open the envelope and read, to my shock, that she was demanding the immediate return of $125,000 which she claimed she had loaned us. She also swore under oath that our home was built entirely with her funds and therefore it, by right, belonged to her. That night she came to the supper table as usual to eat the food I had prepared for everyone, and her expression was jolly.

Curt waved the letter at her. "You are sitting down to eat our food as if everything was normal and happy around here, and yet just this afternoon we received this from you?"

She shrugged matter-of-factly. She was enjoying her little coup and the discomfort it caused.

I was nervous. I had had little to do with lawyers and courts and this sounded pretty ominous to me. Curt, however, brushed it aside as a bluff.

"Look," he assured me, "this is absolutely ridiculous and she knows it. She knows that she did not pay for the whole house, that it was all but complete–except for her quarters–before she came. I have kept all the bills, bank statements and have a record of all transactions, everything we need to prove that her statement is patently false. In fact, she may find herself in big trouble for having perjured herself. So don't worry."

"But I am worrying. She twists things. Last week she argued with me that she had planted our apricot tree three years ago. As you are aware, I had bought and planted that tree with your reluctant help, as well as the apple tree, the year before we started to built–seven years ago. You thought I was pushing things at the time, but I wanted mature, fruit bearing trees as soon as possible. It does look stunted now from having been moved twice; first, when the fill was brought in, and later when the pool was built. But she got this bee in her bonnet that she had provided that tree. It wasn't an important point. What really befuddled me was how she could really believe something that never happened."

"Well, I have all the documents to prove–to the court, if not to her– that she did not finance this house. It's as straight forward as that."

"And what about this loan thing?"

"A scare tactic."

"What if she produces those papers you signed to and uses them to bolster her claim?"

"She won't. She is my mother, after all. She swore to me that she would never use them except if I died and she was put out on the street–something that would never happen."

"Are you going to talk to her?"

"I will. But right now I have to concentrate on putting bread on this table, for her sake as well as our own. I have three bids to get out before the weekend. There is a lot of work involved, and nothing may come of it; there are lots of people buying jobs out there. But that's what I have to think about now."

We contacted our lawyer, a friend named Ed King, and let him know what was going on anyway. He sent a strong letter to her lawyer to inform him of some of the particulars about Trudy, and to help dissuade him from any further proceedings.

In late August, early September, Curt and Mutti had a marathon negotiating session. Mutti complained that Curt spent more time watching football than he spent talking to her. She wept that she had 'lost' him to his wife. She said the pool was too warm for her, and that the apartment was not to her specifications. She gave the impression that she did not understand what was meant in the letter from her lawyer and had only meant it to be a 'shot before the bow', nothing else. Curt let her know that our parish priest was dropping off a little money here and there for food for us, and begged her indulgence, trying to give her a sense of the pressures we were under from the ongoing recession. Despite the hardships we were under, Curt again offered to buy insurance for her to alleviate her feeling of 'insecurity'. In seeming appreciation for his peacefully hearing her out, she agreed to a reconciliation, and she promised to contact her lawyer and tell him that everything was okay now on the home front. We called Ed and told him it was resolved and she had called off her dogs.

On October 24th we received an irate phone call from Ed. "Why haven't you been in contact with me?" he asked.

"What do you mean?" we were startled.

"I have an affidavit sitting here on my desk from your mother."

"Whaaat? She told me she was calling off this witch hunt!"

"Apparently not."

"I have it here in my daybook–yes, September 10, I've got it recorded here; she said she phoned her lawyer that day and told him to drop proceedings."

"September 10? There was no way she could have talked to her lawyer on that day. I had phoned his office that day on another matter and was told he was out of the country."

"Do you mean to tell me that all the time we thought everything was resolved that she has been working behind our backs?"

"It appears so. By the way, has Trudy been seen lately by a doctor?" Ed was pensive.

"What do you mean?"

"Well, do you think your mother could be suffering from.... ?"

"You mean...something like Alzheimers?"

"That's very hard to diagnose," I interjected. "Still, I don't think so. Unless it started at age thirty. And I know for a fact there is no way she would ever agree to be seen by a psychiatrist. She has too much pride."

"If you want a diagnosis," I offered ruefully, "and I have backed away from thinking of her in these terms all these years—but her lack of bonding, her shallow affect, narcissism and flawed conscience development fit the profile of a psychopathic personality. Even her charm and intelligence fit the picture."

There, I had said it. The thought I had never wanted to think, the words I had never wanted to utter. The psychopath is the great deceiver, and hence is very difficult to recognize and very easy to like. Even by me.

Trudy had continued to share meals with us every day, and there had been no new outbursts to alert us that she was up to something. She was perhaps less exuberant than usual, and restrained toward me—but that was not out of the ordinary. At Church she had taken to sitting away from us, but when it came time for the kiss of peace I always sought her out. She was not always pleased about this attention, but I had resolved to love and forgive her no matter what. If not for her sake, at least I had to do it for my own sake. I remembered the injunction that said, "If you would bring your gift to the altar and remember that your brother or sister has something against you, lay down your gift and make peace with your sister or brother and then bring your gift to the altar." I struggled with this week after week, but never so much as on the Sunday following this latest disclosure. In my mind I assented to the need of forgiveness for her healing and my own, but as the Lord's Prayer concluded and the time came to move toward her that day, my body suddenly assumed a will of its own. Sinews and muscles seemed no longer mine to control, as though a circuit had been broken and there was no power left to implement commands. I felt faint, breathless. In amazement I felt my limbs stiffen and refuse to obey the dictates of my mind. My legs were wooden pylons rooted to the floor. My arms were useless rubber appendages, my joints frozen, heavy, and unyielding. My eyes gauged the distance I had to move, and my heart pounded the walls of my chest like relentless surf beating upon a rocky shore. In slow motion I jerked forward, lurching like someone about to fall. Inch by inch I forced my reluctant body to do what must be done. I looked at her stony face and she looked away, pretending not to see me. But I stood there until she began to feel conspicuous and I lifted the great weight of my wooden hand to touch her limp recoiling fingers. If there was peace there, it was only in the steely silence of the will. I felt as if I had met an alien being that day, and it was the body I had been given, the body I had sometimes misused, the body that still resisted the yoke of Love.

In the afternoon a couple of Trudy's friends arrived. They had been friends of mine too. She led them out to the back corner and directed Gustav, a big burly man, to remove the fountain she had installed, and they carried away her garden furniture and put it all on the back of Gustav's truck. Then she ordered Gustav to rip free a cupboard she had had built onto the wooden deck. This too she packed away in the truck. I watched from the family room, wondering what was going on now. Curt walked out the back door and immediately his ears were assailed with a tirade.

"See that man! That's the man I've been telling you about. He's just the way I told you he was. He's trying to kill me by turning the heat off in my apartment, trying to kill his own mother!" she shouted shrilly.

"What are you talking about?" Curt demanded to know in utter astonishment.

"Don't tell me you don't know," she screeched. "For three days you have turned off the heat and I have frozen in my rooms. This too I have told my lawyer!"

"I have done no such thing! Why are you telling such lies?"

Trudy grabbed the arms of her two friends, "See how he talks to his mother? Didn't I tell you? He is his father; he is not my blood!"

"You never told me the heat was off. You have not told me you were cold. Perhaps there has been a mechanical breakdown. Can I be blamed for that? Let me come up in your apartment and I will check it out,"

"Never! Never will you be allowed in my apartment!"

"Then how can I fix it?"

"You cannot help. You only cause me to suffer."

"Gustav," Curt, still bewildered, turned to the big man, "at least you come with me to the basement, as my witness, to see if there is any malfunction down there."

Gustav was embarrassed, but he pulled away from Trudy's grip and followed Curt downstairs. A few minutes later they reappeared, and Curt was still confused. "We have both felt the heating ducts going up to the apartment, and they were warm, were they not?" He turned to Gustav. Gustav nodded assent. "We also felt the ducts coming back from the apartment. They too were warm." Again Gustav nodded. "Therefore, there is heat going up to the apartment, and there is nothing amiss in the basement. Why it is cold in the apartment I cannot know without seeing the equipment up there."

"I will not let you in the apartment," Trudy reiterated with an ugly sneer.

"Then there is nothing I can do to help you. Just as I could not help you if you did not tell me something was wrong." Curt turned on his heel and walked away. Imprecations and accusations followed his retreating shoulders.

She did not show up for supper that night, but the following evening we were surprised to see her standing in the doorway. "My lawyer has said I must let you into the apartment," she said stiffly.

Curt followed her woodenly, grabbing his tool box on the way up. As she unlocked the door to her inner sanctum he felt the rush of cool air pour through the open door. He looked around and glanced at the thermostat. He whooped, "This thermostat is set at 10 degrees celsius!"

Trudy looked startled, and then mollified.

"So what was all that about? Why did you set the thermostat so low? And what was going on with Gustav and Marie?"

"Johanna has told me you will move to the States. I will not go with you. So in the spring I will move out," she said haughtily. "They will keep my things for me. Until the spring."

Angel had followed her Dad and she piped up, "If Mommy said we were going to move, why didn't she tell us too?"

"Shut up, you!" Mutti snapped angrily.

The children became increasingly frightened at Mutti's behavior. They confided in me how she would take them aside and say mean things about me. She also counseled them not to give their sister, Angel, the kiss of peace in Church, because she was "bad". Later we were to hear that Justin's estrangement from her was not all the result of his new adolescent interests. Having gained her confidence because of their close relationship, Justin had become Oma's special confidante. She told him what a terrible mother I was and that she was praying that Curt and I would get a divorce. In fact, she was trying to do what she could to put a wedge between us because Curt should never have married such a "stupid" woman. Then, she said, she would throw Angel and I out on the street and she would have a better life with just Curt and Justin and the others. Anytime she sensed some discord between us, she would call Justin up to her apartment gleefully, shower him with money and goodies, and gloat that her wishes were about to come true. Soon Justin had had enough and he gave her a wide berth. Now it was both Justin and her son that were in her bad books. It must have seemed to Trudy that her plans had gone awry and her world was falling apart. There were new threats, new innuendos.

"Why are you threatening us?" I asked her. "What have you got to gain? Are you trying to punish us? Are you trying to force us to sell the house? What would that give you? It certainly would not give you the money you are asking. The housing market is so depressed right now that we would never get back the money we put into it. So that would mean that any proportion that you might hope to gain would be very little."

"Proportion, nothing!" she said vengefully, "I will take everything!" And she wheeled away, savoring the euphoria of power.

She no longer came down for meals after that, and we no longer pursued her and begged her to come. The children were wary of her and worried when they saw her lurking in our part of the house. To set their minds at ease we got a new lock for the front door and began to use the privacy locks in our part of the house.

Two weeks after the removal of the fountain, at a time when Curt was away in Vancouver, the phone rang early in the morning. It was my neighbor: "Is there something happening?" she asked with concern.

"Why?" I was mystified.

"There are two big moving vans parked in front of your house," she said.

My knees went weak. The knocking on the door was like horses hooves stampeding across my heart. I hesitated. The knocking went on, loud, preemptory. I unlocked the door and opened it just a crack. Trudy leaned her whole weight against it, striking my hip and sending me staggering back.

"Take everything," she commanded the six moving men.

I began to shake uncontrollably. *How cunning,* I thought. *She waits until Curt is out of town. She always said I was too soft, and now she comes, when she knows I am defenseless, to take advantage of the situation. And not one, but two, full sized moving vans!*

I reached far back in my throat to find a voice, "This is my home. You cannot come in here without a court order. You are trespassing."

"Don't listen to her," Trudy said imperiously, trying to wave them in.

But the men knew I was right. They shuffled around uncomfortably, wondering what to do.

I tried to close the door, but Trudy was firmly braced against it and pushed me roughly away.

"If you don't leave I will call the police!"

"Call them," she taunted.

I left her standing inside the door, with the men still milling uncertainly on the doorstep, and walked, through the tremendous fog that flooded my mind, toward the kitchen. To my further alarm, I could barely pick up the phone. I was shaking so hard I could not dial. When I looked at the numbers they were blurry and unreadable.

I must be calm! I told myself desperately. I dialed a number—any number, holding my finger on the button. I thought maybe once she saw me dialing she would retreat. I looked at her. She did not budge. I rubbed my eyes and reached for the telephone book, praying I could read the number for the police. *I have to see! I have to stop shaking!* Finally, after what seemed like an interminable time, I heard a woman's voice say "RCMP headquarters." My biggest problem was to regulate my voice so I was understandable. Squeaking, tremulous, I spilled out my story, and though it was muddled, the woman listening was patient and understanding. She said she would dispatch someone immediately. Taking courage, not wanting to leave the safety of the phone, I tried to remember the name of my lawyer's firm. Then, realizing it was still early I phoned his home phone number. His wife answered. Alarmed to hear me in such distress she said she would leave a message for Ed and come right over. Fortunately she lived near by.

I returned to the door and spoke directly to the men, "You may take anything from her apartment, but nothing from the rest of the house. The police are on the way. The back door will give you direct access to her quarters."

There were thunderbolts in Trudy's eyes, but she could see the men were not willing to enter the front door. Haughtily she led them around to the back.

A tall, courteous police officer had arrived. He surveyed the situation and promised to stay with me the entire morning if necessary. I asked him to watch the upper floor for me while I watched below. Laura, Ed's wife came in, carrying some muffins she had just taken out of her oven. It was such a human gesture in the middle of all that was inhuman. She helped me to pacify the children, who were huddled in terror, and send them off to school. Only Erica remained, clutching onto my leg, her eyes wide pools of fear.

Somehow, while I was on the phone trying to contact my husband, or talking to my lawyer, and the police officer was diverted, Trudy managed to steal the bedspread off our bed, and a painting by Curt's paternal uncle. Gustav and Marie arrived after the furniture was loaded and were hustled into the apartment.

Later, when everyone had left, an uneasy quiet fell over the house. I wandered about aimlessly, trying to slow down my racing heart. I looked at the empty gaping door of the apartment and stepped inside tentatively. It reeked unbelievably of stale smoke. I was startled to see that she had taken down every light fixture in the apartment, leaving live wires hanging everywhere. The medicine cabinet had been taken off the wall of the bathroom and all curtain rods and blinds were gone. Only a church calendar remained with a thick black X prominently marking the day, the 17th of November.

I remembered I had to cook for my family, and tried to marshal my mind back to the mundane needs of everyday life. Wandering downstairs to retrieve something from the freezer, I was sickened to find water swirling above my ankles and boxes floating around the basement.

The time of horror had begun.

CHAPTER 22

"So what does all this mean?" I asked nervously. "What is implied in being served with a writ?"

Curt glanced at his watch impatiently and gave me a look as if to say: "Don't ask too many questions. It's Friday afternoon and I've got to get back to the office yet."

Our lawyer, Ed King, adjusted the blinds beside his desk to filter out the last surge of light of the dying November day. "I presume you have looked through the affidavits I sent you on Tuesday. Basically she is trying to get a court order to retrieve the rest of the antiques she said she loaned to you."

"I'm not terribly surprised after the fiasco with the moving vans. She did not succeed totally in getting her way, and she is not one to give up. But I have several witnesses, both within and without the family, who remember hearing from her own lips that she had given the furniture to us. Some smaller items she is claiming were even gift wrapped and presented to Curt on Christmas and on his birthday."

Ed raised his eyebrows, "The law doesn't allow Indian giving."

"Good!" Curt grunted, "And I hope the law makes that very clear to her!"

"It may not be that easy," I cautioned Curt glumly, "Trudy only believes and understands what will promote her own interests. She seems to have a different understanding of the word "gift" from the average person. Her gifts always have hooks attached. This whole issue is not about ownership anyway. It's about control: what she feels is her right to control us through your grandfather's inheritance. I got my first inkling of this the year I taught Kelli's grade one religion class. There they were, sitting around the dining room table, ten little children as good as gold. It was our only table big enough to accommodate ten children. The table was protected by a sturdy tablecloth, and the children were sitting coloring quietly, when Mutti roared in with the fury of a hurricane demanding that they leave the dining room at once. Her shouting upset and frightened the children, and I was flabbergasted. It was our dining room, not hers. But distinctions like this appear to have no meaning for her. And later when I tried to talk to her about it she simply stone walled me."

"Please take note, Ed, that since the antiques were passed on to us, we have spent over $2,000 upgrading the dining room set, and over $700 refinishing the desk which was full of worms and had to be fumigated and totally restored. I have the bills and paperwork right here," Curt was sputtering with indignation as he handed the bills over to Ed. "I would hardly have spent that kind of money to refurbish borrowed furniture."

"Don't worry", Ed reassured us, his warm brown eyes smiling sympathetically, "I will handle the proceedings myself on Tuesday. You won't even have to attend. Later if she intends to pursue the matter of the alleged loan, that is an entirely separate matter from this one, and with the backlog of cases would take eight to nine months at least to be heard. And before anything like that could come to trial, you would have a discovery day for the mutual disclosure of documents and evidence to help ascertain if there is even sufficient evidence to proceed with a trial. Right now, it's getting late," Ed glanced down at his watch. "Its four thirty already, and the family and I are getting ready to leave for Vancouver for the weekend. I just want to run through her affidavit with you quickly, point by point, to get your comments. I see my secretary has left a couple of extra copies on my desk, so you can grab them and just follow along... Now, see here where it says: "The chattels brought by the plaintiff....""

"Excuse me, can you please tell me where you are reading from?"

"Oh, it is the first point on the page."

"What page?"

"Page one, right at the top."

"I'm sorry, but you must have given us the wrong affidavit."

Ed pushed back his unruly gray hair. "There is only one affidavit," he said crisply, trying to curb his impatience. I could see he was wondering how we could be so obtuse, but I really could not find the section he was referring to in the document in my hand. He looked across the desk at us, lines of fatigue beginning to show in the corner of his eyes. "Let me see your affidavit," he said to placate me. His eyes darted back and forth with increasing rapidity on the page he was reading. His face flushed deep red. "This is a different affidavit," he said, his voice choking. "She must have just dropped off a new affidavit!"

"Why?"

"What's up now?"

Ed averted his eyes, consolidating his emotion under a businesslike crust, "She's combining her actions and is calling for a Summary Judgment on the whole case this Tuesday morning."

"But you said that would take at least eight or nine months? How can she do that? There has been no discovery of documents—we have no time to prepare!"

"She seems to feel you have nothing to contest her claim with. She has enclosed two documents, purportedly signed by you, acknowledging that she has loaned you the money in question."

Curt blanched. I looked at him, all my fears coming to the surface.

"That was under duress," he said hotly. "And as you see, I added a weasel clause 'that these things can be held as true until further notice has been given'. Herewith, further notice IS given!" he shook his head in disbelief. "She said she would never use those papers. Those were just to be her protection if anyone should try to dispossess her after my death."

Our further perusal of the new affidavit indicated that a small, but very significant, alteration had been made from the first affidavit. Now, she claimed to have built the house herself "in whole *or in part*". Our easy, clear defense was shattered.

"See what you can dig up before Tuesday," Ed said tersely.

I felt feverish, panicky. Things were colliding in my stomach.

"What we need to find to put this all to rest is the letter she wrote— you know, the one in which she asked to come to live with us. She was very explicit in it that she was now passing on to us the money and goods willed to Curt by his grandfather." But even as I said the words I had an awful sinking feeling, remembering a pile of her old letters I had found in a bed side drawer during the spring cleaning the previous year. *Why am I keeping all these old letters after all the years she's been with us?* I had asked myself.

"Yes, I remember it well. Find it!"

For the next three days I turned the house upside down, fixated, praying, that this key letter had not been destroyed. I found some old letters in the attic and basement in her handwriting, but I could tell by the dates and addresses that they were not the one I was seeking. I showed them to Curt and he flipped through them quickly and pushed them aside.

"It's not here," he said grimly.

"Translate these anyway," I begged, "One of them might still have some relevant material."

"Forget it," Curt snapped. "It's no use. These are not the right ones. I have no time, don't you understand? I still have to work, too, you know, or how are we going to pay for the legal fees? You'd better get busy getting letters and affidavits from our witnesses."

"It's not possible to get them all before Tuesday," I protested, discouraged. "What about the evidence we need from your Dad in Europe, from your family lawyer there, from Dan down East? I am sure Eva must have told Dan and he would know about your grandfather's will. I am sure your Opa took her aside when she left Europe, just as he did with you, to tell you about his will. I also remember Trudy spouting off about the inheritance and the antiques when Herb and his family visited us in Vienna. Perhaps they would remember...."

The time pressure was crushing. I spent every waking minute and most of the nights to get together what I could. The extended family willingly offered their recollections about the antiques and the inheritance, but Ed insinuated that the judge might consider them biased in our favor. I was weak with apprehension. Lacking so much important documentation I turned to material that would destroy Trudy's credibility. There was a lot of that. I needed it to balance the picture. I was only too aware how Trudy could turn her persuasive charm on and off at will like a tap. Even two days before the moving vans had come to seize the furniture and our possessions she had succeeded in disarming me. Exuding good will she had come to me like the mother-in-law of old, full of graciousness and concern, to show me a small drip she had discovered by the hot water tank in the basement. *Hmm,* I thought, *that was decent of her. She must be thawing out.* As well as I knew her, I still did not suspect that her good cheer masked a cruel plan, already set in motion. Possibly for the same reason, and because he took for granted his role of favored son, Curt watched Tuesday approach with such glib confidence that it could have been a textbook example of psychological denial. Even after everything that she had put us through, she was still his mother. And, idealist that he was, he had no doubt that the John Waynes of this world would always win; the justice system would ferret out the truth. His mother's foolishness was nothing new to him after all. He recalled the time she had taken a swing at him in a fit of anger when he was a teenager. He had ducked and she broke her arm, hitting it against the door frame. Whatever she had done he had always managed to side step it before.

But it would not be so this time. In such a short time, and with dizzying skill, Trudy had charmed the judge, playing the penultimate sweet old lady who had been taken advantage of by her hardnosed, professional son. She denied blatantly that there had ever been a will and flashed the papers that Curt had signed. She pleaded with the judge that she would be forced to go on welfare if the money was not returned, conveniently omitting to mention her healthy bank account, alimony from Europe, and the fact that she was currently living in a luxury three bedroom apartment that was full of priceless antiques. Our pleas for a financial disclosure on her part were treated as irrelevant. Our lawyer protested that through her trickery we had only one working day in which to prepare our defense, but her lawyer parried that we had been aware of the situation since spring. And surely we couldn't forget that in the summer she had demanded her money back, making it payable on her youngest grand child's birthday? In vain did Ed King claim that the documents signed, without witnesses, were not legal, and pointed out the weasel clause Curt had inserted. Her lawyer twisted the weasel clause around to show that it was simply more evidence of Curt's poor faith towards his loving mother. Our lawyer claimed the Statue of Limitations because of the years elapsed. This went unheard. It was her word against ours, and she played her part, the part of a victimized mother, with consummate skill. The attempt of Curt and I to discredit her appeared just like sour grapes. The whole scene was straight from Never Never Land and was over in the scant twenty minutes that had been allotted to it. On twenty minutes of testimony, largely hers, our lives and the security of our children was to be decided. Suddenly, yanked out of our ordinary existence to the musty formality of this dark paneled old courtroom, we had become things to be disposed of: criminals.

The Judge looked down, shuffling the papers on his desk. His expression was inscrutable. After a couple of minutes he raised his eyes, cleared his throat, and announced that he was reserving judgment on this case. The sheriff and the court reporter stood around sharing a joke and deciding where to go for lunch. We no longer existed.

Ed ushered us out, formally.

"When can we expect a decision?" I asked anxiously, hardly managing to speak.

"Probably January. Even late January."

Well, we can at least celebrate Christmas in peace, I consoled myself. *And there still is a chance for a ruling in our favor.*

But the court scene left a bitter taste in my mouth. I felt railroaded, suffocated, strangled, and disillusioned. We had not been heard. We would not be heard. We were not given the time, or the voice, to defend ourselves against her trickery, the sleight of hand she had pulled with the affidavits. From the talk with Curt in August, until Ed had called us about this hearing, she had led us to believe that she had dropped the case. I felt dehumanized, an animal caught and caged. The staging of the whole process conspired to make us look and feel guilty. But of what were we guilty? What had happened to 'innocent until proven guilty'? Apparently that concept is not applied in civil law.

Despite reserving judgment, the judge acted quickly to give Trudy the court order she requested to repossess the furniture, although only the European furniture and artifacts. It did not bolster our confidence in the judge. In vain we presented the affidavits we had accumulated to prove the furniture was part of the estate and was a gift. It did not matter. We pleaded hardship to be without furniture for Christmas. We were overruled. An exultant Trudy arrived with the sheriff on a bleak December day. Accompanying them was Trudy's lawyer, a middle aged man with a red beard. I tried to appeal to him, asking how in good conscience he could be party to this. He looked uncomfortable and moved away from me. The both of them stood in the driveway holding the list of articles while the men struggled vainly to move the heavy furniture, eventually calling in reinforcements. I watched in numb detachment as they removed the great mirror, the chandelier, the dining room furniture, the desk, denuding our home. I would never shed a tear for these things, that were, after all, only things. My tears were reserved for what she was doing to the hearts of my husband and her grandchildren.

Trying to push her triumph one step further, she petitioned the courts to force us to pay her moving costs. This petition failed, but not until it had taken its toll on us.

On a desultory afternoon in January the call came. We had lost the case. In addition to the basic amount she claimed, the courts had awarded her court costs and seven years of compound interest, arriving at a total payable of $235,000. We looked at the figure and blinked, stunned. This was unreal! How could this be happening to us? What had we done to deserve this? Nothing had been allowed for the seven years we had fed and supported her and paid her bills. No consideration was given to the fact that we were struggling to feed five children on an income that had ranged from $14,000 to $17,000 during these years of the recession.

Curt was a wild man. My biggest fear now was not the loss of all our material goods, but the loss of him, of his sanity, of his faith. The denial was over. The truth of what she had done to us had finally gotten through to Curt, and I would continue to live with the fear, day by day, moment by moment, that in his demented fury he would murder her.

That Sunday, after months of absence, Trudy reappeared at Church, anxious to flaunt her victory. As we exited the Church doors we could hear her loud, mirthless laughter reverberating from one end of the parking lot to the other in waves of vindictive joy. I held on to Curt's arm with all the strength I possessed.

We clung to the hope of an appeal. We met in Ed's office. The problem had become now, again, one of money. Ed knew we were penniless. He offered to speak to his senior partners and try to persuade them to continue to carry our case. He did not succeed. But Providence did not desert us. A maiden aunt died suddenly, leaving us an unexpected windfall of $4700. This would help us launch our appeal. Sadly, we watched as the money, which could have been used for so many better purposes, was gobbled up in the voracious jaws of the legal system.

At least, I thought to myself with some relief, *we will be able to present all the evidence that we didn't have time to accumulate before the first court appearance, and everything will be put right.*

We had helpful letters and affidavits from all over Europe and Canada, and I had eventually managed to persuade Curt to translate the old letters I had found. Though none of these were the exact letter we had been looking for, these letters also were clear and explicit in their references to Curt's inheritance from his grandfather; this had always been a favorite topic of hers and she brought it up often. By accident, a hand addressed bank statement in our name arrived at our house as well, and it turned out, in fact, to have been meant for Trudy. Before sending it on, we photocopied it for the evidence it contained that Trudy had perjured herself in the information she had given the court regarding her financial affairs. The funds Trudy was receiving from Europe were far in excess of what she had reported to the courts, and her pitiable financial state was not so pitiable at all. Wasn't perjury a crime? In addition, Curt was convinced from a study of the old letters, that she still had that 'reserve' she had spoken of in one of the letters, probably in a Swiss bank account. There was no other way to explain the discrepancy between the amounts she reported in the letters and the amount she brought to Canada. And where was she getting all the money to prosecute us?

I was soon to have a cruel shock. All our new evidence was for naught. The rules and procedures of the legal system would not allow the introduction of any new evidence during an appeal. The sole criterion for launching an appeal was the possibility that the honorable judge had made an error, or had not properly weighted the evidence he had been given on that one day, at that one twenty minute hearing! The frustration, the overwhelming sense of injustice, grew. We were pounding our fists against a brick wall and there was no recourse for us. Curt spoke angrily of launching a counterclaim. Our lawyer reminded us that to do this we would have to pay to bring our various witnesses from Europe and elsewhere. The cost of one day in court, he informed us, was upwards of $5,000. We would have to allow for about three days in court, and also be prepared for the possibility of deferrals. If we won the case we might retrieve some, or all, of our costs, but we would be required to pay for everything now, up front. I knew we could not do this. Curt knew we could not do this. But the prospect of getting her on perjury and fraud fed his imagination. Although we had no means to carry it through, we had our lawyer send her a notification that a counterclaim was being launched. She reacted with sneering disparagement.

In the meantime, Trudy lost no time in pressing her advantage. She petitioned for the immediate sale of our house, with the proceeds to be turned over to her. As if that was not enough, she kept the pot boiling by launching punitive new offensives, fresh petitions, affidavits, visits from the sheriff on an ongoing basis. She was out for blood. To answer the phone or the doorbell became a daily trauma.

"Who is that, Mommy?" little Erica would cry, clutching me in alarm. "Is that the Judge?"

She had heard and seen what a little girl should never have to hear and see. I was shaking uncontrollably. I could not help myself. What could I tell her? Even to go for the mail was a torment because most days brought bills we couldn't pay, and the inevitable envelope with a legal letterhead. It never failed to be bad news. Trudy was a veteran of twenty two years of legal battles with her husband, and she knew how to use the legal system for her own ends.

Our lawyer managed to get us a stay of execution regarding the immediate sale of our house, pending our appeal. In answer, in a lavish expense account, Trudy claimed her expenses exceeded her income and she petitioned the court that we should continue to support her. The court, in its wisdom, decreed that Trudy did require more to live on than all seven of us combined, and ordered us to supplement her reported income by $400 per month. She was well aware of our financial circumstances. She knew she was squeezing us to death. It was, no doubt, a suitable revenge for us not bowing to her control. Now the courts would control us.

Because of other commitments, or because he was becoming too emotionally involved in our case, Ed turned us over to Simon Chapel, another lawyer in his firm. Trudy had now put a Lis Pendens on our property so that we could no longer sell it ourselves or use it for collateral to borrow money. As we sat in his office, dealing with the ongoing onslaught of petitions and working on our appeal, Simon leaned back wearily in his chair and looked out the window: "Do you see that man walking out of the Safeway's down there?" I leaned over to look. "You have about as much chance of getting justice from him as you do from any Judge in our judicial system."

I was frozen with shock. He was telling us that our situation was hopeless. He explained in meticulous and painful detail that the legal system was not based on laws of morality, truth and justice, but on precedents in judgment made by fallible men. He sat there, looking bleak and discouraged, in the service of a legal system in which he no longer believed.

By now it was evident that we had no money and Curt's income was minimal. Regretfully, we were informed that this legal firm could no longer represent us. Panic stricken, we turned to Legal Aid. It was humiliating to beg, to lay out the details of our private lives on the table of strangers, to be perused like goods in a meat market. And, after disclosing it all, they told us, while we were qualified on the basis of economic need, that they did not have the manpower or the mandate to deal with appeals. Had I committed an armed robbery, I was assured of legal counsel. As the victims in an unjust lawsuit, we were on our own.

"Justice," I thought bitterly, "is only for the rich."

Ed drafted up documents to the court to say that we would be representing ourselves from now on.

I was desperate.

My God, my God, where are you? Have You, too, abandoned us"

I thought of my uncles and contacted them. When they heard of our plight they got together and sent a check for $3,000. My parents had been helping us all along for day to day needs, but there was no way they could begin to field our horrendous legal bills. I even wrote to a philanthropist I had heard of, without a response. It was not enough, never enough. One day, teetering on the edge, a mass of searing pain, I walked into the Royal Bank keeping my head down, as a criminal would do, hoping I would not bump into anyone I knew. I could not trust myself to make a normal social response. So I cringed when someone called my name. Looking up with my red eyes, I saw Helen watching me with concern on her face. Helen, a childhood friend of my mother, was a retired teacher.

"Come have coffee with me and tell me about it," she said kindly, reaching out to me.

I shook my head in acquiescence, not trusting myself to speak. In her friendly eyes I found the greeting of an angel. The floodgates opened on the trauma that no one else wanted to hear. She watched me closely as I talked. Her own life had been strewn with boulders and haunted by poverty. I remembered my mother telling me how she had shared her school books with Helen because Helen's family had no money to buy books. Her winter coat had become so shabby on the outside that she took to wearing it inside out. Today I was the needy person, and she was doing the helping. She sat down and wrote me a check for one thousand dollars. It was a precious beam of light shining through the clouds.

On Sunday, Father Steve handed me an envelope with an anonymous gift of one hundred dollars from someone in the parish. Perhaps God had not forgotten us.

Another unbelievable act of kindness came as manna from heaven. Along with all our other problems, an emergency situation had arisen with regard to Angel's teeth. As her permanent teeth came in we were horrified to see that in some places they were three deep. She had inherited, it seemed, Curt's sister's large teeth and the small jaw that came with my side of the family. Her permanent teeth were grotesquely distributed all over her mouth. It was not simply a cosmetic flaw; it was a disaster. Although they were living in Vancouver now, our friends Peter and Eve continued to keep in touch. On one visit they quickly assessed the situation and promised, if we could get Angel to Vancouver, they would make arrangements for her teeth to be fixed. They were as good as their word. Over the needed years of treatment they quietly saw to this healing miracle. I will be indebted to their love forever.

But for every moment of relief there were endless nights of raw and bitter anguish. I reached out to God and found darkness in my heart and darkness in my soul. But faith was all I had left, as intangible as it was. I went to Church as often as I could manage to in the mornings, and all too often the Host I received at Communion was the Host that had been broken at the altar. In that broken Host I saw God's invitation.

If this is union with the suffering Christ, it hurts too much! I cried. *Heal us and help us, Lord!*

The words of the psalms, sung so glibly before, took on special meaning to me now; their promises fed my heart:

***

"You shall cross the barren desert,
But you shall not die of thirst,
You shall wander far in safety
Though you do not know the way..."

***

Shall we be safe, Lord?

***

"If you pass through raging waters
In the sea you shall not drown.
If you walk amid the burning flames,
You will not be harmed.
If you stand before the power of hell
And death is at your side,
Know that I am with you through it all."

***

Are you with us, Lord, even in this? And with tearful defiance I sang the
words:

***

"Blessed are your poor
For the kingdom shall be theirs.
Blest are you that weep and mourn
For one day you shall laugh!"

To laugh! Oh, to laugh again! I soaked myself in the Divine promises.
It was all I had. Nothing else on earth was strong enough to temper my
pain. We had somehow blundered into, and were caught, and trapped, it
seemed, in some cosmic battle between good and evil?

My mother had become convinced, through some of her own personal
experiences with her, that Trudy was demonically possessed. She was
outraged when Trudy had visited them, attempting to mobilize my own
parents in the battle against me. She flirted blatantly with my Dad. Her
words dripped of honey and venom, pleasing and plausible, excusing her
actions and asking Dad to be her mediator with us. She only wanted peace,
she protested. Dad was flattered. He agreed. She told him, simpering with
pleasure and looking him straight in the eye, that she had just cleared this
idea with her lawyer that very day. Mom was dubious. She immediately
phoned the lawyer–and found that he was away on holiday. Caught in
her lie Trudy turned on my mother, changing instantaneously from the

reasonable, long suffering mother into an ominous being, radiant with hate.

"I will destroy you, too!" she hissed at her.

Was she possessed? I hesitate to use that word. But in her dark moods, her habitual brooding and jealousy, her demands for exclusive attention, her actions against us, she seemed to be working in collusion with evil. The words of St. Paul became alive in my life: "our battle is not with flesh and blood but with the powers and principalities of darkness". Things, strange things, started to happen that appeared to bear this out. One year to the day that she had moved out, the basement flooded again from another failed hot water tank. On another occasion, when I opened the fridge, a flat bottomed serving bowl, sitting alone on the shelf, sailed inexplicably out into the room. Every appliance, everything we owned, began breaking down all at once, as if the object of a malevolent curse. More eerily, on several occasions Curt returned from work and found the house icy cold. Checking the heating, and on other occasions the air conditioning, he found nothing amiss. The cold would arrive suddenly in a freezing avalanche, last for ten minutes or a half hour and disappear as suddenly as it had appeared. But on several other occasions in midwinter we were startled when the house was suddenly filled with the lovely, sweet scent of unseen, unknown, flowers. The mushrooms, of course, continued to grow, but their appearance had spaced out to coincide with religious feasts and events of particular stress. They began to have a negative connotation to me, because, when I would see a new batch appearing I would wince, knowing that their appearance heralded a new crisis.

One of the most hurtful things to me, more diabolical in some ways than some of the supernatural phenomena, was the desertion of our friends. Our problems were so heavy, so oppressive, so never ending, that people stopped dropping by, stopped returning phone calls, afraid of what they might hear. Some told me openly that they did not want to become involved. They neither wanted to hear our troubles nor be in a position to make a judgment or take sides. One friend, Monica, whose friendship I had cherished, and whom I had helped during her own family troubles, became particularly remote. She had experienced irrational, hateful splits within her own family, and she herself had been victimized by misinformation and rash judgments. She used to visit me often in tears and despair, and

I would listen to her and try to comfort her. Now I looked to her for understanding, but she had withdrawn light years away, hidden beneath the veneer of a distant smile. I had been a nun, a respected person, a scholar, a professional, a mother, someone that mattered. Now I was a leper, something unclean, despised, forgotten, to be avoided, in a world that had gone on without me. My desolation and alienation were overwhelming. I was one of the untouchables of India, the colored people of apartheid, a convict, an outcast. Where was my community for me?

Like a match struck in a darkened room, a memorable light flickered briefly into my darkness one day at Mass. Through my swollen eyes I looked up to see a different priest assisting at the altar. With a start, and mounting excitement, I realized it was Father James Daley, the professor from the University of Alberta who had nicknamed me 'St. John'. The last time I had seen him was twenty years ago when I was still wearing a religious Habit. In the crowd of four hundred worshippers he could not see me, of course, and chances were, if he did see me, he would not know me. I stood in his line, nevertheless, to receive the Eucharist from Him. As I stepped in front of him he stopped abruptly in surprise and looked at me with misty eyes.

"I never thought I'd see you again this side of the Kingdom of God!" he said.

His heartfelt words sent a quiver of relief and joy through me, like rain falling on parched ground. Can it be that I still mattered, that I was still remembered? Perhaps I was not an alien upon this earth, but still connected to a wider community, knit into the mysterious web of a Father's Love.

Yet, I walked out of the church into a world in which my life had the significance of a used razor, mere throw away goods, refuse. Trudy built on this with her constant agitating, bad mouthing us within the community, spreading rumors, cultivating sympathy, poisoning Curt's business relationships. The libelous allegations took their toll. Curt was losing work because of her mouth. But she did not stop there. One day Curt was visited by the sheriff at his office. She had obtained a court order to seize his business.

There was nothing monetary for her to gain by seizing our business, and she must have known that. Thanks to her machinations the business had been run virtually into the ground, and its few assets were more than counterbalanced by a mountain of debt. But it was Curt's baby and our livelihood, poor though it was. And it was her crowning achievement to deprive us of everything, pursuing us to the end. Our personal survival on all levels, physical, psychological, and spiritual had become our daily nightmare. As business owners we were not entitled to unemployment insurance, and there was nothing left for us.

The court demanded to see the books. When it gradually became evident that the liabilities exceeded the assets, and Trudy would be inheriting our debts, her interest in the business fizzled out quickly.

There was a bit of a lull as we waited the months for our appeal to be heard. I hugged those relatively calm days to me like treasures. I determined to use these days of early April, as spring transformed the dross of winter with awakening fragrances from the hills, and fresh hope and exuberance filled the air, to restore to my children some sense of normalcy. Their marks in school had plummeted and they were being robbed of the joy of childhood. The consuming nature of our court battles could not absolve us, I realized, from the duties and challenges of parenthood. With tenacity we went through the motions of our usual family customs and celebrations.

Today we were making Easter bread, just as my Grandmother had done so many years ago in my own childhood, those ornate feathery yellow loaves I remembered, lighter than clouds. The sun streamed in the window bathing us in a yeasty peace. Kelli, Christian and Angel sat at the table forming braids and symbols to decorate the bread, each according to their own level of expertise. Erica was playing on the floor, singing to herself, lost in a toddler's self enclosed world. Justin had been over at his friend's house and was still not home.

"Justin, is that you?"

He must not have heard me, because he went straight up to his room.

We continued on with our work, knowing that no one in our house stayed away from the kitchen for long.

The doorbell rang. A tall barrel-chested policeman stood there.

"Have you a son named Justin?"

"Yes." I was flooded with consternation.

"I would like to speak to him."

I called Justin, my heart in my mouth. Justin came down, staring at the floor, a thin, short child-man with fine features and a bushy head of hair.

"You are under arrest," the officer said. "You will have to come with me."

I felt a scream rising in my throat. "What is going on? Justin?"

"Your son has been accused of assaulting another juvenile with a bicycle chain."

"What? What happened, Justin?"

Justin's face was dead, despairing. "Don't worry about it, Mom. I'll handle it." Justin was struggling to be brave, to be a man, but there was trauma in his eyes. I knew that he was afraid to load still more on my shoulders.

I felt ripped open when the officer took Justin away. I did not know it was possible for a heart to feel so much anguish.

I waited interminably, scarcely breathing, waiting for Justin to be brought home. His shoulders were sunken under a great weight when he walked in the door.

"Tell me," I asked softly, holding his shoulders.

Justin sank down on the couch. "You remember the day you answered the phone and some guy swore at you? He was one of the jerks from Okanagan Falls who have been phoning me and threatening me."

"Why, Justin?"

"I don't know. They are just a bunch of bullies. Their idea of a good time is to go and vandalize a school. I don't know them well. Martin's folks and their folks are friends."

"So, what happened?"

"They came to Martin's house while I was there. It was okay while we were all in the house, but when I went outside to leave, they followed me. Jake, one of the guys tried to kick me in the groin, and the other punched me. I grabbed a bicycle chain that was lying on the driveway and swung it."

I caught my breath. "How bad?"

"Cut him on the forehead, above the eye. We took him to the hospital for stitches. The nurse called the cops. Their Dad wants to press charges." Tears started flowing down Justin's cheeks.

Angel had walked up, silently. "Those guys are creeps, Mom. I've heard lots of stories about them from Martin's sister. They are always in trouble."

I phoned the police officer. He was off for the next three days. How could I wait that long with this burden on my heart? I phoned Ed.

"Leave it with me," he said.

I was beside myself. As I sat, meditating, praying, it occurred to me that this must be what Mary went through when her son Jesus was arrested and unjustly condemned. It threw a whole new light on the story I had heard so many times.

Ed, meanwhile, was having a good chat with the boys' father. However much the father was aware of his sons' activities, he came out of that talk much better educated. He decided it was in his family's best interests to drop the charges.

Boundless relief and thanksgiving filled my heart. We had survived for one more day.

Through everything, I still managed to fulfill a commitment to teach a religion class at the Church, along with Danylo Tims, Monica's husband. Now I needed to talk to someone, to hear a kind word, to get some vestige of encouragement. I decided to approach Danylo.

"How are you," he mumbled a cursory greeting rushing by me.

I stood stock still. "I'm hurting," I said, in such a way that he had to turn his head. "I need to talk."

He looked uncertain for a second. "Come here," he said abruptly, leading me around the corner to a quiet room. "What's going on?" he asked grimly.

"She wants everything, Danylo. We're breaking apart. Our family is collapsing. She is trying to get our house, our possessions. She's sent the sheriff to seize Curt's business. Everything. She makes no secret of the fact that she wants us out on the street."

"Give it to her then," Danylo said icily.

I looked up at him in disbelief, bitten by the wintry blast of his voice, locked out by the gray steel of his eyes. Is there no end to this horror? Does she speak now through you, my friend?

"How can you say that?" I faltered. "You think I should put five children on the street?"

"You are a Christian are you not? If someone asks half of your cloak, give him the whole...."

"But she's not in need," I cried in utter desolation.

Who was this stranger who had gone by the name of friend? Can this be the same man who sat in my living room two years ago and told me, "Johanna, you are the warmest, most loving person I have ever known." Have you now no glimmer of compassion, no light, no warmth for me?

Why?

Have you, foolishly, put me on a pedestal, and have I let you down? I am not an icon for your idealism. You knew me in days of strength, but now I am a wounded person, besieged by hell. Have you no kind word for me? If not for me, for the Christ suffering in me?

What do you want of me? In your idealism, have you yourself given everything to the poor? Am I called to sacrifice my family to her vindictiveness? Is this a Christian thing to do? And even if I could do this, Curt would never do it. His volcanic rage is my greatest burden, my most awful nightmare.

I stared at him in silence, and he rebuffed my gaze.

"Think about it," he said.

Think about it? What else have I been thinking about these past twenty months? In the middle of the night I awake and cannot sleep, imprisoned always in the dark streets of my thoughts. This is a bloodless death, every day renewed. Except for the welfare of my children and husband I would welcome death. With Job I cry out to you: "Have pity on me, at least you, my friend, for the Hand of the Lord has touched me!" Only, it is not the Hand of the Lord, but the claw of Satan who has scratched me with his wrath. Oh, I am not innocent, surely; my soul has walked in his domain. Is this, O Lord, my expiation? And yet, You have promised, "The bruised reed I will not break."

But why have you, my friend, drunk her poison? Have you no better beverage for your thirst?

I looked at him hopelessly. He turned on his heel and walked away.

To whom shall I go, Lord?

Are You here? Have you gone from me, too? It broke my heart yesterday when Kelli said to me in her thin, little girl voice, "We have prayed so much, Mommy. God will surely hear us!" If You do not answer, her faith will be destroyed!.

Today in Church, in this early morning, I look at the altar and struggle to pray. The priest begins the Mass. He leans over and kisses the altar of sacrifice. We ask forgiveness. We listen to the Word. We ask that our sacrifices be joined to the great Sacrifice. My eyes are drawn to the slanting windows behind the altar where strings of power lines are joined to a pole holding a transformer. Blackbirds cover the entire length of the power line, facing me, as if they too had come to pray. The priest begins the words of consecration and the birds begin to shake their wings and tail feathers.

"This is My Body.... This is My Blood of the new and eternal covenant which is being shed for you...."

The priest lifts the chalice, and in one motion the birds sweep towards the window as if they too would drink from the chalice of Life. I am fascinated.

The next day, and the next, I watch for the birds and they are always there. When the priest utters the words of consecration they become excited, or swoop down to the window. Do they, who have attended no great universities, know more than we know?

On the fifth day there is a difference. In the midst of all the dark colored birds there is one only who is snowy white. Today again they venerate the coming of the Lord among us, and the snowy white bird leads them down to the window. After this day, they come no more. But I am satisfied.

Ed phones the next day. Though he had prepared the documents for the court to say we would be representing ourselves, he wants to make a suggestion. He has taken it upon himself to talk to some lawyers from other firms, and he advises us, if there is any way we can manage it, we should be seen by two separate lawyers. He gives us their names. He feels this is the way to go from now on. My heart sinks. *Two new lawyers? Double the expense? Starting from square one with them? Extra money while they familiarize themselves with our case?* I tell Curt. *Yet how can we hope to go it alone through the legal minefields? We must have help.*

Gary Smith looks across his desk at me shrewdly, measuring me with his eyes. I tell him my story and can feel his skepticism. He has heard a lot of stories. I am just another face. He doesn't promise me anything, but he seems sharp and tough; a Kojak with hair. He tells me that the strategy for our appeal will focus on separating Curt's defense from my own.

"You have never signed anything. You have never had any agreement with her. There is no reason why you should have been named in this suit."

"That's odd. I never thought of it that way. I guess, being married, our joys and our sorrows have always been joined together as one. But you are right. I have never had any monetary relationship with her."

The Court of Appeal agreed. In a unanimous decision they agreed that the honorable Judge had erred in including me in the suit. They ordered that Trudy recompense me for the $13,000 it had cost me to mount my defense. It dismissed her cross appeal. In a two to one decision however, the court upheld the judgment against Curt, and did not allow the entry of our new evidence.

On the day we received this judgment, Trudy wasted no time. Before the afternoon was over she had again dispatched a sheriff to demand the immediate sale of the house so that the judgment in her favor could be executed. But now she had a big obstacle in her path. Me. She could no longer order me to do anything. And I was not about to accede to her demand to sell the house, because I was joint owner and tenant of it. Gary Smith warned me, however, that she had several avenues to take, and could eventually force me out. In the meantime we had the weight of the counterclaim to defer execution, as well as the rights of the children to live in the house until age fifteen. But there was small victory in all of this. She would leave us no rest. She ignored the lawyers continuing demands for discovery of documents leading to the counterclaim. She seemed to flaunt the law and get away with it. And in the meantime she kept us sitting on edge and bled us financially. At several points the lawyers made a bid for an out of court settlement, but she would have none of it. Or, in one case, in a supercilious show of good will, she made demands that were clearly impossible.

Curt consulted a bankruptcy lawyer. We felt this was the only club we had. The lawyer made the point, that given all our debts, if she pushed us in this direction she would gross almost nothing. But that did not deter her. She continued to harass Curt. She had always wanted a hatchet man. Now the law was her toy. No matter that she pleaded poverty and the only payoff she could expect was revenge. It was enough. That was what she wanted.

I felt constantly ill. The continuing phone calls through the night did not allow us to sleep. Fear plagued our days. Someone came in through the second story window of the apartment during a birthday sleepover, while the children huddled in the bathroom in terror. We saw a yellow truck with a ladder driving away. How could we give our children a normal existence when life was like a war zone? How could I tell them not to hate in response to this ongoing hate? We were up against a wall. There was no way out. After two years in the courts, no end was in sight. And nothing we could do would wipe out the judgment against Curt.

I was swimming in my usual pond of despondency the day Pat Frazer phoned. A friend from a long way back, she had decided to check up on me. After I told her the story she asked me, "Have you thought of going for prayer?"

"Prayer? That's all we've done, Pat. That is all we can do. I look at the miracles God has sprinkled along our way to assure us of His care. But so far this looks like a victory for evil. There just is no human solution for it," I sobbed.

"What about prayers for healing? Or an exorcism?"

"Funny you should say that. My mother is convinced that Trudy is possessed."

"Well... I'll give Fr. Don a call. Shall we do it at my house?"

The prayer session was set up, and I was rushing around getting ready to leave when the phone rang.

"Hi! Father Bernie here. I've been having this strong feeling that I should give you a call."

I did a lightning recap. I hadn't heard from Father Bernie for years. "And so I am just out the door now to go for prayers of healing and a possible exorcism."

"Yes, from what you've told me the demons seem to have been playing hardball with you. Did you know that I am the designated exorcist for the diocese of Calgary?"

I caught my breath. "Then, please help," I begged.

I could feel the comforting smile in the voice of my old friend from Cursillo days, a man who looked like a latter day John the Baptist with his wild dark beard and disheveled clothes.

"Go, and be at peace," he said.

Father Don was a little disconcerted when I told him I would like him to say some prayers of exorcism. He protested that he was not the priest designated in our area for exorcisms–this was a long and formal process.

But, somehow, he happened to have some prayers with him whose deep and moving words called on the Christ of Calvary to break the hold of the spirits of darkness within our lives. Then he went on to pray for the healing of my husband and our family. This was on a Thursday night.

On the following Monday night there was a loud pounding on our door. As always, I recoiled in fear when someone came to the door. It was pitch dark, and this did not help my churning stomach.

I tiptoed quietly into the bathroom and opened the window a crack to see who it was. Our house was like a fortress with all the dead bolts my father had installed. But I was still afraid. There are no dead bolts to protect the heart.

To my amazement, Danylo stood outside.

"Can I come in?" he asked, with a trace of his old country accent. "Is Curt here too?"

"Listen," he said earnestly, once we were sitting at our table. "This thing is tearing our community apart. Something has to be done. Too many people are hurting."

We looked at him bleakly. "What do you think we've been trying to do for over two years? She won't let it stop! We've tried every avenue we know. We're up against an unassailable wall."

"I think if I talked to her we could come to some agreement."

Curt began to scoff. I grabbed his arm. "No, don't act like that," I remonstrated with him. I turned to Danylo. "I would be willing to try anything. I agree with you that this has got to stop!"

Curt was unconvinced he could help.

"I don't know what Danylo has in mind, but let him try," I begged. "It can't hurt, and maybe it could be the miracle we've been praying for,"

Curt shrugged.

"Go, then, talk to her. Do what you can," I implored him.

"What if she asks for money?" Danylo asked.

"We have none."

"Could you get a mortgage?"

"Not with the Lis Pendens she has on our title. She would have to remove that first. It is also doubtful that we could get a mortgage because our income is so low."

"I'll see what I can do," and Danylo disappeared into the night.

I remembered how much Trudy had liked Danylo and I wondered if I dare hope. He was the only one I knew who could out charm her, and she lapped it up like a kitten drinking milk. I sat on the edge of my couch, waiting, praying.

In about two hours, Danylo returned. "I've got it!" he said triumphantly. "But you will have to come up with some money. She suggested $55,000. She has agreed to remove the Lis Pendens so you can try to get a mortgage."

"That's too high," I said, dejected. "Don't forget that we have many thousands of dollars in lawyer's bills to pay as well. The lawyers will not discharge this thing until they are paid out. And there is the $13,000 in lawyer's fees of mine that the appeal court ordered her to pay, but of which she has not paid one cent."

"I will return to her with a proposal of $35,000 if you will throw in your lawyer's fees as well. I know that issue particularly galls her."

Curt was still grumping. "You realize," he said, "that by rights we do not owe her a cent."

I leaned over and rubbed Curt's arm. "Don't let us blow a chance to settle this." I begged. "I can't stand any more of this!"

Curt nodded slowly. "How do we know she won't double cross us like the last time?"

"The lawyers will make it air tight."

The next week was occupied in working through the legalities. As I feared, the bank would not consider us for a mortgage, even considering the value of our house. Just as it looked like things were slipping away again, another lawyer friend phoned me and offered his help to try to come up with something for us. He did. It was a non-conventional mortgage at a less attractive rate, but it was the key to the end of our nightmare. We took it.

It was over. Just like that.

I walked outside with what seemed like a new body. I ran my hand along the rough bricks of our home, feeling solidity again. I lifted my face to the warmth of the sun and heard the shrieks of children at play. I smiled at the lazy gyrations of our cat, rolling and stretching on the warm cement. Our cherry tree was radiant in bloom, dazzling in the sun, a sea of white blossoms. In my heart I had discovered Easter.

CHAPTER 23

Silly conversation drifted back and forth between the family room, where Kelli was studying biology, and the kitchen, where I was preparing a barbecue. Angel was toiling away, creating chocolate chunk cookies.

"Imagine! The giant earthworm of Australia is more than two meters long. Yuck!" Kelli announced to no one in particular.

"Christian," I remonstrated with my twelve year old fisherman, "you are going to have to be careful where you dig up your worms in future. The garden is all planted now, even if not much is showing yet."

"Okay, Mom," Christian was studying the fridge. "When are the cookies going to be ready?" he demanded of his sister.

I sighed. If Christian followed in Justin's footsteps, I would have to put a bed in the fridge so he could rest between eating.

"The way you like food," I suggested to Christian, "you had better learn to garden so that you can feed yourself when you grow up."

"Nah, that won't be necessary," Christian declared loftily.

"Oh?" I said, cocking my eyebrow at him. "And why not?"

"Because I'm going to marry a girl who likes gardening," replied my mischievous son.

"Did you know that the snail exudes a sticky protein filament like epoxy to glue himself to the sand?" Another bit of invaluable knowledge from our resident biologist.

"Just what I needed to know," Justin quipped sarcastically as his head joined Christian's in the fridge.

"Hey, as the guy who did his toilet training in Dad's slippers, I'd say you can use all the educational upgrading you can get!" Kelli taunted him.

Justin ignored the jibe. He had grabbed Christian, and holding him over his head like a torpedo, was racing headlong toward the family room where he would slam him onto the big floor pillows.

I shuddered. Normalcy: blessed, insane, normalcy. My eyes misted with the realization that my world had been given back to me. Relief! Blessed, most incredible relief! Our family was now on the road to recovery. With the inborn resiliency of children, they lost no time in putting the trauma behind them. My husband's face bore a new softness, and he looked on his family with fresh tenderness and appreciation. My spirit, besieged, battered, almost annihilated, breathed in like an asthmatic having a good day, grateful, so grateful, for every healthy breath. All the little things of life were profound luxuries to be enjoyed. With a sense of unspeakable deliverance I sank into a chair and felt my taut muscles releasing the terror of the past years. What a simple, undervalued pleasure, just to relax in a chair. Food, too, no longer filtered through me in a river of sickness. Now, instead, too much of it was sticking to my hips! I groaned as I looked at the bathroom scale.

But now, more than ever, I understood how fragile we are, and the utter insufficiency of this world to bring us lasting joy. How dependent we are on so many factors of health and good will and circumstances. I am grateful for today, but I want more! I want the God of Joy!

"Are you crying again?" three-year-old Erica looked up at me with concern.

"No, no," I hugged her silky head to me. "I'm not crying because I am sad. I'm crying because my heart is moved."

Startled, her blue eyes reached up to mine: "Your heart is moved?" she asked in alarm, "Where is it moved to?"

Her older siblings guffawed in glee.

"You'll have to learn," said Justin patting Erica on the head, as he reached for another cookie, "Mom was born with leaky plumbing. She breaks down every time she watches a sad movie."

"Yeah," added Kelli, "She cries if they open up a new Walmart."

I glared at them. While they were enjoying their joke with great zest, I grabbed the tray of cookies.

"Hey, Mom!" they wailed, chasing after me.

There was some truth in what the children were saying. Some call it the gift of tears; but the gift of tears has never been given the good press afforded the gift of tongues or the gift of prophecy. It has just been profoundly embarrassing.

But now these tears were healing tears; for myself, and for my family. These tears came to wash away sorrow and fear. Oh, the fear would never be completely erased, especially on the part of the children. Years later, when they were to marry they would keep their engagements secret and vehemently resist the suggestion that they put a wedding announcement in the newspaper. Even then they feared that their Oma would somehow see it and come back to destroy their happiness.

The way in which our experiences had burrowed into their unconscious was graphically illustrated by a repetitive dream that plagued Kelli.

In the dream Kelli saw the apartment as Trudy had left it, with the hanging wires, and the calendar with the thick black X. The family, brothers and sisters, had gone up to visit the echoing rooms with a sort of somber curiosity, suddenly having the freedom to explore what was out of bounds to them before. Poking into the walk-in closet that opened under the eaves, Kelli found that a loose board had been left against one wall. On moving the board she was astonished to see a steep stairwell that went down further than her eyes could see. In fascination, holding on to her brothers and sisters for support, she descended deeper and ever deeper into a place of eerie gloom. Finally, in the murk, in a flickering greenish light, she saw a throne, in a place she guessed was hell. On it, smirking, sat Trudy.

In a follow up dream, Trudy arrived at our front door with two small children in tow, a small blonde boy and an adorable tiny girl. The children were cowering and afraid, and each time either of them spoke or made a noise, Trudy would hit them. The little girl especially was the recipient of the cruelest, and most continuous blows. Kelli felt touched by the suffering eyes of the children and lashed out at Trudy. Trudy shook her fist in Kelli's face and dragged off the hapless children. Kelli found herself scratching and kicking, trying in vain to rescue the children. With a sickening feeling it came to her that the little boy was her Dad and the little girl was Eva, his sister.

My body, too, was still habituated to horror. I went downtown reluctantly, and only from necessity, when papers had to be signed or details taken care of at the lawyers' offices or at the bank. As the car would near the familiar intersection, and the courthouse would come into view, I would break out into a cold sweat and my stomach would heave in nausea. The threat was over but my body continued to respond like a dog too often kicked.

Lord, heal me. Love me into wholeness! I begged.

My psyche was still robed in dread. My sinews and reflexes were habituated to fear. When I went shopping at the Mall I was so sensitized to Trudy's presence that I would always know when she was there, and my knees would grow weak and I would feel faint and wobbly. I needn't have feared that she would acknowledge me in any way. She would raise her head haughtily, pretending she did not see me or the children, and march by us as if we were invisible. I would force myself to look at her. Something within me would not allow me to capitulate to her, to let her know how deeply she had invaded my existence. And I could not allow her to further rock the security of my children. They needed me to be strong, unafraid, someone they could lean on. So, although I was quaking, I composed my face and looked at her. Amidst the crowds milling about she could have been just another innocuous old lady, albeit attractively dressed in her hot pink tailored suit, immaculate white heels, gloves and purse, and her elegantly styled coiffure. But to me she was the embodiment of every fear I had ever known, of ultimate annihilation.

O Lord, my spirit cried above the busy mayhem of the bustling mall, *I am not yet healed. Love me into wholeness!*

Though my husband would continue to be swamped by debt until old age, I was grateful that she had relinquished her control over us, and that we could at last sleep again in peace. Had it been the prayers of exorcism that had broken down the impregnable wall? I felt I should show some good will for her compliance, for her signature on the legal papers that spelled an end to our nightmare and the beginning of a new peace. As Christmas approached I wrestled with myself, striving to muffle my repugnance, to find the higher road. I did not want myself or my family to be left poisoned by the residue of her hate. I wanted to acknowledge in some way that we were not bound by that hate, that we appreciated the fact that she had finally abandoned the witch hunt against us. I looked for the most neutral Christmas card I could find, one that would wish her well without being guilty of insincerity. It took a lot of searching. Then, I signed it simply from 'the family'. Two weeks later a letter arrived for me, with my name misspelled on the envelope. In it was our Christmas card, returned, with the cryptic message scrawled across its envelope: "I have no family."

Lord, love me into wholeness: it would continue to be my prayer.

Challenges continued. Angel began to recover from her bleeding ulcers, but the sharpness of her pain still spilled out in biting words and barbs. How can I soften the harshness in her soul? She has every right to be angry and hurt, but it is not right that her heart be contaminated by hate. I can only pray that God, who is everything good, will provide such a counterpoint of love into her life that the pains of these years will fall from her like autumn leaves in a kindly wind. The children had gone into our photo albums and removed and defaced her pictures. It was their way of trying to excoriate her from their lives. My husband tries to forget. Mostly he concentrates on his work, which is now increasing after the long recession, and he no longer speaks of her. But an inadvertent question by a stranger, or a chance remark, is enough to unleash an explosive torrent of bitterness.

"Because of her I have to work seven days a week, and every night, just to get out of debt. I have no life, and nothing to show for it. God help her if she ever tries to cross my threshold!"

"She signed an undertaking before the court that she would not."

"But if she did, I would turn her away, even if she was starving."

"Curt, for our own good, if not for hers, we must try to forgive her and leave her in God's hands. If she succeeds in making us hate, then she has won after all—and she has succeeded in destroying us."

"I don't hate her. I could care less about her. But what I am afraid of, is that God will somehow forgive her. And I tell you, if she goes to heaven, I don't want to go there." Curt's voice is razor sharp, like the cry of a wounded wolf.

I am stunned; sorrowful. I understand his feeling, of course, but it makes me shiver with fear for him. "Curt," I feel my way cautiously, "the way I'm handling it is by simply putting her, and my feelings, in the hands of God for Him to handle for now. We know that if she deserves the justice of God that she will not be able to escape by deceiving and manipulating that ultimate court. She cannot fool God. She will have no lawyer to defend her then. But, if God still finds some spark of love in her which He can fan, and because of this she is able to change, this will not be the Trudy you and I have known, but a creature renewed and re-created, and we will all be the richer for it."

Curt scowls. "I just ask God this, and I think He will not subject me to a temptation beyond my strength, that I never run into her. I cannot trust myself how I would react."

I bow my head. *Lord,* I whisper deep in my heart, *help us not to be tainted by the same bad blood. At least, help us to pray for her. May your will be done in her regard, whatever that may be. Why was it that she finally conceded the battle after stonewalling for two years? Was it the exorcism? Has your grace somehow touched her? I must leave the door open to the possibilities.* At least, my spirit tells me so. My emotions are still buried in the trenches.

"Curt," I said. "Do you remember what they told us at marriage encounter? Feelings are neither moral nor immoral. They simply ARE. Emotions alone aren't love. Emotions alone aren't hate. Love is a decision. Hate, too, is a decision. You don't have to be best buddies with your mother but.... "

Curt shouted, interrupting: "Don't call her that. I have no mother!"

I snapped. "Curt! If you persist in hating, you may end up being her roommate in hell!"

Not just now, but all our married life I have battled the artesian well of his anger, fed by the icy kiss of his early memories, which, even as a child, he recognized as evil. It must be that in the earliest days of innocence he had glimpsed a vision of the upright Adam, and he has always found this world thereafter a foreign and disappointing place.

Curt was angry now, but I knew he would think about it later. Like Jacob we all have our angels to fight before we can find that ladder up to the stars. My voice softened: "Think of it this way, Curt. Someday her shoulders will bend. Age must inevitably bow her head. She will lose control of her own life, and have then to bear the consequences of her chosen isolation from family. How many years has she got left? It cannot be many. And what will she have then? Her possessions will be cold comfort. They will not give her love, acceptance or youth. And one day her strident voice will be stilled by a power greater than she can withstand. She is the original straw man, Curt, more to be pitied than hated."

"But she has destroyed my life!"

"No, she hasn't! You still have a home and a family that loves you—these are lasting riches. But she—it is she who is destroying her own life. Remember Gustav and Marie?"

"Of course. Marie was Trudy's henchman."

"Not really. Marie is basically an upright person. She was just taken in by Trudy."

"Well, some friend she was. She wouldn't even talk to you. And there she was driving her to court all the time, helping her to move...."

"Now, listen! After these years of silence from her, I accidentally ended up at the same table with her at the Church tea last week. I was nervous, but as casually as I could I asked her, "How is Trudy these days?" In clipped tones she replied: "Strange, strange woman!" That was all. Someone volunteered the information later that there was a big falling out between them. Trudy turned on her for leaving her out of a family picture or something. Typical. But that's the sort of thing I mean. Given enough time Trudy's colors come through and step by step she will alienate herself from everyone. She will create her own hell. She doesn't need us to hate her. I don't think it is God Who damns us. I think we choose that road ourselves."

Curt was pensive. "I'm so tired," he said, hanging his head. I leaned over and held him close.

"The graffiti of our times is written upon our souls, Curt. We can't escape it. Our walls have all been dirtied and desecrated. But our Christ promised; "Though your sins be as scarlet they will be made whiter than snow." All we need to do is forgive—like we say in the prayer we recite daily—'Forgive us, Father, as we forgive those who trespass against us"? And, "in the measure you measure it will be measured unto you"? It also says, in the Book that you and I profess to believe in, that "the sufferings of this time are not worthy to be compared to the joy to come that will be revealed in us". We live in the womb of time, Curt, and aren't our trials just the labor pains of our birth into eternity?"

Erica trundled into the room. "Tell me a story," she demanded plaintively, tugging at my knees.

I looked at Curt.

"Yes, tell us a story," he said, smiling wanly.

I thought for a moment. Erica laid her head on my lap and lazily dangled a piece of wool in the face of a sleeping kitten. The cat's whiskers moved spasmodically until it sat bolt upright with the wool grasped firmly between its teeth and bounded out of the room. Re-energized, giggling and shrieking, Erica bolted after him.

"So much for the story," Curt grinned and shook his head.

"Not so. You asked for a story and a story you are going to get; a fairy tale! When I was growing up I read lots of fairy tales. I read them over and over."

Curt wrinkled his face.

"No, really, fairy tales are very important. They cross our cultural boundaries like an underground stream. I think they carry some down home basic truths about our existence. Imagination? I don't think so. Our fairy tales tell us who we are and what destiny we are called to." I pirouetted in front of him. "Because, you see, I am Cinderella. I am very poor–and growing old–and I am attired in rags, at least emotionally. The world around me is inhabited by wicked stepmothers and nasty stepsisters.... (It could be that my own disposition is not so hot either...!) But I have heard that there is a Divine and heavenly dance to be held, and some song in my heart tells me that I am called to go to this dance... Despite the fact that the world tells me I am unsuitable, lack finesse, fine garments, superior breeding. And so I formulate the wish–the impossible dream–only God knows why– that I might be called out of the drudgery and suffering of my position in life to this heavenly dance. In response to my wish–for all wishes are heard somewhere in the Kingdom of God–help comes. I am given what I was too poor to have on my own. I am adorned like a princess; because only a princess can sit at the table of the Prince. And the Prince represents–and IS–every dream of love we have ever dared to dream. And more!

I am also the Sleeping Beauty. I was not always sleeping, but the power of evil made me sleep, missing out on the greatness of the life to which I was called. But a Prince comes–he has sought me long and hard–he has had to fight to get to me, to battle brambles and thorns and suffering. Because love is worth any price. He comes armed with only the power of love and He gives me a kiss. And I awaken to the glory of Life.

My name is Snow White. I was created beautiful, but evil has poisoned me–the evil of pride and jealousy, bad thoughts, bad habits. The violence and depravity of the world continue to poison the apple I have eaten. But Love still exists, and because that is what Love is–unmerited sacrifice, unmerited giving–Love comes to seek me out and awaken me from my stupor to new possibilities, new life. My Prince always comes, the Prince of Peace; over tall mountains, deserts, paying every price, every sacrifice. My Prince is not a fairy tale."

Curt was staring at me with a bemused, but enigmatic look.

"God is our hope," I whispered to Curt earnestly. "Love will be our victory."

Curt still said nothing, so I continued, "We love to sit in an armchair and read a book, to immerse ourselves in the trials and conflicts of some hero or heroine. We read because we like to share the vicarious thrill of overcoming obstacles and dark forces, of surviving against the odds, of solving mysteries, of finding love. Right now you and I are living out our own novel, Curt; the only novel we will ever be called upon to write. We, too, must solve the great mysteries of life, face the mystery of suffering, the mystery of evil, the mystery of God. You and I are invited to be heroes and heroines. Real ones. Are we going to make it?"

We were not the only ones, at that moment, who were working intensively on our novel. During the sultry days of that August my mother was called to write the closing chapters of her life.

Twenty months earlier my mother had found herself in combat with the dragon of cancer, with the nemesis she had defeated so many years before. This time her colon was blocked by a tumor, and her body erupted in pain. The ambulance screamed as it rushed her to the hospital. Her tumor was removed in a shiny, efficient operating room, and the doctor assured us that she would be fine. The operation was a success. During Mom's convalescence we began surreptitiously to prepare for Mom and Dad's fiftieth wedding anniversary. Unknown to them, we invited relatives and friends from all over Canada for the long May weekend. We dug out Dad's old air force uniform, and found the pale blue dress with the white collar in which Mom had been married. With the young grandchildren in the starring roles, we reenacted the story of the love that had become the foundation of a far flung family. It would be the best and the last anniversary we were to celebrate together.

As the cool winds of late October stole away the last vestiges of summer, Mom began to experience some foreboding stomach distress. "The flu," she said; "a stubborn flu."

I still hear her voice , with its bell like clarity, when she phoned me that day, ten days before Christmas.

"Johanna, I have bad news. The cancer... I am afraid it is back. I have tumors in four or five places in my liver. It is terminal." Her words were solemn, tentative, resigned. "It's funny, but it passed through my mind when we made perogies two weeks ago that it might be for the last time."

For the last time! For the last time! That refrain kept playing through my mind. Everything was for the last time. I drove past the Bay where Mom and Dad had lunch on their shopping days, and I thought; *for the last time.* I picked her some saskatoons, and brought her a bouquet of lilacs for Mother's day—*for the last time.* One of her recipes that she wrote out for me bears the notation *'the last recipe from Mom'.* Tremulous and in awe the whole family gathered for Christmas, nervous and profoundly moved, knowing that Mom was on the threshold of her great Eternal Christmas.

I'll be an orphan! I told myself, feeling surprised that at age fifty I still had the vulnerability of a child.

Mom had never wanted to die suddenly. She said she wanted time for all her goodbyes, time to put her affairs in order, to finish her tasks. She was getting her wish. Of course, she did all she could to prolong her life, taking various remedies, clinging to hope, making a virtue of the normal routine of life, participating fully. We watched her, and her days were measured out like the steps of a dance.

It was the prayer of everyone who knew her, our common urgent prayer, that Mom not have to go through pain. She had suffered enough pain, both physical and mental, in her lifetime and we prayed that God would spare her.

But, on the evening of December twenty-third, Mom was gripped by such an intolerable pain that she didn't know what to do with herself. Nothing she took did anything to mitigate her agony, and she rocked back and forth and paced, all in vain, striving to say the rosary that had been such a comfort to her through so many earlier nights of pain and sleeplessness. Nothing helped. Finally, her panic stricken eyes fell on a bottle of water on the mantle-piece that an aunt had brought her from Lourdes, the apparition site of Mary and the place of miraculous healings. She struggled with the lid, and drank half the bottle. Her pain began to recede gently, like a wave returning to the sea. From that time to the time of her death eight months later, although she grew weaker and was occasionally nauseous, she had no need of pain medication. Only once do I recall her asking for a single dose of morphine.

She remained at home, as Dad and she had wished: there was nothing that they could do for her in the hospital anyway. In those last months I watched Dad's brusqueness, his roughness, give way to gentleness and tenderness as he became her arms, her legs, and her comfort. This finally was Dad's university and his devotion to her became the climax of their married life. It was not easy. As she lost mobility he was up with her often during the night, wrenching his back helping her to the commode, and on more than one occasion they fell, remaining in a heap together on the floor until the dawn.

Now the rays of the August sun filtered through the Boston fern, and the plant called 'the Crown of Thorns', and fell upon the leather couch where Mom lay, her pasty colored legs swollen and itchy from un-discharged fluid that her kidneys could no longer deal with. We rubbed her legs vigorously with a prescription ointment to help alleviate the itch and to stimulate circulation. Only the week before, Dad and I had struggled to put her in a wheelchair, then in and out of the car, a woman obviously dying, who still insisted we take her to the dentist to get her new dentures adjusted. Still, at the edge of death, the eternal woman!

Paradoxically, this time of dying became also a life giving time. My aunt Rose, who had dropped out of our family sixteen years before, afraid to face Dad after she had divorced his alcoholic brother, reappeared quietly in our time of need, with her much valued nursing skills. It was Rose that provided special medicated swabs to keep Mom's mouth moist, a sheepskin to make her more comfortable and to help prevent bedsores. She taught us how to move Mom, and instructed us to put a soft pillow between Mom's knees when we laid her on her side to ease pressure points. So many things we needed to know!

Mom spoke very little now. It cost too much effort. But two days before, with the end coming, amid a procession of visitors coming to say goodbye, she opened her tired eyes and they twinkled still with her characteristic wry humor:

"Who's next?" she quipped. "The Pope?"

Inside her spent body, that now hung around her like a useless rag, her spirit still shone. She was still 'Mom'. She had taught us how to live; now she was teaching us how to die.

"How long.... ?" we all wondered. Even the Doctor couldn't say. How much lower could she go? Her eyes were dull and yellowed now and she lay quietly without moving, drifting in and out of sleep, sometimes making strange droning noises.

Aunt Rose plumped up the pillows around her head and wiped off her brow. "I think I'll go home now for a couple of hours," she said. She turned to me briskly, "Come here and help me turn her before I go?"

As we pulled back the blankets to rearrange Mom, Rose suddenly pointed to Mom's back, where the skin had become mottled. She looked at me intently. "This is it," she murmured, "Her circulation is shutting down." She sat down again.

Someone went to call the other members of the family. I sat down, helplessly, praying, holding Mom's limp hand. Dad hovered anxiously. Rose leaned over her compassionately, stroking her forehead and caressing her hollow cheeks.

"It's hard to be born and it's hard to die, isn't it?" she asked her, searching her face for a reaction.

"Yesss," Mom's quiet voice sounded from deep in her throat.

"Do you have any pain?"

"Nooo," Mom's voice was barely audible.

I wondered, with apprehension and dread, if Mom would have the death rattle that nurses talk about. But her breathing was not labored. It just became sparser and sparser, quieter and quieter. Suddenly as I looked at her, though there had been no perceptible movement, no sound, no indication that I could put my finger on, everything had changed. Like a light that had fled this earth, her spirit had fled her ruined body. What was left was no longer her. *She is free now*, I sang in my heart, *and now forever young*. I could not begrudge her that. I had cried so many tears in the months leading up to this moment. Now there was no sorrow, only a breathless tranquility.

Two months after she died I had a dream, in which I came into the kitchen and found her sitting at my table as usual. Typically, for she had devoted the last years of her life simply and purely to being love, she was comforting my youngest daughter who was bent over in a chair crying. There was a soft light that surrounded her, and I, curious, fascinated, ever doubting, walked behind her chair to check if there was a ready explanation and source for the light. There was not. And as I continued to gaze at her peaceful loving face the light grew gradually brighter and brighter until she finally disappeared into the light.

Her presence hung, at first, like an invisible gossamer curtain in her home, and around us who were hers, encircling us still with continuing warmth. But now when my spirit reaches into the infinity of God to find her, I sense her presence as a fragrance next to my being–not a scent perceptible on the physical plain, but in some uncharted, unknown way, real. This is most curious, because, although my mother wore perfume on occasion, I never associated her with any perfume. And yet, her essence and being is expressed in this way, and from her tomb the fragrance of her heart embraces us still.

And there is also the mystery of the rose...a special gift from her to her still grieving husband. Dad had let the yard go to rack and ruin after she died. Two years later he picked up a shovel to remove a climbing rose that had died with Mom, and had been an anniversary gift Mom and Dad had given each other. To his surprise, he found a single leaf on the long barren stem, and so he let it be. It soon flourished again, and in amazement he called me one day to show me a single rose growing out of the heart of another rose.

CHAPTER 24: EPILOGUE

It was Erica's least favorite time of day.

"Hurry up, Erica! It's bedtime!"

"Just a sec, Mom."

"Get on your pajamas, please!"

"Can't find the bottoms. Just a sec, Mom."

"Erica, are you out of bed again?"

"I need another drink of water. Just a sec!"

"No more secs!" I bellowed at her in frustration.

Her older siblings howled. I looked at them in irritation. "What's so funny?"

"Mom," Angel squealed between giggles, "would you care to repeat what you just said?"

Sometimes it's hard for a mother to maintain her dignity.

Erica grabbed me imploringly by the arm, "Why do we have to go to bed anyway? Why do we have to sleep?"

"Because you need to grow, you need to rest...."

"I don't need to rest. I'm not even tired!" she protested vehemently.

"Well, I'm tired. And I don't want you cranky for the big trip."

As I burrowed my way into my own pillows, I wondered if I had really answered Erica's question. Why do we have to sleep? A legitimate question! Of course, our bodies need to repair and rejuvenate. But our minds never really stop—even in our sleep they play in the streets of our dreams, reliving, creating, musing, but always aware of our own existence. If sleep serves to rest the body, what service does it render the spirit? It is a tantalizing question. If we spend a third of our lives sleeping it must be for a reason. I roll over in bed in a tangle of sheets and wonder if the answer begins in what I have learned about myself? During the times in my life when '*I did it my way*', as Frank Sinatra used to sing, I always found myself dissatisfied and in the end, incomplete. A solo act didn't enable me to meet the terror of my yesterdays. It doesn't feed my eternal hunger.

Judging from the outside, most people would say that I have achieved all the goals that most humans scramble for: a beautiful home, an advanced education and profession, travel, and an intact and loving family. But it isn't enough. It isn't that I don't value those given to me to love, inextricably woven into my life as they are; my husband, family, friends, and companions on the road. They are part of the canvas of my life, my color, my singing. They are comfort, challenge, and the textbooks of my life. But they are as limited and floundering as I am. Like rivers we flow together, side by side, sometimes mingling, sometimes apart. Yet they are not my raison d'etre. They are not my source. They are not my destination.

When night comes and I lay down the playthings of the day, I surrender to another reality, another need. Has God, perhaps, imprinted in us the reflex to surrender, a plan for our spiritual passage, so that we might open our beings to His peace, recovering innocence in His loving arms?

Nature, too, calls us, after our beginning years, to give ourselves to another. Is surrender not implicit in our lovemaking, our fantasies, even in some perversions?

It strikes me that Napoleon and Alexander the Great, even as they chose the route of domination and power, had to lay down their heads, as we do, at the end of each day and surrender their egos to the need to sleep. They, too, were just creatures. How often have I unclenched the hand of my child, still gripping a toy, as sleep washes over him? Each night the Father also disengages us from our preoccupations, in recognition that we have another destiny, another calling. To be united, to answer that need for oneness with Another, there is need for a personal surrender. For by ourselves, we are less than the dust of the desert or a coyote's howl on a lonely moor.

I have found it to be so. *When I do not feel your presence, God of my spirit, everything on earth tastes flat and all color fades away. There is no music to lift my soul. Without You I have no wind for my sails and I sit helplessly, becalmed on my own Sargasso Sea, bereft without and within, as barren as sagebrush, trapped in a land of scorpions. Without You, trouble claims me, and I find no water for my thirst, nor has the earth a liniment for the ache in my spirit.*

I am empty.

In the darkness of my room, my heart resounds like an echoing cave. Memories creep into my mind of another cave of long ago. As a child I heard the Christmas story and was aghast that no one would give the weary couple a room so Love could come into the world. *I would have given Him a room!* I protested vigorously. But often in the years that came, my room was let to other guests, less worthy. And now, as a shaft of moonlight cuts a swathe across my wall, I understand that God can only dwell in us when we make space within ourselves.

My room is vacant, Lord, awaiting in hope that Life which is my beginning, and my everything.

I have read Your love letters in the winds, in the stars, on mountain peaks, in the solitude of my own garden. I have marveled at how the delicate snowdrop and tulip pierce through the heavy, frozen, lugubrious soil to emerge unsoiled and beautiful. How can things so weak escape their formidable prison of darkness? By what strength do their fragile stems reach through the dead leaves of a summer past to embrace life? Even so, do we. You give us Life.

Fill me, Lord, who have only you. Love me into wholeness. There is no wholeness outside of You.

The tranquil night is nudged out by a morning as clear as crystal, and a flurry of activity ensues as we prepare to leave on a very special trip, our first family holiday in fifteen years. An airline price war is enabling us to visit Justin, who is now teaching diving on the Cayman Islands.

We fasten our seatbelts. Seattle.... Detroit.... With the whir of modern travel we are in Miami and are scooped up above the clouds for the final junket. We fly over the lush greens, the bays and the coral reefs of Cuba, and the endless shimmering sea. We circle and descend. The airport is small, with a banana grove to one side. Coconut palms dot the landscape willy-nilly everywhere.

A large disgruntled Jamaican woman leads us to her taxi which looks like a prototype retired from the fleet of Rent a Wreck. We pant for air in the incredible heat.

"Oh, it's hot!" daughter Kelli begins a non stop monologue. "I have never been so hot in my whole life. Even in the sauna. I can't believe this heat. I feel like I'm sitting on a cooking element. Pass the barbecue sauce. Where is the air? This car has no air conditioning. This is like breathing chicken soup...."

By the time we disembark the taxi lady is grinning foolishly. I have the feeling that we have provided the fodder for her dinner table conversation that evening.

We rent a red jeep and maneuver gingerly, unaccustomed to driving on the left hand side of the street. Our son leads us through Georgetown, the banking Mecca of Grand Cayman. Quaint and pretty green and white colonial buildings flank the shoreline and jostle with the sophisticated modern architecture inland. In no time we have circled half of the small island, stopping to visit the turtle farm and a place merchandized as Hell, due to its strange and desolate, jagged, black rock formations. We have our pictures taken and send postcards from Hell. Later, as we eat turtle soup on a patio outside a grass hut cafe, tiny tropical fruits, unfamiliar, but resembling litchi nuts, drop on our heads from the trees above, and splash into our soup. Erica is enthralled with the pleasant sweet fruit and scurries around gathering it all up.

But the focus and the highlight of the trip takes us down by the rocky shoreline, past a clapboard clubhouse, where Justin's special pride awaits us. Looming above the water, gleaming and white, its lower deck hung on all sides with scuba gear and littered with dozens of tanks of air, the 'Cayman Princess' lolls idly on the gentle surf. Tomorrow, he tells us, he will take us out in this boat which he captains. But first he must school us in scuba diving in the safety of the hotel pool.

We pass our lessons, and for our reward we lean into the spray stinging our faces as the boat rumbles into full power. We take turns in the captain's chair, voyeurs of Justin's world, until the slow putting of the engine signals us to don our ungainly gear. At the ramp, Justin demonstrates how to roll backwards into the warm turquoise waters of the Caribbean. The bubbly clear world that we drift down into is a wildly colored universe of incredible beauty. An artist's brush has gone crazy here, with neon and fluorescent fish of every hue and design gliding by between undulating purple flora. Some of the fish look like cartoon figures, with markings on them that appear to be the work of mischievous angels. It is a world that stretches the imagination, a harmony of motion and color whose very silence becomes music.

"Tomorrow," Justin promises us, "I will take you to Sting Ray City. It is a shallow sandbar off the coast of Grand Cayman, where the sting rays will eat out of our hands."

We look at each other apprehensively.

"Aren't sting rays dangerous? I've seen programs on TV about them and their tails are lethal!"

"Don't worry. We've never had any trouble with them. Five or six ships a day stop to feed them, so they are accustomed to being hand fed and are very friendly."

Still, striking up a relationship with a sting ray has never been high on my list of priorities.

But exhilarated and quivering, the next day we find ourselves standing in shoulder deep water, with about thirty sting rays making a bee line straight for us. It appears we are the only action around. A large impressive yacht and a barge are just departing. My stomach tightens. I edge behind Curt. Up to five feet in diameter, they glide toward us looking like eerie black space craft, as flat as dinner plates, with ominous hooded beady eyes and tails that look like long horse whips. Everything about them is other worldly, sinister, and threatening. I move in the direction of half a dozen baby sting rays who are hugging the sea floor, making no attempt to approach us. Later Justin informs me that these small ones are not babies: they are the males!

Justin grins behind his mask, the smile of experience. He gesticulates toward us to follow his lead, and my brave husband holds out some pieces of chopped squid in his hand. A huge sting ray, followed by several more, bear down on him, and as the first one approaches it lifts one side of its body to reveal a white underside with a toothless, dolphin-like mouth, as mild and inoffensive underneath as it is foreboding from on top. Still, I keep a nervous eye on the deadly tails after which they are named.

We needn't have worried. The sting rays have only one concern, and that is the free lunch, and they are generous in their appreciation, lifting up one side to rub against us.

"Johanna," my husband calls me enthusiastically. "Feel their undersides. They are as soft as down!"

Erica holds on to my hand, transported with joy, bobbing up and down in excitement. She reaches out her other hand gingerly, but when a friendly sting ray rubs half its body against her to give her a cuddle, she loses it. She shoots like a torpedo over to her father, scrambling up monkey fashion to sit on top of his head. Her screaming echoes and resounds across the waters in continuous volleys until we return to the boat. I feel a bond of solidarity with her as I stand riveted like a wooden statue while another sting ray offers me its gesture of grateful endearment.

The following day we are invited for supper aboard a luxuriously refurbished trimaran, which is making its inaugural voyage. It is a graceful vessel, with sweeping lines, whose sails spear the sky with majestic authority. All day we cruise lazily, eating and drinking, and as the early tropical night falls like a golden curtain, the gentle sea stretches out to the horizon gleaming like an amber plate. Reflecting on its still surface is the boundless immensity of the sky, a fiery temple of glory. A hush of awe falls over the guests.

"It doesn't get any better than this!" exclaims a husky young man stretched out on the deck, clutching his beer.

Oh yes it does! I murmur quietly within.

This wonderful family opportunity is pure refreshment for senses and emotions stripped bare, yet the tranquility of this tropical night points beyond our sight to the Author of this Beauty. My hungering spirit tiptoes into His presence, and reaches gratefully like a child for her Father's caress. I know now that He has never left me, even in the greatest darkness. My heart overflows and speaks with boldness, familiarity and trust. I, who have been tormented by fear, racked by inadequacy, obscured by sin, am at peace. *Who is this new, forthright person that I am?*

Then one night my house of cards collapses. How inappropriate all this is, some voice mocks. You are just putting it on. It is all imaginary; wishful thinking, inane and insane, a boundless delusion. *How can I, a creature cowed by fear, riddled with weakness, tilting with shadows in the safety of my room, how can I pretend to a courage I do not have? How can I presume to have formed a friendship with He Who is infinitely beyond me? In actuality, my love has the endurance and strength of a flickering candle in a Northern wind. Where will my rejoicing and my confidence be when I actually stand before His power, He Who willed the energy of a billion suns, Who fashioned the quark and stands astride the mountain as if they were grains of sand? Where will my bravado be then; I who am tongue tied before mere men? My tongue will dry like cork and lie inert. I will be paralyzed like a novice actress looking out on a hostile crowd. Naked and ashamed, I will shrink before that high court.*

I slink away to my empty corner, desolate and alone. Days pass and take me prisoner, chaining me to nothingness.

I know, of course, that God is Love. But what measure of love have I to give in return? His Love is of a different order of being. "As far as the heavens are above earth, so far are my ways above your ways." His words mock me.

But, yet again, if I cannot talk to Him, to whom can I talk? It is He who gave me voice. If I cannot yearn for Him, for whom can I yearn? If I am born to surrender, to whom can I surrender this flickering flame? To no one I know. And if He cannot accept me, who will? Does it even matter?

A suffocating oppression hangs over me, like a thick coating of tar, stifling and demoralizing me. The weeks reduce me to psychological pulp, leaving me without intelligence, feeling, or light. Again I am the little girl vainly trying to buy a dog license, the child at the birthday party who can not get near the table with the puzzle, the teenager whose loves are swallowed up into disappointment. I am all the wars I have fought and lost.

I meander through endless hours, life hanging drably on my shoulders like a shapeless worn out coat. Lent arrives again. Not a time for a lot of jolly ho ho ho's anyway. The children, restless and resurgent, take hold of the day. They have put behind them their flame of gratitude for the crisis resolved, and are heavy into some petty nit picking, flicking aggravations around the van like a desultory game of ball. I scold them. Curt threatens to stop the van and make them walk.

"I didn't do anything."

"Yes, you did!"

"No, I didn't. She did."

We arrive at Church drained and dissipated. This would be another routine Mass. I have noticed since I was a child, that if any day was likely to go wrong, if tempers were to flare and discontent be aired, it would be on a Sunday. It seems that the powers of darkness, always interested in high profile targets, hold reveille each Sunday morning, joining forces to dim the light of the Lord's Day. Despite this, we do muster our forces and attend Church faithfully. For as far as I know, God has not rescinded His commandment to "keep holy the Lord's Day", and since I cannot pretend to be in His league I cannot quibble with His reasons. Besides, it only stands to reason that if we promise our human loves to be faithful in good days and in bad, this same faithfulness and commitment is necessary in our relationship with God. If we want His presence, we must give Him ours! I also believe, despite the dryness of my spirit, that the mystery of God is present in this assembly, not only in His Spirit, but also in His Body. I have experienced so often how, in the midst of a 'routine' Mass, my reality has been transformed, enlarged, renewed. God is a God of forever new beginnings. I have gone, stagnant and purposeless, and found light and direction; heavy with conflict and found courage; hurting and have found peace. All my growing, my leaps of understanding, the nudges that have led me from desperation to inspiration, have happened in the context of this community of faith. Here is healing, forgiveness, and understanding. But here is also the human condition with its inadequacy, its discordancy, its needs. Sometimes patience and forgiveness are asked of me here. In gratitude for the human and timeless gifts which I have received, gifts without number, it is only fair that I give something in return, if only my faithful presence. Is not giving without expecting return the test of maturity? But what have I got to give? This is the most disturbing question of all. It seems impossible that the God of the universe would find any useful role for me. And yet I am His, the work of His hands. He does not make junk. As a mother I hang up the unskilled drawings of my children on my fridge, recognizing their smallest efforts. Can it be that He, who is the archetype of fatherhood and motherhood, also takes joy in the scribbling of our spirits? Perhaps He, too, takes our feeble efforts and hangs them on the 'fridges' of heaven.

But today, I just hold on to the robe of Christ, as did the woman with the hemorrhage in the Scriptures, not seeing His face, but trusting in faith that He will give me vitality and what I need.

The Church is only half full when we arrive. I seek out my father's solitary figure and squeeze into his pew beside him, along with my husband and those three of our children who still remain at home. Kneeling, I reach around in my mind for some semblance of a prayer. I notice as Father Gord, looking slightly agitated, hurries down the aisle, speaks to someone in the choir, and heads back.

He stops beside me. "Are you a Eucharistic Minister?" he asks.

"No," I answer with a sudden stab of regret. I did bring Communion once to my mother when the usual Minister of the Eucharist was away, but that was an extraordinary occasion. My mind retrieves the memory of that day with longing. Christina had dropped off the pyx at my house before she left town, and I had held the little gold medallion shaped container to my heart in awe and reverence. I wondered if some atom remained of the physical presence of Jesus. Moved, shaken, privileged, I wore the pyx over my heart as I slept and felt God was very near. The next day at Mass I received the consecrated Hosts I was to take to my dying Mom and housebound Dad. I was very conscious of my precious cargo as I drove to their house. Somewhat awkwardly I read from Scripture and prayed, and gave my mother one of the last Communions of her earthly life. But that day passed, and the memory and feelings faded.

Years before, when the children were all small, our former pastor had invited me to be a Eucharistic Minister, but I had declined without batting an eyelash, sure that my efforts would be better spent exerting mob control over my brood. But now...now...suddenly my chest feels crushed with a great longing.

Why did I answer "no"? Well, I had to.... It was the truth. I was just being honest...and yet.... In any event, it is too late now. Father has left, returning to the back of the Church to vest, and, no doubt, to ask someone else to serve. But why am I feeling like this? I have never cared before. Why am I now so fiercely drawn to this august ministry?

Suddenly I yearn for the magnetic Christ with a power that shatters me.

Why is this happening? I ask myself incredulously, riveted to the pew in acute pain, an ache that fills me everywhere, body and soul. It is an agony of loss, stronger than anything I have ever known, searing me inside with a merciless fire. *This is ridiculous,* I say to myself. *So often I have received Communion with a soulless tedium, ho-hum, distracted, blasé. What is happening to me now? I am burning with longing!* I reflect that perhaps this experience is akin to the suffering of the souls in purgatory, those departed ones who cleanse themselves in the fire of longing, reaching for the love response to rise above the petty idolatries, the lost opportunities that are holding them back? Like a song once heard, they strive to recapture the melody of Love sung to them in the dawn of their creation. Now it is like food out of their reach, the effort of atrophied, crippled limbs crashing through a wall of pain to run toward the most important and joyous encounter of their entire existence. I understand. I hurt, and I understand.

Five minutes pass—or is it five hours? Six minutes. Seven. I am caught in an airless limbo of yearning, burning with invisible flames.

As unexpectedly and inexplicably as he had come the first time, Father Gord returns to my pew from the back of the Church.

"There is nothing to it," he says abruptly, with almost an undercurrent of impatience in his voice.

"Yes!" I cannot say another word, just "yes". Joy explodes in me. It is indescribable.

With five hundred people in the Church, why has he come back to me? My father is sitting next to me. He had been active as a Eucharistic minister for years.

Trembling from head to foot, tears running down my face, I approach the altar.

"This is My Body," Father Gord is saying, and the words electrify me. "This is the Blood of the new and eternal covenant that will be shed for you and for all men for the forgiveness of sins. Do this in remembrance of Me."

I have accepted these words all my life, but it has been through faith that I have seen the physical reality of Christ in the tiny Host, the same kind of faith it takes to plant a nondescript seed in the ground and know that a flower will bloom. In the annals of history, from the earliest Church to the present, recorded consistently in all the extant writings of the early and later Church fathers, the incarnate presence of Jesus in the Eucharist was recognized and accepted. Unbelievable? A mystery? Of course. But when has God ever fit into any of our little boxes? The first time in Scripture that Jesus spoke of eating His Flesh and drinking His Blood, His listeners knew exactly what He meant and they were horrified. Because of this most of His disciples and followers left Him that day. But He didn't call them back and say, "Oh, I'm sorry, that's not what I meant; I was speaking symbolically, metaphorically!" He meant what He said. He is that mysterious "Bread from heaven", the new manna, Who nourishes us even today with His presence. In the Old Testament, why did God make the sacrifice of an unblemished lamb the central act of worship for His chosen people? What meaning could the sacrificed flesh of a mere lamb have to a God who is pure spirit? And what a strange understanding of sacrifice this! At Passover, the lamb would be slaughtered and its blood would protect the owner's dwelling from death, but then the family was commanded to eat it. The lamb that was sacrificed to save them from death then became their food for the journey through the desert. All generations were to repeat this sacrifice, such was its importance. But as a mere animal, the lamb possessed no power or significance in itself. Yet God used this humble creature to direct our minds, to prepare us, to lay the foundation for an act that is mind boggling. This lamb, then, becomes God's redeeming signature written across our history, pointing to Jesus. Jesus IS Passover.

Yet, my cerebral faith remained on the back burner of my life, a seed waiting to bloom in eternity. I have slipped over it, glossed over it and demurred trying to explain what is beyond all explanation. Yet, to have faith is to believe in the trajectory of the arrow that flies beyond our sight.

But today is different. Suddenly, I am invited to a Divine nuptial! The hole inside me that I had sensed so early in my life is filled. The Love that drew me as a teenager caresses me. The God I had served as a young nun gives me His Heart. The One who had sent me mushrooms, quail, a calendar, today gives me much more. He gives Himself, the ultimate gift! I stand, holding the greatest Miracle that could ever exist, within my own hands. It is He! It is He! So sweet, so wonderful that nothing in my life before can compare to it, not human love nor any earthly joy. I look at my fingertips, and He is there, as He is everywhere within me, and my hands are His Hands. Stunned, breathless, swept into ecstasy, I feel I know Him for the first time.

You are with me! You are in me! I cry in stunned realization. *You are the eternal Dawn!*

I know now, in the power of His intimacy, that all the wars of my history have already been won. I am seized by the timeless embrace of God. It seems that my soul will flee my body; my body cannot withstand and hold this rapture! It cauterizes the pains of the past with a sublime kiss. "And God will wipe away all the tears from your eyes...." Revelation says. It is so! How can I describe the universe of love and light that inundate me? What words can I use? The experience lies beyond the boundaries of all that I know. Joy? Peace? Awe?. A gratitude that can be only expressed in adoration. I realize, suddenly, that up to now I have never understood what it means to adore. At fifty years of age I am a slow learner! Today I experience adoration, and from a well in my spirit leaps a cry of praise and surrender. Infinite horizons open. Today I see through a wide angle camera where before I saw through a pinhole. Understanding flows like electricity filling a light bulb. How different God's reality is from ours! In His Kingdom my joys, my victories, are yours, and yours are mine, as in a shared banquet, unity in the greatest diversity. All over, in color which is also music, which is the eternal dance, are groups of people, each with their own radiance, sharing the blessings, the victories, the special joys of the lives that have budded on earth. I understand that like the moon, each of us possesses no light of ourselves, but we are like mirrors who reflect Him Who is Light. Unlike this earth where we war with one another, compete with, and denigrate each other, in heaven the light of your mirror will increase the light in mine, and the light in my mirror will shine on you, increasing exponentially your joy. Insofar as any of us have grown and become all that we can be, we will enrich the experience of heaven for each other, joined in ecstatic love. The answer to the question of my teenage years about Perfect Goodness is now before me. I see that in my life I have shrunk God to my human perceptions, encapsulating Him in all the failures of love that I have experienced. I could only project onto Him my own stinginess and imagine Him standing on the sidelines with His big stick, doling out love with a slide rule. My experience now is of a different order. It is as He promised the lowly Samaritan woman at the well, whose quest for love had culminated in five husbands: "I will become in you a fountain of living water bubbling up unto life everlasting". Today I am filled with the glory of this reality. I understand that, when Christ prayed so repeatedly for unity at His last supper, it was not like me saying to my children "Okay, kids, get along!" It was in actuality an invitation to be one with each other and with Him in a nuptial feast, enclosed in the Trinity, the Love that is Existence Itself. What is the fragmentary, limited union of married love after all, but a foreshadowing of Divine intimacy? If the nature of love is to give, perfect love gives absolutely; He gives us Himself. Because we are creatures of flesh as well as spirit, He becomes incarnate in our mortal flesh to embrace our reality and lead it to resurrection. It is in following this human Jesus, the God-man, that all the possibilities of our humanity open up to us. The Divine Food is indeed a nuclear fusion, capable of transforming our disunity; healing and enfolding us into the Love for which we were created.

God dignifies us with choice. With blinding clarity I see that He has left Himself defenseless before this choice, so utterly open, non-threatening, vulnerable to our coldness, to our neglect. He is Love that does not seek to overwhelm us, but simply invites us to an answering love. With a trembling of my spirit I behold His total self giving in the Bread and Wine in my hand, the Covenant of Himself. He Who is Everything has emptied Himself of Everything to offer it to me. He has walked my walk, suffered my pain, left me a road map to get through the minefields of this world, and becomes the Food for my journey. What other love has given me so much?

I drive home down the back roads, and I see everywhere copious blue clouds of bachelor buttons growing in wild profusion in the ditches along the roadway. Crafted by God, they call out in their beauty, a constant reminder that God is the eternal bachelor, always seeking our love.

Two years have passed. My life revolves around my Eucharistic service and it remains, by far, the greatest privilege of my life. I laugh. I cry. My knees shake. It is as if time and gravity do not exist. I live my days mostly in ecstasy. Prayer is a joy. I look forward to stealing away to be with my great Love. I long always to be with Him. I pray now in a new way. I come before Him simply as a receptacle, a chalice, a channel and He flows into me to fill my emptiness. But as He is gift, I am also to be gift. Whatever He gives me must course through me to His Body, His people. Like a wind instrument I must play His music in the hollows of this world.

I find that my life long hang up with authority has melted away. In the Fatherhood of God I have found a more tender and loving camaraderie with my earthly father, as well as a new appreciation of the sacrifice made by that Father. I still flinch to remember the excruciating pain of seeing Justin arrested and taken away, and I begin to realize, and I am in awe, of the utter giving of the Father Who allowed His innocent Son to be taken, abused, tortured, murdered, to redeem us and bring us back to the Fatherland. Had we been a flawless people it might be more understandable. Even we humans make costly sacrifices for our children. But His sacrifice was for the unworthy, the unloving, those who scorn and spurn the ultimate Gift, who remain cold, slow of understanding, and ungrateful. Yet, He calls us to union with Him, giving us the means, the wings, to transcend this passing world. Even the death that comes to us as suffering, in Him becomes Life. Suffering becomes, not a meaningless, purposeless thing, but part of our Divine patrimony, the insignia of a family born to redemptive Love.

With dread, sorrow, and resignation, I realize that I cannot remain always here on my Mount Tabor. As Peter and John and James had to leave the glory of the Mountain of the Transfiguration, I too will have to return to the grit and despair of His needy world, where the discordancy of evil jars the soul. I will have to return to my own shadows, to my own fragility, until my growing is complete. I will return to a world that is full of the sound of blather, where TV and radio with their blustery cheerfulness prostitute our senses with the allures of a passing empire. Articulate thieves, they rob us of ideals, and silence, and fill our emptiness with trivia. Here, at the crossroads of the information highway we are deafened with the concourse of words and images. Words ram us, batter us, beguile us, deceive us, flatter us, disturb us. In the end we become automatons, absorbing and reacting, but desensitized and separated from what is most real and enduring. We become stoic consumers of a world we find mostly meaningless.

Yet, in the midst of this wasteland, where the pillars of language have been eroded, polluted, degraded, and jargonized, where love and morality have been compromised and democratized into ambiguity, the Word still becomes flesh. My life stands in testimony that the power of God still speaks His living Word into our hearts and experiences. The Scriptures are dead for me today unless His Word is clothed in my flesh, enervating my unique reality, shaping my growing pains, calming my storms and healing my soul. As Mary was pregnant with Christ, I am called to bear Christ and give Him birth in the cradle of this new millennium.

In the quiet of an early morning weekday Mass, I look with new eyes, new love, on a nondescript sea of ordinary human faces: others, like myself, who have been touched and called by the Divine Mystery to love and be His Body. Each of us have our own stories, our own reasons, our own crosses. By no human power or urging, and for no enticement of earthly gain do we gather here together, strangers and brothers alike. In the pallor of the morning there is little hint that behind youth and wrinkles, throat clearings and sagging shoulders, is hidden a universe of God's splendor.

A woman who I have seen now and then, but whose name I don't know, touches my arm as we exit under a cloudy sky.

"You have such a beautiful face. I can't stop looking at you," the woman says to me earnestly.

I am utterly taken aback! Me? I am only too conscious these days that the beauty of youth is long past. Even in youth my beauty was not perfect. I worked hard at looking good and managed reasonably well, despite a profile that was less than classical, and legs that were a bit too ample. But now? Now I have a double chin, an age spot on my nose, and my teeth, which were never straight, are a rather disenchanting yellow. My figure has ballooned past middle age and by every standard of beauty of this world I am definitely over the hill. Shopping for clothes is my current nightmare. So how can this be? On other days, strangers approach me to tell me that I have a wonderful smile. Does everyone around here need their glasses upgraded?

I know, despite the strong messages coming via our media, that physical appearance should not limit who we are. My grandmother and my Superior, who in their mature years were not raving beauties, were in no way diminished or hampered by the lack of classical profiles and hour-glass figures. Nor would I have loved my parents, and other important people in my life, more had they conformed better to Hollywood's standards of youth and attractiveness. If I were asked what I would change in the ways they looked, I would have to answer, "Nothing." Each is a unique facet of a living diamond, irreplaceable, another wonderful refraction of God's light. Each is a nuance, a fragrance, a special flavor like one of the hundred different flavors of ice cream in the donut shop I frequented as a child.

Still, I am stunned at being approached by people in this way. As I muse about it I recall an account given by Josyp Terelya in his book, 'Witness', where he speaks of the phenomena accompanying recent apparitions of Mary, the Mother of Jesus, on the steppes of the Ukraine. He describes how her appearance is heralded by a great soft light. On one occasion, Josyp looked around at the thousands of milling people and was struck by the fact that in that heavenly light everyone looked beautiful—the toothless old babushka to the ungainly peasant with three days growth of beard.

So I accept that in the radiance of the Light of God we are, each of us, beautiful. Though my biological clock is winding down, inside my spirit has no arthritis, no pain, no age. I ride on the shoulders of my Father, whirling like a gypsy on the hills of time. Tomorrow my Father will take me to visit His galaxies and watch new universes coming to be, a Father sharing with His child the power of that creative Love by which all things have come to be. In Him is found every dream of love I have ever dreamed, and in His Heart where all is tenderness and ecstasy, I am made new. My heart echoes with Mary: *My soul magnifies the Lord, and my spirit rejoices in God, my Savior.* Every day I am one day closer to the Supreme Joy.

I stand now before a lifetime of memories, emptied and strewn like abandoned toys; gravestones awaiting the final resurrection. What can be distilled from all of this? What remains? What is my legacy to pass on? Only the power of faith to clear the clogged arteries of the spirit. The glory of God among us. The primacy of Love.

This is my Last Will and Testament.